MANTHROPOLOGY

The science of why
the modern male
is not the man
He used to be

PETER McALLISTER

ST. MARTIN'S PRESS 🜲 NEW YORK

MANTHROPOLOGY. Copyright © 2009 by Peter McAllister. All rights reserved. Printed in the United States of America. For information, address St. Martin's Press, 175 Fifth Avenue, New York, N.Y. 10010.

www.stmartins.com

Library of Congress Cataloging-in-Publication Data

McAllister, Peter, 1965–
    Manthropology : the science of why the modern male is not the man
he used to be / Peter McAllister.—1st U.S. ed.
       p. cm
     ISBN 978-0-312-55543-6
   1. Men—Anthropometry.   2. Men—Physiology.   3. Masculinity.
4. Women—Anthropometry.   5. Women—Physiology.   I. Title.
   GN59.M4M53 2010
   305.31—dc22

                                 2010031717

First published in Australia by Hachette Australia

First U.S. Edition: November 2010

1 3 5 7 9 10 8 6 4 2

MANTHROPOLOGY

contents

Acknowledgments

No book would ever see the light of day without the dedicated efforts of a team beyond just the author. In *Manthropology*'s case those instrumental people include the wonderful staff at St. Martin's Press, particularly Yaniv Soha, whose deft editing will undoubtedly receive the ironic but highest of accolades—it won't be noticed. My sincere thanks go also to my agent, Peter McGuigan of Foundry Media, who saw the project through from beginning to end with unfailing faith and good humor. Gratitude is also due to the many people, expert and lay, who gave freely of their time in interview and conversation. I must also, finally, thank my good friend Richard Shapcott, without whose idle suggestion, made over coffee, this book would never have been written.

prologue:

the worst man in history

If you're reading this, then you—or the male you have bought it for—are the worst man in history.

No ifs, no buts—the worst man, period.

How can I be so sure? As a paleoanthropologist (Greek roots: *palaeo* = ancient; *anthro* = man; *logy* = science) it's my job to study people, including men, from way back in our evolutionary past until today. It's been my work for many long years to mark them, measure them, research them, and describe them—and those years have convinced me that all is not well with the male of our modern species.

Not well at all.

As a class we are, in fact, the sorriest cohort of masculine *Homo sapiens* to ever walk the planet. And, since any man reading this—or woman reading it about him—is by definition a modern one, I confidently repeat:

You are—or he is—absolutely the worst man in history.

I know, I know—such sentiments aren't exactly helpful right now. In these times of masculine crises—of falling sperm counts, accelerating job losses, waning libidos, and fading masculine relevance—men are not looking to be challenged. They are looking for a messiah. A savior. Someone who will soothe their battered egos, re-store their lost virility, and set them back up where they think they once belonged: at the top of the gender chain.

Sorry. I am not that man.

In the words of another man, one who really *was* a messiah, I have not come to make peace among you, but war. I have come to turn father against son, brother against brother, and friend against friend. I have come, with the sword of science in my hand, to dem-onstrate that every terrible little doubt you have ever had about yourself is completely and utterly true.

I have come, in short, to rub it in.

In my defense, it wasn't always so. I didn't set out to destroy the image of modern males when I started this book. Far from it. As a paleoanthropologist, and a man, I love my brother males—every single one of those who, like me, carry the mark of our stunted, mutant Y chromosome on their brows. It was that love, believe it or not, that started me writing. I read everywhere that my fel-low men were suffering—from feminization, ornamentalization, emasculation—and I decided to help. I would use my research into the evolution of our species to prove that men today are *not* weak, contemptible commitment-phobes who can't hold down their end of a meaningful conversation, let alone a snarling cave bear, but gods on earth whose heroic abilities would make Zeus himself sneak back to Mount Olympus to work out on his Abdominator in shame. I would write an ABC of the virtues of *Homo masculinus modernus,* comparing him to earlier men to prove that he is—we are—the crowning glory of humanity's long evolutionary struggle up from our inauspicious beginnings as leopard food on the Afri-can savannah.

As you will see, I failed.

In fact, I didn't even get past B. I discovered, to my horror, that it's impossible to write a book about the superior achievements of modern males, because we haven't made any. From battling to boozing, babes to bravado, there's *nothing* we can do that ancient men, and sometimes women, haven't already done better, faster, stronger, and usually smarter.

Typically, that knowledge dawned on me slowly. Like any challenged male seeking to cover up a gnawing sense of inadequacy, I started by picking on a girl: a Neandertal girl, to be precise. I decided that demonstrating how strong modern men are compared to our ancient brethren (thanks to fitness science and superior nutrition) would make a great beginning, so I calculated the average upper-arm strength of several winners of the World Arm Wrestling Federation Championships since 2000 and compared it to that of the Neandertals who lived in Europe in the Upper Paleolithic roughly 40,000 years BCE (before current era). I must have already sensed I would need to stack the deck a little, since for some reason I decided to start with a Neandertal woman. That did me no good, however, for a troubling inconsistency quickly emerged.

She was stronger.

I checked and rechecked the data, but there was no mistake. Incredibly, it seemed that even a random, anonymous Neandertal female would slam the big men of the WAF to the table every time.

That, admittedly, was disturbing, but I felt that it had to be a statistical anomaly, what scientists sometimes call an outlier. So I moved on confidently to a surer field of inquiry: sports. Competitive athletics are widely considered the proving ground of modern physical superiority—witness the succession of smashed Olympics records last century, culminating in the dizzying, drug-fueled heights of the 1980s and 1990s. A rough calculation shows over 80 percent of current Olympic athletics records were set between 1984 and 2000, and have remained unbroken since. Surely modern men of the track and field would leave their ancient rivals trailing in the strength, speed, and agility stakes?

To my intense disquiet, the answer was no. As I went deeper into the research I uncovered a succession of startling facts. I found Mongol bowmen in the twelfth century who shot with higher accuracy than modern Olympic archers, over distances *six times greater*, and from galloping horseback to boot. I found ancient competitors in the Greek Olympics who won three grueling events on a single day's competition, in one case repeating the feat at four successive Olympics. I found other Greek athletes who set long jump and triple jump records, unassisted by modern technology, that would have stood until the 1952 Olympics. Not to mention the bravery and commitment of competitors such as the boxer Eurydamas of Cyrene, who swallowed his smashed teeth during a match to disguise his injuries from both his opponent and the judges.

The further back I went the more calamitous the news became. Archaeological research from a fossil footprint site in the Willandra Lakes region of southwestern New South Wales shows that twenty thousand years ago Australian Aboriginal men regularly ran at speeds rivaling, and probably exceeding, the top speed of the current one-hundred-meter world record holder, Usain Bolt. Going back beyond the dawn of our own species, the picture is bleaker yet: even *female* chimps, gorillas, and bonobos, our closest living relatives, not only carry much higher ratios of lean muscle to body mass than modern men, their individual muscles are up to four times stronger than those of any male *Homo sapiens*.

By this time I was seriously shaken. In desperation I widened my focus; if we modern males couldn't compete on speed and strength I would simply find a field in which we could—such as brains, or beauty, or even the bardic arts for God's sake. But it was no good. Wherever I turned I found humiliatingly high historic and prehistoric achievers. In the manufacture of their intricate "Levallois" spear points, Neandertal flintknappers from the Lower Paleolithic display an understanding of stone fracture mechanics beyond that of most modern-day geology graduates. The beautification routines of modern metrosexuals wouldn't get them into the starting line-up of a Wodaabe male tribesmen's "Gerewol" beauty pageant. The wittiest and most grueling freestyle battle rap between superstars such as Kanye West and 50 Cent couldn't match the drama and duration of a traditional Eskimo song duel, let alone the poetic feats of medieval Slavic bards who frequently free-rhymed for days on end. The final straw came when I read of the extraordinary parenting feats of Aka Pygmy fathers in Central Africa (who spend 47 percent of their waking time in close physical contact with their children and even sometimes grow breasts to suckle them). That was it. Suddenly even the very last refuge of the modern incompetent male—being *good with the kids*—was no longer safe.

It was then that I crossed over to the dark side.

If I couldn't write about the virtues of *Homo masculinus modernus,* I would instead record his failures. I would document in meticulous and humiliating detail every modern male weakness, inadequacy, or vice. I would lay *Homo masculinus modernus* bare to the world in all his feeble, cowardly, and unlovely lack of glory.

An extreme reaction, to be sure, but in my defense it was driven as much by my shame as a scientist as by my shame as a man. The statistics quoted here have mostly been available for years (in some cases centuries), and it strikes me that many a male researcher before me must have drawn the same conclusions from them as I did, but then recoiled in horror. No doubt they dumped them deep in some dusty, forgotten cabinet drawer to grow moldy and never *ever* assault us with their appalling implications again, just like I was tempted to. But some last shred of self-respect, a rebellious desire to prove that if nothing else one of our pathetic breed could at least once look the truth squarely in the eye, *like a man*, stayed my hand.

Here, then, are the grim fruits of my inquiry into the life and times of *Homo masculinus modernus*, the infuriating, insulting, demeaning, and ultimately fascinating conclusions of a new science of masculine inquiry; a science I call manthropology.

Brawn

If you really want to see the trouble modern men are in, just drop in on an action figure (definitely *not* action doll) convention such as, say, "JoeCon 25"—the 2007 gathering for collectors of Hasbro's G.I. Joe. The pointers aren't so much in the audience—those grinning Gen-Xers from across the country who bought the "American Hero" registration package and have now packed into the Atlanta Marriott atrium to await the forty-seven-floor parachute drop of three hundred eight-inch Cobra Red Ninja figurines. The trouble lies with Joe himself.

A series of scientific papers at the turn of the millennium unearthed a disturbing fact about G.I. Joe: he's growing steadily, absurdly hypermuscular. The modern G.I. Joe "Sgt. Savage Extreme" figure, for example, is three times as muscular as his 1982 counterpart. The trend is particularly striking when "Sgt. Savage" is compared to real, living males. The average modern man has a biceps circumference of about eleven-and-a-half inches. If the 1982 "Sgt. Savage" had been scaled up to a living man's height his biceps circumference would have more or less equaled this, at just over twelve-and-a-half inches. The biceps of "Sgt. Savage Extreme" in 1998, however, would have ballooned to almost forty inches if he had been likewise supersized. Not even steroid abusing bodybuilders ever get this big: the largest biceps in the modern world belong to bodybuilder Greg Valentino, who 'roided his up to a grotesque, but comparatively meager, twenty-eight inches. Even such not-so-hyper-masculine figurines as Luke Sky-walker and the Mighty Morphin Power Rangers now equal this. Mattel's Ken—to quote one final, humiliating example—has not escaped unpumped either. Barbie's inoffensive arm candy now sports a chest circumference attainable by just one in fifty real men.

G.I. Joe's bulging biceps are a testament in ABS plastic to our ac-celerating obsession with male muscularity, and he's not alone. Another scientific paper found that the nude male centerfolds of *Playgirl* magazine have gained an average 26.4 pounds of muscle over the past quarter-century, and lost 12 pounds of fat.[1] A survey of American male university students found that most wanted to emulate these magazine man-muffins, stating a preference for 24 pounds more muscle and 7.5 pounds less body fat than they actually had.

All across the Western world men are packing into gyms, pumping iron, and swallowing ever greater quantities of legal and illegal supplements in the quest for buffed, bulked physiques. The number of weight-training gyms has ballooned and legal muscle-building supplements are now a $1.6 billion per year industry. Il-legal steroid use is rife, too, with 70 percent of bodybuilders, and 12 percent of American high school boys, admitting to taking them. This has led to a predictably dramatic explosion in male muscula-ture: one scientific paper found that Mr. America winners from the pre-steroid era averaged a fat-free muscle mass (total body weight minus fat, bones, and connective tissue) of 158 pounds, while body-builders in the post-steroid era average 176 pounds. (This doesn't sound like much, but an extra eighteen pounds of pure muscle is a *big* increase.)[2] Even this, however, doesn't seem to satisfy us. A recent article in the *Harvard Review of Psychiatry* estimated that a million American men now suffer from Body Dysmorphic Disorder—a syndrome whose major symptom is the obsessive desire for a more muscular body.[3] Even women are not immune: several surveys of American university women found that the majority of them secretly wished their boyfriends were more muscular.

Rock of Ages

The ground shook figuratively, as well as literally, when Iranian weightlifter, Hossein Rezazadeh, slammed down the 580-pound barbell after winning gold in the clean-and-jerk event at the 2004 Olympics. Not only was it an Olympic record, Rezazadeh also won, by popular acclaim, the title of "Strongest Man in the World." A little history, however, shows the title to be too late—twenty-six hundred years too late, to be precise.

Nineteenth-century archaeological excavations on the Greek island of Thera uncovered a 1,058-pound boulder, dated to the sixth century BCE, bearing the inscription "Eumastas, the son of Critobulus, lifted me from the ground." This is classified as a deadlift, in which event Rezazadeh has recorded a lift of 836 pounds (the world-record deadlift, 1,006.5 pounds, is held by powerlifter Andy Bolton). True, Eumastas probably didn't lift the boulder up to groin height, as modern deadlifters do, but weightlifting historian, David

Willoughby, points out that the difficult grip of a boulder, compared to the ease of a barbell, renders the feat probably unattainable by almost any modern weightlifter.[4]

Nor is that the only superior ancient weightlifting feat. Another sixth century BCE boulder, this time a 315-pound stone found at Olympia, bears an inscription to the effect that an athlete called Bybon lifted it overhead, one-handed, and threw it. No modern weightlifter has been able to even lift this weight overhead one-handed since the German strongman, Arthur Saxon, in the late nineteenth century—and not even Saxon managed to *throw* it.

But if we modern Hercules so easily outmuscle the men of fifty years ago, how might we fare against males of the truly distant past: those ancestral members of our genus *Homo,* such as *Homo erectus* and *Homo neanderthalensis,* who have populated the world at various times over the past 2 to 3 million years? As a paleoanthropologist, that was my burning interest, so I decided to test it. Since the focus of our current obsession with muscularity seems to be on the arms (one paper found that almost 75 percent of tenth and twelfth grade American schoolboys specifically desire bigger biceps[5]), I decided to compare upper arm strength between modern and ancient humans. In the interest of a fair fight, I decided to have them slug it out in the one modern sport in which arm muscles are undeniably king: world championship arm wrestling.

Competitive arm wrestling is a surprisingly popular sport these days. In the pantheon of modern strongman events—such as truck pulling, refrigerator carrying, and car wheelbarrowing—arm wrestling has been near the pinnacle ever since Sly Stallone's 1987 movie *Over the Top* showed a down-at-heel trucker, Lincoln Hawk, arm-wrestle his way into his son's heart and win the world championship along the way. The World Arm Wrestling Federation boasts 85 member countries and hundreds of thousands of enthusiastic participants in events such as "Arm Wars X" and the annual "Riverboat Rumble." The big names, however, are the winners of the world championships—men such as Travis Bagent, premier left-arm wrestler in the world, and multiple world championship winner, John Brenzk (who actually wrestled in Stallone's movie). To represent *Homo masculinus modernus* in this matchup, however, I've chosen one of the biggest, strongest men to ever bend the arm in professional combat: 2004 World Arm Wrestling Federation champion, Alexey Voyevoda. At 255 pounds with a 22-inch bicep (10 percent bigger again than those of Arnold Schwarzenegger at his peak), Voyevoda is the man to give *Homo masculinus modernus* his best shot at claiming the title in this interspecies grudge match. We're going to need him, too, because for Voyevoda's opponent I've chosen the toughest, most muscular species of ancient human to ever walk the earth.

The Neandertals.

The Neandertals were a type of human (or hominin, as all such member species of our genus *Homo* are called) who flourished in Europe, the Middle East, and Central Asia between three hundred and fifty thousand and twenty thousand years ago. *Homo neanderthalensis* males and females were comparable to us in brain size (in fact, some Neandertal brains were much larger), but their bodies were far more muscular. Neandertal males, for example, though they averaged a mere 5'5" in height (around four inches smaller than modern male *Homo sapiens*) are thought to have carried 20 percent more muscle than modern men. One possible reason is their cold environment—a thermoregulatory principle known as Bergmann's law predicts that people who live in arctic environments, such as modern Inuits, or Eskimos, will have greater mass and more spherical body shapes to reduce surface area and retain heat. Another possibility, however, is that hypermusculature was an adaptation to the violent lives Neandertals lived. Thirty percent of all male Neandertal skeletons found, for example, have traumatic head and neck injuries, a level reached only by rodeo riders among modern populations. It's probable the Neandertal men received their injuries from the same source the riders did—close encounters with enraged bulls and beasts—since the archaeological evidence shows, incredibly, that they hunted prey as big as woolly rhinos by ambushing them up close with thrusting spears.

So muscular, in fact, were the Neandertals that I began to take pity on poor Alexey Voyevoda. Anxious to give this champion of *Homo masculinus modernus* a fighting chance, I stacked the deck slightly in his favor: I decided that instead of having Voyevoda square up to a hulking, rhino-hunting Neandertal male, I would send him into battle against a *girl*. A sweet, demure, coquettish Neandertal girl—the five foot, 176-pound beauty with the unfortunate name of La Ferrassie 2 (taken from the French cave site, La Ferrassie, where she was discovered with several other buried Neandertals in 1909).

Comparing their biceps strength was difficult, but not impossible. (It does involve a little calculation, unfortunately, so if that bores you just skip ahead four or five paragraphs.) The force a biceps muscle produces per square inch of cross-sectional area (called CSA and measured perpendicularly across the muscle) is known—it is 62 pounds. Fortunately, this doesn't seem to vary between men and women, though obviously the total area of their muscle does.

Measurements of Alexey Voyevoda's total biceps CSA are, unfortunately, not available, but the average for a comparable group of modern males, elite bodybuilders, comes in at approximately 3.5 square inches. Multiplied by 62 pounds per square inch, that gives a hypothetical force of roughly 220 pounds for Voyevoda's biceps. But how, then, to estimate the CSA of La Ferrassie 2's biceps, given that all that survives of *her* arm is bone?

Surprisingly, it can be done thanks to a rule known as Wolff's law. Wolff's law, named after German military surgeon Julius Wolff, states that bone carries a record of the muscular load placed upon it because it grows larger over time in response to mechanical stress. In crude terms, the size of the muscle can therefore be estimated from the cortical area, or CA (a cross-sectional measure of thickness similar to muscle CSA), of the bone it was attached to. Since we have measures of bone CA for both La Ferrassie 2 and a representative group of average (non-bodybuilding) modern males, all I had to do was calculate the ratio between the two and multiply it by the average, non-bodybuilding male's biceps CSA (1.8 inches square).

That, however, was where the first surprise hit me.

Despite the fact that modern males have 50 percent more upper body muscle than modern females, La Ferrassie 2 had bigger biceps than any average man alive today. The CA of her upper arm bone, or humerus, was 0.34 square inches, compared to our puny 0.3 square inches. Her biceps CSA was therefore probably around 2 inches square, around 16 percent larger than our 1.8 square inches. Multiplied by 62 pounds, that gave La Ferrassie 2 a hypothetical biceps force of around 124 pounds. Now, while this was enough to slam the average male pub challenger (with 112 pounds) to the table, it was a long way short of Voyevoda's 220 pounds. I had not yet, however, corrected for the effect of training—one couldn't be so unchivalrous, after all, as to let La Ferrassie 2 wrestle without a prolonged weight-training program to mirror Voyevoda's. Several studies of elite female bodybuilders have shown that women's muscles can grow, or hypertrophize, by approximately 31 percent in response to prolonged strength training. An increase of this size would bring La Ferrassie 2's biceps CSA up to 2.6 inches square and her force output to around 162 pounds. Impressive as this is, it's still just 75 percent of Voyevoda's biceps output. At this point, it seemed, the Russian champion would have been counting his prize money and basking in the gratitude of vindicated modern males everywhere.

Except that La Ferrassie 2 had a nasty little surprise in store—two in fact. One was a trick of leverage and the other a quirk of Neandertal muscle anatomy. Put together they would have left Voyevoda regretting he'd ever been so stupid as to take her on.

It is widely acknowledged, among arm-wrestling champions, that a short forearm is a serious advantage. This is because the forearm is a third-class lever. Levers generally increase the amount of work that can be done as they grow longer, but third-class levers don't—they *decrease* it. This is called the lever's "mechanical disadvantage," and its number rises as the lever lengthens. A short forearm, therefore, means a lower mechanical disadvantage. (The Neandertals had such short wrists because of another thermoregulatory principle, Allen's law, which states that organisms living in cold environments will have dramatically shortened arms and legs, again to reduce heat loss.) My calculations show that Voyevoda's forearm would probably have a mechanical disadvantage of 6.145, while La Ferrassie 2's would be lower—around 5. If you divide each contestant's absolute force by their mechanical disadvantage, it turns out that the amount of power La Ferrassie 2 delivered at her hand (the end of the forearm lever) would be just short of Voyevoda's—roughly 33 pounds compared to 36.

By now the sweat beading the burly Russian's forehead would no doubt be as much from relief at his close escape as from effort. But La Ferrassie 2 had a final, cruel anatomical trick to play. In Neandertal forearms, both male and female, the point where the biceps muscle was attached was located much further around on the radius bone than in modern humans, making Neandertals immensely strong in *supination,* or rotating the wrist counterclockwise, since full biceps contraction could be maintained through the whole movement. They likewise possessed much more highly developed muscles attaching to the other forearm bone, the ulna, giving them great strength, too, in clockwise rotation or *pronation.* These two features would have made La Ferrassie 2 an unbeatable dominatrix at two winning techniques in arm wrestling: the hook, where the wrist is *supinated* to get inside the opponent's arm, and the top roll, where the wrist is *pronated* to get over the opponent's wrists and bend his fingers back.

Once La Ferrassie 2 got her 10 percent bigger brain around those little numbers, Voyevoda's pathetic 7 percent advantage would disappear in the snap of an upper-arm bone (fractured humeri are surprisingly common among arm wrestlers; see below). Of course, the beaten Russian could always cry foul, adding the title of "sorest loser" to the bulging trophy case of modern male failures. But the prospect of La Ferrassie 1—a fully grown male Neandertal bulging with 50 percent more upper body muscle than La Ferrassie 2—wading in to restore her honor, would probably dissuade him.

■ it's all fun and games until someone loses an arm

Though popular, arm wrestling can be dangerous. One study from the Department of Orthopedic Surgery at the Keio University Medical School in Tokyo, for example, reported forty cases of broken arms from arm wrestling over a period of twenty years.[6] The injuries were invariably the same: a spiral fracture from twisting of the humerus (the upper-arm bone).

Surprisingly, the majority of injuries occurred in men who fought weaker or evenly matched opponents, rather than stronger ones. Alcohol, predictably, was a factor, but so was inexperience: 60 percent of victims had never arm wrestled before the bout (usually against a friend) in which they were injured.

Doctors concluded that the injuries came from inexperienced wrestlers trying to push their hand, arm, and shoulder in the same direction—a natural, throwing motion. The drawback is that this simply added to the torque, or twist, that the opponent was putting on their upper arms. This overloaded their rotator muscles, prompting a sudden switch from concentric contraction (in which muscle fibers shorten to provide resistance) to eccentric contraction (where they elongate and *add* to the opposing force).

This phenomenon probably explained why the "Arm Spirit" arm

wrestling arcade game had to be withdrawn in Japan after three players broke their arms on it. The bone-breaking game *should* have been a pushover—contestants progressively wrestled a French maid, a drunken martial arts master, and a chihuahua!

In any case, Voyevoda's performance in this interspecies grudge match might actually have been even worse. These calculations all assumed that the individual muscles of ancient hominins were exactly the same strength, pound for pound, as those of modern humans. There is considerable evidence, however, that they may have been much, much stronger. Most of it comes from anatomical studies of our very close relative, the chimpanzee. The two species of chimpanzee—*Pan troglodytes,* the common chimp, and *Pan paniscus,* the bonobo or pygmy chimp—are not our immediate ancestors, but they are direct descendants of whoever was. It is highly probable, therefore, that early human males at the time of our separation from chimps (about 5.5 million years ago) were exactly as strong as male chimpanzees are today.

So how strong is that?

Exceptionally strong, as it happens. Scientists who work with chimps often remark on the animals' phenomenal physical strength. Jane Goodall, for example, told a Canadian TV host that she frequently saw chimps manipulate branches six times heavier than a man could. Given the savage attack suffered by the unfortunate Charla Nash, a Connecticut woman whose face and hands were almost ripped off by her friend's pet chimpanzee, Travis, in early

2009, this seems more than plausible. Much scientific data also testifies to chimps' incredible strength. A study of bonobos, the smallest chimpanzees, found they could jump, from a standing start, almost three times the height an average man could, and almost twice as high as any elite high-jump competitor despite the fact that their leg-muscle mass is just one-third that of humans.[7]

Why *are* chimps so phenomenally strong? Muscle bulk does seem to be part of the answer. Despite the fact that chimps' overall muscle mass is lower, the level of it relative to their reduced body size is quite high. One study of dead chimps from English zoos found that every one of their muscle groups (except the quadriceps) was significantly larger than those of humans when scaled for limb length; their biceps were almost *twice* as large. But sheer muscle bulk can't be the whole answer. For, as a fascinating 1926 experiment showed, common chimpanzees, even female ones, really are over four times as strong as human males, weight-for-weight.

There is a delicious irony about John Bauman's early twentieth-century chimp strength tests at Muhlenberg College, a small Pennsylvanian university. The researcher tested his three chimps using a dynamometer: a lever connected to a two-thousand-pound-capacity steel loop spring and a dial to register the maximum pulling force. The machine had been provided by the Narragansett Machine Company to Muhlenberg (a Lutheran college) for the purposes of anthropometry—recording the physical strength of male students—a craze that swept American universities in the late nineteenth century as part of the "muscular Christianity" movement. Instead of aiding the development of the perfectly masculine Christian man, however, Muhlenberg's machine would, in Bauman's hands, prove just how feeble that man really was.

Bauman used the dynamometer to test the pulling power of

three "anthropoid apes . . . of suitably vicious disposition" against that of five "husky farm lads" attending the college. To his astonishment, the chimps dramatically out-pulled the men, without really trying.[8] Suzette, a female circus chimp who'd been donated to the New York Zoological Park on account of her "increasing treacherousness and meanness," made a random pull of 1,258 pounds—four times the college students' average. (Interestingly, the only student who, at 127 pounds, weighed *less* than Suzette, pulled the highest human total: 460 pounds.) Bauman's male chimp, Boma, made a single-hand pull of 847 pounds, again over four times the strength of the male students' single-hand pulls. Bauman drew two conclusions from these results. First, that the individual fibers in chimp muscle must be roughly four times the strength of human fibers. (In fact, later research has shown that chimp muscle fibers are not individually stronger than ours; instead they are recruited en masse in one explosive contraction, in contrast to our more staggered firing. It is this that gives chimps their super strength.) Second, that this strength must be genetic and inherent, rather than conditioned. Bauman pointed out that his farm lads were fresh from a season of strenuous farm labor, while the chimps had been idling their years away in tiny cages.[9]

Here Bauman had stumbled onto a theory that would later become important in evolutionary explanations of human origins: that *Homo sapiens* is simply a kind of degenerate ape. Several lines of evidence support this idea. Some of the genetic mutations that differentiate us from the chimp and our common ancestor seem to involve a simple loss of function—put simply, our version just doesn't work anymore. Then there are our visible differences in body form, or phenotype. Though we have roughly as many hair follicles as chimps, our hairs (except on our heads) are pathetic remnants by comparison. Our kids grow more slowly than chimp children do: so slowly, in fact, that the chimpanzees adult humans most resemble are the juveniles, leading some anthropologists to label us "neotenous" organisms—ones that become adult in their juvenile stage. We are, effectively, a bald chimp that never grows up. A bald, *weak,* chimp, according to Bauman.

◼ HOMO pugilistus

Paleoanthropologists have long wondered how our earliest ancestors defended themselves on the harsh African savannah, home to such nasty predators as leopards, hyenas, and lions. Early humans lost their large canines as soon as they left the trees, and effective spears didn't become available for 2 million years. So how did they fend off ravening carnivores?

Remarkably, they might have punched them senseless.

We humans are natural-born boxers. Like our chimp cousins, we were originally brachiating (or branch-swinging) apes, with shoulder joints adapted to an almost 360-degree range of motion. When we shifted to bipedalism, however, this meant we also suddenly acquired the ability to throw vicious jabs, hooks, and sweeping haymakers.

Chimps still use these to devastating effect today. Anthropologist Richard Wrangham describes witnessing a male chimp, Hugo, punch out a male baboon, Stumptail, that had canines as long as a lion's:

As Hugo approached, Stumptail reared [and] bared
his fangs . . . but before he could close to biting range,
Hugo swung his arm in a wide arc and punched Stumptail in the belly. Stumptail crumpled . . . looking sick.
Moving like a prizefighter, Hugo quickly landed a second
punch . . . snapping the baboon's head backwards.
That was it. Stumptail retreated . . . and Hugo, taking his
place among the delicious palm fruits, ate for a peace-
ful half-hour.[10]

So much for Stumptail, but could our tiny ancestors (they averaged
between 3 and 4 feet tall) really have punched out leopards and
hyenas? Well, maybe. Consider, for example, the *Homo sapiens*
boxer, Rocky Marciano. Engineers tested Marciano's punch in the
1950s, reporting that it generated enough force to lift an 1,100-pound
weight 12 inches off the ground, break facial bones, and smash its
victim into instant unconsciousness. Now consider the fact that our
earliest ancestors were probably, like their chimp brothers, about
four times as strong as Marciano. Put this way, a punch from early
Homo pugilistus could have knocked any 110-pound spotted hyena
out of the ring . . . and then some. ■

But why should such degeneration have proven so successful, evo-
lutionarily speaking? Surely natural selection should have weeded
out ninety-eight-pound weaklings like us long ago? Evidence from a
2004 study on another human muscle, the jaw, may tell us why it

didn't. That study, by the Pennsylvania School of Medicine Muscle Institute, found that the fast-twitch fibers in human jaw muscles are now just one-eighth the size of their chimp counterparts, thanks to a mutation in the genes encoding for the myosin protein that provides muscle-fiber bulk. It's the same condition that expresses itself in bodily muscles as Inclusion Body Myopathy-3 (IBM3), a wasting disease, and means our jaws generate just a fraction of the bite force that chimp jaws do. But this loss of function may, paradoxically, have been indispensable to the enlargement of our brains. It may have reduced the need for a thick, low braincase with a heavy, bony crest—such as chimps have, to which their powerful jaw muscles attach—thereby freeing the skull up for the first round of hominin brain expansion, which in fact took place shortly after this jaw weakening mutation appeared around 2.4 million years ago. It's possible our loss of general body strength carried similar benefits, such as trading off strength in our muscles for fine motor control—useful for such things as making tools and throwing stones and spears.[11]

It's hard to see, though, what benefits came with our next trophy in the masculine Hall of Shame, for, as it turns out, we're not only weaker than just about any male human who ever walked the earth, we're also *slower*.

The evidence this time is written into the earth itself. In 2003 archaeologists from Bond University discovered a series of human footprint trackways preserved in a fossilized claypan lake bed in the Willandra Lakes region of New South Wales, Australia. The twenty-three trackways date back twenty thousand years and feature almost seven hundred individual footprints. The most interesting are those of six adult men, probably hunters, who seem to have been running to outflank a prey animal. An analysis of the men's speed (calculated from their stride length) shows that all were running fast, but that the outside individual, the 6'5" "T8," was achieving incredible speeds. The record of his athleticism, written into the dried hardpan of an Ice Age Australian lake bed, raises serious doubts that any modern sprinter can honorably claim the title "Fastest Man on Earth."

Take Usain Bolt, currently the world's fastest man. Bolt set the 100-meter world record of 9.69 seconds at the Beijing Olympics in 2008. His top speed, measured at peak acceleration near the 60- to 70-meter mark, is approximately 27 miles per hour. He achieved it by running at maximum effort on a prepared track with the aid of spiked shoes and strict training backed by decades of scientific research into how to crank the maximum speed from the human body. He is also an elite competitor selected from a pool of many millions of men alive today, and has the lure of glory and a lucrative career to drive him.

T8, on the other hand, was sprinting barefoot through a shallow, soft, muddy lake edge, with nothing but a possible meal of kangaroo or waterbird to spur him on, and he still managed to clock 23 miles per hour. Since the energy cost of running through mud or sand is 1 to 2 times that of running on a solid surface (let alone a rubberized track) this implies T8's real speed was around 27.6 mph. Given that this may not have been his top speed (his lengthening strides show he was accelerating) and that he was just one of possibly 150,000 Aboriginal men alive at that time (and probably not even the fastest), it seems likely there were many prehistoric Australian males who could, if they trained, have regularly clocked 28 miles per hour and taken out every Olympic sprint in which they competed.

How was T8 able to run so fast? Australian Aboriginal men and women have many enviable sporting achievements today, but nothing to equal this. It is tempting, given how far back in the distant past T8 and his comrades lived, to put it down to genetics, like the superior strength of the Neandertals. But T8 was essentially the same feeble species of man as today's *Homo sapiens*. Besides, he was not the only incredibly high ancient achiever. Fast forward seventeen thousand five hundred years, and slip across to the Mediterranean, and you'll find another group of super-athletic males whose achievements confound science to this day—ancient Greek trireme rowers.

Greek triremes were 132-foot wooden warships driven by the oars of 170 rowers arranged vertically on three decks. Thucydides, the famous Greek historian, records that in 427 BCE the Athenian Assembly hot-headedly ordered that the men of Mytilene, a colony 211 miles away on the Aegean island of Lesbos, should be put to death, and dispatched a trireme with the command. The next day they repented, sending another trireme to rescind it. The first trireme had a whole day-and-a-half start, but Thucydides records that, by rowing for 24 hours straight, the second ship caught up with the first and canceled the murderous order. Even allowing for exaggeration on Thucydides' part, this puts the second trireme's sustained speed in excess of 7.5 miles per hour, or almost 7 knots. This is an impressive pace, but one that was, according to other Greek writers, commonly maintained by even mediocre trireme crews. Such statements have caused many a modern historian to wonder— could today's oarsmen achieve such speeds? Thanks to a British exercise physiologist, the Greek navy, and a dash of Olympic nostalgia, we now know the answer.

They can't.

As part of the opening ceremony for the 2004 Athens Olympics, the Olympic flame was towed into the Athenian port of Piraeus by a trireme named *Olympias,* which was reconstructed by the Greek navy in 1987 from pictures of triremes on ancient lamps and paintings. Harry Rossiter, an exercise physiologist from Leeds University and a racing oarsman himself, took the opportunity to test the endurance of trained modern rowers in a real-life trireme. The results were dismal. Rossiter reported that the modern rowers could, after several months of training, get *Olympias* up to nine knots for a brief spurt; but they couldn't maintain that speed, or even just seven knots, for any sustained period. Rossiter measured the rowers' metabolic rates and discovered the reason: the modern crew just wasn't physically capable of the sustained aerobic effort required.

"The Athenian oarsmen's endurance was extraordinary," said Rossiter's coresearcher, historian Boris Rankov. "In that respect, compared to anybody you could find today they were super athletes."[12]

What makes the ancient Greek rowers' achievements even more remarkable is that they were small men. Champion rowers today average 6'3", giving them a reach advantage with the oars, but ancient Athenian males averaged a mere 5'6". Remarkable, too, is the fact that Athens seemed to have so many of these superb athletes, at one stage fielding a thirty-four-thousand-strong army of rowers for the city's two-hundred-trireme fleet. The rowers were apparently paid and fed well, but their diet was nothing special, consisting of simple barley meal kneaded with olive oil and wine. So why then are modern rowers so weak by comparison?

Part of the answer seems to lie in training. Elite rowers training for the Olympics today row about one hundred miles a week, which corresponds to between twelve and fourteen hours at the oars. But Thucydides makes it clear that trireme rowers often went on training voyages that lasted for days. Races were also held to keep them at peak fitness. (The Romans, who also used oared triremes, even made their crews practice rowing on land, according to the Greek historian Polybius.) This can't be the whole story, however. Modern studies have found that increasing aerobic endurance training generally only raises performance in already-trained athletes by around 4 percent. Was the secret behind the incredible aerobic capacity of the trireme rowers, then, also genetic? Again, this is an appealing explanation, but one difficult to believe given that just three thousand years separates the heroic Athenians from their sluggish modern counterparts. Evolutionary change, via natural selection, generally works on much longer timescales than that. The answer probably lies more in our modern-day bone idleness. To find it we need to actually look at those bones, for it is there that the full story of our feeble sloth is written.

Studies comparing our bones to those of fossil humans reveal that we have lost about 40 percent of our bone mass and strength over the past 2 million years. This, too, could be chalked up to genetic causes, except for one telltale sign: the articular heads of our bones (the bulbous ends that form joints such as the knee, hip, and elbow), whose growth definitely *is* genetically controlled, are still almost exactly the same size as those of *Homo erectus,* who lived from approximately 2,000,000 BCE to 1,000,000 BCE. Our loss of bone mass has mostly been from the shafts of our long bones— the femur, humerus, tibia, fibula, radius, and ulna—the components known to be those most responsive to Wolff's law. The cause is the declining levels of muscular load placed on them over the past 2 million years. Proof of this can be seen in modern athletes' bones, which grow thicker in response to repeated muscular stress.

Some modern tennis players, for example, display a cortical thickness in their upper-arm bones almost equal to that of *Homo erectus*.[13]

This then is the *real* secret of the Ice Age Australian runners and the Athenian trireme rowers: their incredible athleticism was not genetic, but *ontogenetic*. Ontogeny is the process by which an organism grows by interaction with its environment. While genes might fix the limits of its potential development, whether or not it reaches them is governed by the environmental stresses placed upon it. Effectively, therefore, those historic and prehistoric men were superb athletes because of the working toughness they had developed over harsh and demanding lives. Not only was the Athenian trireme rowers' training drastically tougher than that of modern oarsmen, their work as shepherds and farmers formed a grueling, lifelong program of bone, muscle, and tendon toughening. Ice Age Australian runners, similarly, probably trekked and ran substantial distances daily. (Studies of a comparable hunting population, the Kalahari Desert Kung, have found that male Kung hunters run an average of 18.6 miles on every antelope hunt.) Importantly, both groups probably also began this constant exercise from a very early age, a crucial help in developing bodily toughness. Those scientific studies documenting bone thickening in modern tennis players, for example, found that the greatest expansion took place between the ages of eight and fourteen.

Examples of how much working toughness historical men had compared to *Homo masculinus modernus* are available even closer to home. Laborers in the rip-roaring early days of the Industrial Revolution, for example, often performed feats unthinkable today. One *New Scientist* correspondent reported that bridge builders in the mid-nineteenth century toiled all day with forty-pound sledgehammers;

today's hammers weigh fourteen pounds. English railway navvies in the 1850s were expected to shovel, by hand, twenty tons of earth daily. In the Sheffield steel mills men chained themselves in gangs of forty to drag glowing iron plates weighing twenty-five to thirty-five tons from the furnace to the "Demon Hammers" for stamping, draping themselves in wet sacking to survive the hellish heat. Remarkably, these super-strong working men were also much smaller—at an average 5'6" around four inches shorter—than their weakling modern counterparts, who, as we have seen, now average 5'10" in height.

Again, an early start to a tough working life seems to have made the difference. Young boys employed as runners in British glassworks apparently ran between 13 and 17 miles a day, ferrying blown bottles to drying rooms. Lads with the unenviable job of "pusher-out" in a brickworks (dragging cartloads of bricks from the moulder's table to the kiln) were thought to shift between 12 and 25 tons a day. While such abuses, thankfully, went the way of witch burnings after the Earl of Shaftesbury's report showed a revolted British public that naked five-year-olds were pulling carts like beasts in deep and deadly coal mines, it is worth noting that such grueling work isn't always as crippling as we assume. Porters in the Nepalese mountains—another group of small men at an average 4'11" and 110 pounds—routinely transport punishing loads of 200 pounds (almost twice their body weight) up to 60 miles, on foot, along steep mountain trails. They, too, start at an early age (usually twelve) but seem able to keep working well into their seventies without noticeable degeneration in either spine or joints. Chinese cycle hauliers, similarly, crisscross Beijing daily with loads in excess of 1,100 pounds, and seem able to keep it up without ill effect into late middle age.

Perhaps the most striking examples of working toughness in action are the careers of the old-time strongmen. The circus and sideshow performers of the strongman golden age (mid-nineteenth to early twentieth century) are often ridiculed as leopard-skinned lard tubs with a nice line in facial hair and fakery, and little else besides. Their failure to reach the impressive records of modern weightlifters, such as the 580-pound clean-and-jerk of Iranian super-heavyweight Hossein Rezazadeh at the 2004 Olympics, is held to be evidence of their lack of real super strength. Yet this does these remarkable characters an injustice. In fact, much of the increase in weights lifted today is due simply to improved technique and standardization of events. Old-time strongmen dabbled in a crazy variety of feats beyond the two basic lifts of Olympic weightlifting—neck lifting, back lifting, chain breaking, card tearing, and coin and horseshoe breaking, to mention a few. Actually, the real evidence shows that some of the historical strongmen were just that: very strong indeed.

Louis Uni, for example, who used the stage name Apollon in his late-nineteenth century Parisian performances, was a 6'3" giant weighing a muscular 260 pounds. He was so strong that the pranks other performers played on him—secretly swapping his weights for supposedly unliftable amounts—often backfired when Apollon failed to notice the change. At an 1892 show at the Varieties Theatre in Lille, for example, a friend switched Apollon's 220-pound barbell for a 385-pound version (almost 70 percent of the modern-day clean-and-jerk record): the strongman not only lifted it, he held it up in one hand (while standing on one leg), then tossed it up and caught it in the crook of his elbows. Apollon also used to lift a set of solid train wheels, which have been raised by just three weightlifters in the 80 years since his death. There is now an official event called "Apollon's Wheels" on the American strongman competition circuit, in which competitors attempt to lift a replica.

Importantly, many nineteenth-century strongmen worked in tough, physical occupations before they became professional performers. John Marx, "The Luxembourg Hercules," famous for his 3,968-pound harness lift, in which weights were lifted by straps from the shoulders, worked as a blacksmith from an early age, and hefted full beer kegs throughout his teen years as a brewer's assistant. Martin "Farmer" Burns, a light-heavyweight (187 pounds) wrestler who lost only seven of his 6,000 wrestling matches in the late-nineteenth century, and who often hung himself from a seven-foot drop to demonstrate his tremendous neck strength, passed his grueling childhood in Midwestern lumber camps. The upbringing of all three men clearly formed an ontogenetic finishing school for their later phenomenal feats of strength.

A one-armed Tarzan

Those ferocious lions that Johnny Weissmuller wrestled in numerous *Tarzan* films were, luckily for him, all stuffed—not even the strongest Hollywood stuntman could have handled a real *Panthera leo*. Yet there is at least one genuine account of a man taking on, not a lion, but a leopard, hand-to-paw. This was the incredible fight between Belgian anthropologist Jean Pierre Hallet and a full-grown male leopard—a battle from which Hallet emerged victorious.

Hallet, at 6'6" tall and 254 pounds, was a giant of a man, yet he was also hampered by having just one arm (he'd lost the other while dynamiting for fish to feed starving African Pygmies). This proved no obstacle, however, when a leopard attacked his team of porters on an expedition in 1957. The gargantuan anthropologist simply jumped on the attacking cat's back and locked its limbs with his own arm and legs. What followed was an epic 20-minute struggle as Hallet fought to stop the furious beast disemboweling him, and to simultaneously strangle it with his one arm. Even Hallet, however, wasn't quite strong enough for that, so it wasn't until a terrified porter threw a knife near him that Hallet was able to prevail. Even then it was another 10 minutes of violent fighting before the Belgian Tarzan could roll the leopard over to the knife, release its neck and front legs, and grab the knife to deliver the death blow.

Which is not to say, however, that there wasn't room for an occasional, genuine, genetic *freak* among their number. One such prodigy, apparently, was Thomas Topham, the famous strongman who thrilled London audiences with his performances in the early eighteenth century. Topham stood a mere 5'9" tall, and weighed just 195 pounds, but his strength far outstripped that of much heavier men. He once, for example, lifted an obese (385 pound) English vicar overhead using just one arm; two-handed he was reportedly capable of hoisting a horse over a farmyard fence. On another occasion he bent, and unbent, an iron bar three inches in diameter (the unbending being the most difficult, since the muscles used are weaker). He also frequently broke ropes of 2,200-pound capacity and could smash a tobacco pipe by holding it lightly in the joint of his bent knee and simply flexing his tendons. Topham had been a carpenter in his youth, but it seems his incredible strength was not, this time, solely a matter of working toughness. As the pipe-breaking feat shows, Topham's rock-hard muscles and tendons bulged to an unusual degree, meaning there was something different, probably genetically, about them. One observer confirmed this, stating that Topham, when stripped, appeared to be "extremely muscular" with armpits and hamstrings "full of muscles and tendons." It could be that Topham's muscles simply had a much greater cross-sectional area than average. Or it could even be that his genome carried some reverse mutation making his musculature closer to that of chimps and our common ancestor. Sadly, we'll never know.

Topham's case does raise an interesting question, though: what is the genetic future of male muscularity? We humans often think evolution and natural selection only happen to animals, or possibly to earlier versions of ourselves, yet a recent scientific analysis drawn from the international HapMap project (a study of human genetic variation, or haplotypes) found that the pace of genetic change in *Homo sapiens* has actually accelerated since the development of agriculture.[14] Might muscularity be in for radical changes, too? Now that *Homo masculinus modernus* has achieved the couch-sitting, labor-shirking nirvana he has always lusted after and the selective pressure for muscularity has eased, might muscularity not eventually wither, like the residual eye-spots of cave-fish or the vestigial leg bones of whales?

Two conditions would be necessary for such an outcome. First, muscularity would have to be at least partly heritable. Second, there would need to be some selective mechanism by which a tendency toward muscularity could be either retained, or eliminated, from the gene pool. As it turns out, some aspects of muscularity (such as biceps circumference and jumping ability) do seem to be as much as 80 percent heritable—so, too, is the ability to add muscle through training. And, as it also happens, there *are* two selective agents operating on the level of muscularity in male humans: sex and death.

The first of these, sexual selection, is the dirty little secret of our craze for male muscle. Many authors seem puzzled by our muscle obsession, putting it down to the influence of either ancient Greek art (in fact, the nineteenth-century father of bodybuilding, Prussian strongman Eugen Sandow, often *did* mimic muscular Greek statues in his public performances, coating himself with white powder for a marble effect) or, as Susan Faludi did in her book *Stiffed*, to an overcompensation for the loss of masculine relevance in physical work. There is a simpler explanation, however: instinct. The giveaway is that it is not just Western men and boys who obsess about muscularity—all males do. One study of Fijian boys, for example, found that nearly all aspired to a big, muscular build.[15] Another found that even male Ariaal nomads of Kenya wanted more fat-free muscle, even though their real problem (given their chronic malnutrition) is a lack of fat.[16] The preference also shows at a remarkably early age. A 1967 study of English schoolboys aged six to ten, for instance, found that by the age of eight over 80 percent wanted to grow up muscular, describing such ideal men as "strong," "brave," "friendly," "smart," "neat," "honest," and even "good-looking."

There is a very good reason for all this instinctual craving for bigger muscles—women, which brings us back to sex. Those university-age men who reported a desire for 24 to 26 pounds more muscle said it was because women find muscularity attractive. This is true, but only partly. Other studies do show that many women find muscular men more sexually attractive than their scrawny counterparts, but only for certain sorts of sexual encounters. A survey of 286 Californian university women, for example, showed they preferred less-muscular men for long-term relationships, but more-muscular men for short-term ones.[17] This was because they found muscular men more dominant and attractive, but also assumed they were therefore less trustworthy. Most of the women reported that their last short-term partner had been more muscular than their last long-term one. The women also slept with the short-term, muscular men much more quickly—within an average of 1 week, as opposed to 12 weeks for the less-muscular, long-term partners. These results seem to back up two of the report's other findings, which otherwise might have been dismissed as mere macho boasting: that muscular men reported more sexual partners overall, as well as more encounters with women who were already mated.

Why should male muscularity be so sexy? It's not just because it signifies physical strength in the hunt and war, though that principle does operate. Big male muscles are also what is called an "honest" sexual signal, similar to the male peacock's tail—an unfakeable indicator of how good the male's genes are because they show he can afford their cost. Big muscles are expensive not just because of their energy cost, but also because the testosterone that builds them suppresses the immune system. This means that the disease-fighting system of any healthy, muscular male must be exceptionally strong, simply to remain functional in spite of such high testosterone.

Thus, it makes perfect sense, from a mating-strategy point of view, for women to prefer muscular men for short-term liaisons, simply to access those genes. But therein lies the modern rub: thanks to contraception, those liaisons no longer have as many reproductive consequences. Sure, women's instincts may still drive them to steal away for illicit pleasures with the occasional passing beefcake, but they save their reproductive potential for their tamer, less attractive but thoroughly-better-with-the-kids partner waiting patiently at home.

Sexual selection by modern women really might, therefore, be acting to remove male muscularity from the human gene pool. But what then of the second selective agent, death?

In this case the muscularity genotype may be in trouble from an unlikelier source—its owners. Muscular men are frequently more aggressive than less-muscular men. Interestingly, this is *not* because of their high testosterone levels; in fact attempts to link testosterone directly to aggression have largely failed. In pre-agricultural societies, where survival depended on individual strength, this aggression tended to spread genes for muscularity, since their aggression both won them female partners and eliminated male sexual rivals. One study of the hyperaggressive medieval Viking berserkers, for example (see BATTLE chapter), found that these violent warriors left more children and grandchildren than their less aggressive compatriots.[18] Now, however, in urbanized societies governed by the rule of law, that aggression has turned back on its owners. Highly aggressive men are significantly more likely to die through violence in their youth, thereby removing themselves from the gene pool. They are similarly likely to be imprisoned while young, and to then commit further crimes incurring even longer sentences—again tying up their prime reproductive years. In the United States they even possibly (thanks to the end of the leveling effect of the draft in 1973) enlist for military service in greater numbers, making them statistically more likely to die through war.

Locked up in prisons, dying on foreign battlefields, or on urban back lots in gang turf fights, the genetic muscular legacy of *Homo masculinus modernus* might well be slowly disappearing. It will be up to those of us left behind—the weak who've inherited the earth—to face the indignities of our coming decline bravely.

Are we up to the job?

At first glance the answer appears to be yes. If medal counts are anything to go by, modern men are actually getting braver and braver. The number of medals awarded to U.S. soldiers, for example, has generally doubled or even tripled in every war this century, up until the first Gulf War. Medal counts, though, are not much help in comparing modern to ancient male bravery. (True, tribal males did have some, like the "counting coup" decorations of the Great Plains tribes in North America. We don't, however, have precise enough data to fairly compare Cheyenne wearers of the coyote tail or eagle's feather with modern Victoria Cross and Congressional Medal of Honor recipients.) We must look beyond the horrors of war, therefore, to the unbelievable horrors that some prehistoric men faced just in their everyday lives, to properly gauge their bravery. Try not to squirm, then, as we take a bloodcurdling tour through Australian Aboriginal penis mutilation; Kayapo Indian "man vs. wasp" fights; platform torture among native North Americans; and the finer points of Stone Age "trepanation" (open-skull surgery performed without anesthetic and while conscious).

I don't know about you but I'm getting the heebie-jeebies just thinking about it.

Bravado

One clear, sunny morning in 2005, rail commuters in Hanau, a small town near Frankfurt, witnessed an amazing spectacle. As their InterCity Express (ICE) bullet train left the station, a black-clad, bandannaed figure leaped ninja-style onto its rear windscreen and attached a vacuum-grip handhold. For the next 20 minutes the man, a twenty-something train surfer known as "the Trainrider," held on for grim, buffeting death as the ICE cranked up to its cruising speed of 155 miles per hour. Convinced he'd be killed, passengers shot hurried emergency calls through to the Federal Border Guards, who arrived just as the ICE reached its last stop. Incredibly, however, the Trainrider was uninjured—he even escaped a possible 10-year prison sentence by the simple precaution of having bought a valid ticket.

The Trainrider was lucky; an investigation by Humboldt University's Institute of Legal Medicine reported that in the six years between 1989 and 1995, forty adolescent males were seriously injured, eighteen fatally, while train "surfing" on Berlin's S-Bahn and Underground lines.[1] Surfing trains has become a worldwide phenomenon among daredevil young men, but techniques seem to vary: in Europe and the United Kingdom the aim is to mount the roof and ride freestanding without falling off; while South African thrill seekers sling themselves under slower-moving trains and perform the "gravel" maneuver—paddling their legs through the gravel fast enough to prevent them being torn off. The thing they share is an extreme disregard for danger. The Humboldt University report found that falling off, though gruesome enough and usually fatal, was not even the major cause of death for train surfers; most died from massive trauma after high-speed collisions with power poles, signal masts, and even other trains.

What makes young men so needlessly risk their lives? The Humboldt authors dismissed the simple urge to show off, instead wheeling out familiar suspects such as alienation, the search for recognition, and lack of facilities and positive role models, among others. Yet, curiously, they failed to note that most of these in fact *confirm* the thesis that young males universally experience strong instinctual urges toward reckless displays of courage. Why, for example, would anyone search for recognition through such foolhardy acts unless others found them impressive? In fact, what young male daredevils like the Trainrider demonstrate is what an evolutionary psychologist might call "conspicuous bravery"—bravery specifically aimed at communicating one's evolutionary fitness and courage to one's peers. Another word for it is the much maligned term *bravado*.

getting your
kicks, sioux style

Adolescence is a time for young males to show their courage. Portuguese teens go on rampages through their neighborhood backyards, while American boys indulge in extreme sports such as wave jumping, snowboarding, and "vert" skating. None of these, however, is anywhere near as extreme as the games nineteenth-century Sioux boys played. Brule Sioux chief Iron Shell, for example, described for one chronicler his tribe's "swing-kicking game," in which:

> ... two rows of boys faced each other, each holding a robe over his left arm ... after the ... stock question, "Shall we grab them by the hair and knee them in the face until they bleed?" ... using their robes as a shield, they all kicked at their opponents ... [who] once down ... [were] grabbed at the temples with both hands and kneed in the face ... until [they] could fight no longer.

Even supposedly gentler Sioux games took considerable nerve to play. In the "buffalo-hunt" game, one boy was required to hold up a cactus leaf, representing a buffalo's heart, while the others shot

At first sight, bravado presents a puzzle to an evolutionary anthropologist. Recklessly putting yourself at risk of injury or death, for no reason, hardly satisfies the cardinal rule of natural selection: that an organism's attributes and behaviors should tend to propagate its genes. It seems, in other words, to be maladaptive. Rational bravery, on the other hand—where individuals expose themselves to danger in pursuit of a goal—suffers no such ambiguity. Be the goal either hunting a dangerous animal for food, or swimming a crocodile-infested river to mate with an attractive female, the effect is the same: the courageous act brings reproductive rewards that outweigh its risk. Even apparently unrewarding acts of bravery can still be rational, particularly if they display altruism. Brave behavior performed for another's benefit can, just like the big muscles mentioned in the previous chapter, function as an honest and unfakeable sexual signal to a potential mate—look how capable and fearless I am, and how willing to use that strength to help others! A recent University of Maine study into the mating preferences of American university women confirmed that altruistic, or heroic, bravery is seriously sexy: roughly three-quarters of the women expressed strong preferences for heroic risk-takers as boyfriends.[3] Bravado, however, was right out—almost as many women stated they wouldn't even date, let alone marry, a man who indulged in risks that weren't altruistic.

To add to the mystery, young men don't seem to have the foggiest notion that their bravado so signally fails to impress women. Another phase of that same University of Maine study, this time aimed at university men, revealed that they grossly overestimated how attractive their non-heroic risk-taking was to females (though they accurately predicted how attractive their heroic risk-taking was). Similarly ignorant was Lebohang Motsamai, a famed South African train surfer who told the BBC that he performs the "gravul" and other tricks because "when I do this they [the girls] are going to love me. They are going to say, eish, this boy is clever."[4]

Why *do* young males maintain this mistaken belief in the sexual appeal of their reckless displays? A subsidiary survey in the University of Maine study gives a clue. That survey found that although swaggering bravado was unattractive to women in either a mate or a same-sex friend, it was highly desirable in a same-sex friend for males. This suggests that the real target of male bravado is other men. By advertising their willingness to take risks when nothing is at stake, men are simultaneously underscoring their worth as a formidable coalition partner for other males when something *is*. This is important because male-male bonds (the "band of brothers" phenomenon) are a central organizing principle of most human societies that have been studied ethnographically.[5] Indeed, from the evidence of chimps and bonobos, it seems to have been inbuilt since at least the time of our last common ancestor, around 4.5 million years ago.[6]

A final piece is still missing from the puzzle, however. Male bravado might well be aimed at other males, but the logic of natural selection still demands it have some positive reproductive consequence in order to persist. Is there any evidence it does? In fact, there is. Frans de Waal's primatological survey at Burgers' Zoo in

Holland recorded some intriguing details about the reproductive effects of male-male coalitions in chimpanzees.[7] De Waal noted that Yeroen, an older chimp who had been overthrown as alpha male by younger rivals, still managed to get the lion's share of mating opportunities by judiciously forming coalitions that pitted his rivals against each other. Even when these arrangements collapsed and Yeroen became subservient to a single dominant male, Nikkie, he still received a share of mating opportunities as the price of his support. This seems to tally with anecdotal evidence that modern human males who associate with attractive, high-prestige men greatly increase their own reproductive opportunities—as in the case of those roadies described by *SPIN* magazine who scored sex from "ramp-rat" groupies by hanging around with rock stars.[8] Swaggering young men like Lebohang aren't, it seems, so deluded after all. Their braggadocio *does* get them girls, just not in the way they think. (This, incidentally, neatly illustrates the distinction between *proximate* and *ultimate* causes in evolutionary theory: the proximate cause of young men's bravado, besides instinct, is their mistaken belief that it appeals to women; but the real, ultimate, cause is probably its role in establishing male-male coalitions.)

If we modern men are, then, dancing to an ancient tune in our love of braggadocio, the question remains: how well are we dancing? How brave *are* we? We obviously think enormously so: both in heroic bravery, if the upsurge in post-9/11 films extolling patriotic bravery is any guide,[9] and in non-heroic bravado, if the rash of reported adolescent copycat fatalities following TV shows like *Jackass* is to be believed.[10] But how, I wondered, would we fare in the harrowing ordeals of courage and masculinity that ancient male members of our species had to undergo: the initiation rituals, tortures, terrifying medical treatments, and dangerous wild-animal hunts? Luckily, each has a modern equivalent, so the answer seemed to lie in a simple comparison.

Initiation rituals, for example, are still a feature of male in-groups such as military units, school cohorts, and criminal gangs. In 1997 a furor erupted in the United States when film footage surfaced showing Marines being stabbed with badges as part of a graduation hazing ritual at the Corps' training school for airborne warfare. The graduates writhed in pain, shirts bloodied, as instructors jabbed their golden graduation wings (backed by two half-inch spikes) repeatedly into their chests. This, it turned out, was a traditional Marine induction ritual called "Blood Pinning" (also known as "Blood Wings" in the Army airborne training school), which reportedly dates back to World War II. The then Secretary of Defense, William Cohen, called the practice "disgusting" and demanded the Corps eliminate it, but history was apparently against him—hazing seems to have long been, and to be still, an inevitable feature of male (and sometimes female) in-groups. A similar scandal, for example, shook the U.S. Naval Academy as long ago as 1905.[11] The modern Russian army, similarly, has several brutal equivalents as part of its *Dedovshchina* ("rule of the grandfathers"), system, including the "dried crocodile," during which conscripts are forced to hang upside down from a top bunk while the *Deds*, or "grandfather" soldiers, beat them savagely. One medical study, as well, reported that over two hundred and sixty thousand American university athletes surveyed had suffered from hazing incidents, and that for sixty-five thousand of them the hazing had included violent and illegal activities such as beating or kidnapping.[12] Far from being isolated incidents, brutal initiations are, it seems, part and parcel of the universal male experience.

Nor are they the regrettable invention of bored modern grunts and students. Acts of bastardry such as Blood Pinning are simply imitations (and generally pale ones) of rituals that are tens, and possibly hundreds, of thousands of years old. Romanian religious philosopher Mircea Eliade described the heart of these ancient rituals as "the ordeal"—a brutal experience that the uninitiated underwent to qualify for graduation into the group. The purpose of the ordeal seems to have been threefold. First, it provided a test of the would-be member's strength and courage. Second, the violence of the initiation rituals seems to have symbolized the death of the uninitiated male's earlier self, and his rebirth into the world of the group's men. Third, the cruel abuse seems, paradoxically, to have strengthened in-group bonds by heightening the uninitiated male's need to belong to the group. The ordeals themselves always featured one or more of the following elements: extreme pain, bodily mutilation, or the performance of extraordinary physical feats. How, then, do our modern initiation rituals compare on these three scores?

Blood Pinning, for example, is clearly painful, but probably mild compared to the rituals of urban American gangs, to which entry is often gained by being "jumped in"—beaten by existing members in a mass attack. (Gang researcher Mike Carlie Ph.D. described a ritual called "Freein' Hoover," in which would-be members had to pick six pennies off the ground while suffering multiple bashings by initiated gang bangers.) Even these, however, are a shadow of the torments endured by ancestral *Homo sapiens* males during initiation. One of the most painful was (and is) the initiation ritual of the indigenous Maués people of Brazil. Young Maués males don a palm-fiber mitt into which hundreds of stinging bullet ants—so-called because their sting hurts worse than being shot—have been woven, stingers facing inward. Bullet ants have the most painful venom of any insect alive, yet the fourteen-year-old Maués boys must wear the glove for ten full minutes, resulting in blinding pain, paralysis, and days of uncontrollable shaking.[13] Luiseño boys of prehistoric California possibly had it even worse, being made to wallow in a pit filled with stinging ants during the *heminuwe* puberty ceremony, and whipped afterward with stinging nettles.[14] An even more astonishing use of dangerous insects was in the "wasp fights" of the Brazilian Kayapo, in which adult Kayapo males ascended ladders to assault—with their bare hands—huge nests of highly aggressive wasps until the enraged hornets stung them into semiconsciousness. An adult Kayapo man might engage in a dozen of these fights throughout his life. Hornets were also used (and probably still are) in the initiation ceremonies of the Keyo, a Kalenjin-speaking people of Kenya. Here, though, the real pain was inflicted with plants: during the hornet ordeal young Keyo men were also forced to crawl through tunnels woven from stinging nettles, and to have the same plant rubbed into their genitals.[15] Even more sadistic ritual use of plants was (and still is) recorded among the Sambian men of New Guinea: not only do uninitiated boys there have stiletto-sharp blades of *pitpit* cane thrust repeatedly up their nostrils to cause profuse bleeding, they also have three-feet-long loops of vine forced down their throat to induce vomiting, then their glans penis slit with bamboo blades.[16]

This genital surgery leads us neatly into the second element of Eliade's ordeal—mutilation. The main function of bodily mutilation appears to be not just extreme pain, but also permanent advertisement of the initiate's endurance and membership in the initiated group. One of many modern examples is the hot-iron branding used by some African American college fraternity males to advertise their solidarity.[17] A more extreme one is the severing of finger segments, used as both a punishment and initiation ritual, among the Japanese *boryokudan*, known to Westerners as the *yakuza*.

Another ritual of the *boryokudan,* incidentally, confirms a curious fact, alluded to by the Sambian initiations: that male mutilatory rituals frequently center on the penis. Twenty percent of incarcerated Japanese *boryokudan* examined in a survey by the Kumamoto University Department of Legal Medicine, for example, were found to carry a peculiar genital modification: penile balls. This mutilatory ritual, called pearling, sounds excruciating—the subject, or a fellow prisoner, penetrates the foreskin with a sharpened toothpick or paperclip, gouges out a tunnel, then pushes a "pearl" of glass or melted plastic deep into the wound, leaving it there to heal in situ. Yet even this gruesome procedure is a cakewalk compared to the savage penile modifications endured by men in prehistoric times.

Modern circumcision, for example, is often denounced as a barbaric and primitive practice, even generating its own protest group: the International Organisation Against Circumcision Trauma (INTACT). Modern medical circumcisions of adult males, however, are performed under anaesthetic—usually a dorsal penile nerve block—in a ten-minute, low-invasive surgical procedure. Tribal circumcisions, however, often were, and are, excruciatingly long operations performed with no pain relief—this was, in fact, their point. The Keyo circumcision ritual, for example, was not only the culmination of the abusive ceremonies already described, it also required the initiates to stand stock-still while *boiyot-ab-tuum* (the "old-man-of-the-rite") skinned their penis from halfway down its shaft using the *kibos* ("bald-headed knife"), then sliced off any remaining skin and connective tissue with a razor blade;[18] finally, the remnant penile skin was yanked forward, a transverse cut made, and the bloodied shaft forced through to make it sit up permanently in semi-erect mode. Incredibly, very few young Keyo males failed this ordeal, though apparently death from blood loss and gangrene were common. Even Keyo circumcision, however, pales beside the sub-incision rite practiced by Australian Aboriginal men throughout the continent's desert regions. In this rite, still practiced, the underside of the young man's penis is slit deeply from tip to scrotum (depending on how much pain the initiate can bear) using either an extremely sharp, traditional quartz knife or (these days) a razor blade. The penis then heals open, urethra exposed, leaving it looking something like a pitcher plant flower. How clearly this is a means of permanently advertising status can be seen in the custom of some South Australian tribal men who, on meeting the men of a strange tribe, would press their penises into the palm of each stranger to demonstrate their initiated status.[19]

■A medal, or a chest to pin it on?

The large number of military medals handed out these days seems to give comfort that modern male bravery is alive and well. Only, however, if we assume one not-quite-indisputable fact: that every soldier who gets a medal deserves it.

Some critics point out that, in the United States at least, military decorations show unmistakeable signs of inflation—the tendency to grow until just about everyone gets one. In some cases this is literally true: every U.S. soldier who fought in the first Gulf War got a medal just for showing up, and more medals were handed out for the invasion of Grenada than troops who actually participated.[20] It is also now the case that every U.S. soldier who completes boot camp gets a medal for doing so. Even the most revered decorations have not proven uninflatable—one U.S. paratrooper in the 1989 invasion of Panama received a Purple Heart for getting heat stroke.

Interestingly, medals awarded for ultra-heroic bravery—like the Victoria Cross and the U.S. Congressional Medal of Honor—have bucked the trend, going down rather than up. The United Kingdom, for example, has awarded just 14 Victoria Crosses since World War II, compared to 1,340 in the 90 years before that. The United States, similarly, has given out just 7 Congressional Medals of Honor (the highest military bravery award) since the Vietnam War, compared to 245 in that conflict. Similarly, 20,000 soldiers in the Vietnam War won Silver Stars (the third-highest award), while just 400 have in the years since.[21] The pattern is so striking that the economists who authored the paper revealing it asked, quite justifiably, "Where have all the heroes gone?"

To be fair, heroism is definitely harder for the modern soldier than his World War II comrade. Charge an IED (Improvised Explosive Device) in Iraq, yelling like a banshee, and chances are you'll wind up dead before onlookers even have a chance to download the Medal of Honor application form. It's also true that military brass have become deliberately miserly with these awards, partly as a reaction against the free-for-all with lesser medals. Yet the paper's authors point out that the main cause is a far less noble one.

> Rising incomes and affluence have vastly increased the "opportunity cost" of dying through heroism. Put simply, modern soldiers have much more to live for than soldiers of their fathers' generation, and so take the rational, sensible, and completely cowardly decision to make sure they stick around to enjoy it. ■

Though also a simple cosmetic option for both men and women these days, tattooing remains another body-altering ordeal often used to assert masculine identity. A survey of American military men with tattoos, for example, showed that they considered theirs to both promote in-group solidarity ("all Marines have tattoos") and advertise the wearer's ability to suffer the ordeal of getting them ("they !@#$% hurt!").[22] Ancient tattooees, however, would have laughed at such pretensions. New Zealand Maori full-face *moko* tattoos, for example, were hammered into the tattooee's skin using bone and stone chisels (which also featured special spatulas to wipe away the copious blood flow) leaving deep, permanent furrows. The process was so painful that several attendants were required to hold the recipient down, and it often left the tattooee so injured that he had to be hand-fed through a funnel for weeks. Traditional Samoan *tataus* were even more brutal, utilizing inking combs of sharpened human bone that were bashed into the skin with a heavy coconut-palm mallet. Since their main purpose was to demonstrate the bravery of their wearers, they often featured plain areas of solid color from navel to knee as part of their intricate designs, leading early explorers to report that Samoan men wore strange, tight silk breeches. Given that these breeches involved weeks of painful pounding and piercing of the anus, scrotum, penis, and perineum, and the very real threat of death through infection, we can readily acknowledge their wearers were extremely brave. Even the *boryokudan*—whose association with traditional *irezumi* tattoos is so marked that many Japanese swimming pools expressly forbid tattooed swimmers so as to keep gangsters out— are wusses in comparison to their painted predecessors. Modern-day *yakuza* get their full-body *irezumi* done in Western-style parlors using high-speed inking machines and Western inks. Traditional *irezumi*, however, were hand-pricked into the *boryokudan* gangster's body with iron needles over a period of years by a *horishi* (tattoo master). The cadmium-based inks used by the *horishi* apparently caused such extreme pain that even the most stoic of early *yakuza* could only bear an inch or two of coloring in one session.

Eliade's third element of initiatory ordeals, the performance of physical feats, is often still part of modern male rituals, too. Mike Carlie describes the "blood-in, blood-out" rule by which prospective American gang members must commit a murder, or other act of violence, to gain entry to the gang (they also, as the name implies, must commit one to get out). This sounds ferocious, yet in the age of firearms such feats are often tame, drive-by affairs posing little risk to the shooter (Carlie reports that even just shooting up an enemy gangbanger's house-front was often acceptable). Some Papuan tribesmen of the New Guinea highlands in the colonial era, by contrast, could not even marry until they had committed their first murder—by hand, with a ceremonial bone dagger—after which they wore a special homicidal insignia that marked them as initiated killers for the rest of their lives.[23] Numerous other tribes and societies historically had even more dangerous initiation tests in which young males had to single-handedly kill savage beasts. Alexander the Great, to quote a famous example, was not allowed a spot on the couch at the Macedonian royal court's regular drinking symposium until he had speared a wild boar (*Sus scrofa,* specimens of which reach 550 pounds and can disembowel a man with their ten-inch tusks) without the help of a net. East African Maasai boys initiated into the *murran* warrior class faced even greater perils. During the *olamayio* ritual (in fact not solely an initiation rite) they often killed, by hand, full-grown lions. Remarkably, these ritual hunts still take place, and still using spears, though the Maasai have presumably had access to guns for decades now.

If modern male initiation rituals are a shadow of the tortures endured by ancestral males, what about *actual* torture? How well would modern men withstand the terrifying, grievous mistreatment that males historically endured, either from tribal enemies or cruel overlords? Most of us seem to believe that the new millennium has ushered in a depraved, brave new world of fiendishly refined torture, along with ever more scientifically advanced methods of resisting it. In 2005–06, for example, a scandal erupted in the United States when it emerged that psychologists from the military's SERE (Survival, Evasion, Resistance, and Escape) program, which trains U.S. soldiers to resist torture in the event of capture, had played a role in the creation of the "enhanced interrogation techniques" used on detainees at the U.S. Naval Base in Guantánamo Bay, Cuba. According to critics, the sleep deprivation, hypothermia-inducing cold, waterboarding, and stress positions constituted a barbaric new development in the sordid history of torture, though an intriguing rock engraving on the walls of the Addaura Cave in Sicily, dated to approximately 10,000 BCE., clearly shows two men who may be captured warriors bound in a classic stress position, with legs and neck tied together to forcibly arch their backs.[24] The SERE-program schools (there are six, distributed between the U.S. Army, Navy, Marines, and Air Force) also boast that graduates of their grueling program of confinement, deprivation, and abuse are better prepared than any other soldiers in history to withstand ill-treatment at the hands of an enemy. Yet, without taking anything away from the suffering of modern POWs, how tough are SERE graduates really?

How, for example, might they fare in comparison to Native American men in pre-contact North America? Native American warriors had a reputation for showing extreme bravery in the face of torture; they had to, since they were also some of the premier torturers of the hunter-gatherer world. (This is sometimes disputed: scalping, for instance, is frequently described as a European import rather than an indigenous Native American practice. A 1980 investigation by William Sturtevant, curator of ethnology at the Smithsonian Institute, however, pointed out that the evidence of a Native American origin of scalping is overwhelming—many pre-contact Native American skulls bear scalping cut marks, and the word itself was not even a verb in English until white settlers saw the practice in America.[25]) Scalping was not simply a painless procedure inflicted solely on dead enemies. Records show that it was also a torture technique. Jesuit missionaries in the Great Lakes area during the seventeenth century reported that villagers there tortured war captives by scalping them and then heaping hot coals onto their scalped heads. But this was just part of several extensive torture "complexes" that anthropologist Nathaniel Knowles described among eastern Native Americans (torture was not as common on the plains and in the west), differentiated by how the victim was secured for abuse—on a frame, a platform, a pole, or a stake.[26] Methods were fiendishly inventive and included: hanging red-hot metal hatchets around the neck; tearing out beards; slitting ears, noses, eyes, and tongues; pulling sinews out of arms; skinning alive; outright burning; burning cords bound around the body; and pin-cushioning with burning pine splinters. Knowles reported that one Seneca chief had been tortured by the Cherokee by having the soles of his feet burned, hard corn pushed into the blisters, and then being forced to run a gauntlet of warriors attempting to club him to death. Other captives had multiple cuts sliced into their bodies and embers pushed inside the wounds, or were slowly dismembered and disemboweled.

Given such bloodcurdling treatment, defeated Native American warriors might have been forgiven for blubbering all the way to their gory ends. The evidence is, however, that they met them defiantly. The European explorer, trader, and historian James Adair, to give one example, described the firebrand torture of an Iroquois man that he witnessed, saying that the man:

> . . . having unconcernedly suffered much sharp torture . . . told them with scorn they did not know how to punish a noted enemy, therefore he was willing to teach them . . . Accordingly he requested of them a pipe and some tobacco, which was given him: as soon as he lighted it, he sat down, naked as he was, on the women's burning torches that were within his circle and continued smoking his pipe without the least discomposure.[27]

Similarly, in cases of Iroquois platform torture, which often lasted for days, missionaries reported that victims were expected to, and did, sing and dance the entire time. These "death songs" might be simple, lyrical farewells to the world the victim was shortly to leave, such as the haunting Choctaw song recorded by the poet Jim Barnes (himself part-Choctaw): "When I pass, this prairie will hold my tracks as long as the wind sleeps."[28] More commonly, however, they combined boastful accounts of the war deeds of the victim himself, scornful assertions of his lack of fear, and threats to his torturing enemies of the vengeance his tribe was shortly to wreak. This last—the intense sense of corporate, tribal identity—is probably the key to the incredible endurance of these tortured Native American warriors. Modern SERE instructors, too, emphasize in-group bonds and a sense of shared ordeal as essential for their graduates to withstand enemy abuse.

Whether those same graduates could endure the attentions of an Iroquois platform torturer is, fortunately, a question rarely asked.

Strong corporate identity also helped another group of victims withstand extreme torture—the Roman Christian martyrs (though here religious consolation probably played an even greater role). These were those early adherents of Jesus who, in the four centuries after his death, faced harsh persecution from the Roman Empire. The empire's torture methods were uniquely brutal. Roman scourging, for example, used bone- and metal-fretted whips like the *horribile flagellum* ("horrible whip"), which tore off so much flesh its victims often died of blood loss. Criminals and unrepentant Christians might also be sentenced to wear the *tunica molesta* ("annoying shirt")—a serious misnomer given the *tunica* was a naphtha-soaked garment that was set aflame once donned. Similarly, most people are aware of *damnatio ad bestias*—the practice of throwing Christians to the beasts—but not of what it actually entailed. In addition to being fed to lions, victims of *damnatio ad bestias* might also be tied to wild boars and gored, staked out in front of an enraged bear, or netted and thrown to a leopard. Women were treated particularly cruelly: as well as being gored by wild bulls they were, according to one writer, also sometimes smeared with the vaginal fluid of cows so as to be raped by them.[29] If written accounts are to be believed, however, the early Christians frequently refused to buckle under such torture. The *Ecclesiastical History* of Eusebius, the scrupulously reliable fourth-century church historian, lists examples such as that of the youth Apphianus, who was racked for twenty-four hours, scourged so hard the bones of his ribs and spine showed, and then had his feet soaked in oil and burned to stumps; he still refused to renounce his faith and was drowned in the sea. Another man, Sanctus, had the book of Roman tortures thrown at him, being subjected to such heavy scourging, racking, *damnatio ad bestias,* and burning from hot brass plates fastened to his body (and particularly, his genitals) that he became "one continued wound, mangled and shrivelled, that had entirely lost the form of a man to the external eye"; he, too, held firm, being finally roasted to death on an iron chair.

◻ʀaging bulls

Screen boxer Rocky Balboa beat all his opponents with his heart, not his muscle, according to his wife, Adrian. But ancient Tahitian boxers needed the hearts of lions just to get in the ring, so deadly was their version of the sport. The reports of missionary and author William Ellis leave no doubt about how brutal the Tahitian ring could be:

> ...no time was spent in sparring or parrying the blows... [which] were generally straightforward, severe, and heavy; usually aimed at the head. They fought with the naked fist, and the whole skin of the forehead has been at times torn or driven off at a blow...

Predictably, the injury and death toll from such savage pugilism was substantial. Ellis recorded that Tahitian boxing champions "were proud to boast of the number of men they had maimed and killed."[30]

Very few modern males, of course, will ever be subjected to waterboarding at Guantánamo Bay, let alone *damnatio ad bestias*. But there is one form of torture almost every modern man undergoes: medical treatments. Several studies confirm that the clinical arena is another prime one for displays of masculine bravado. The 2004 General Household Survey of the United Kingdom's Office of National Statistics, to quote one, reported that English women were twice as likely as men to see a doctor in response to pain.[31] Of those men who did go, most expressed supreme confidence in their own stoicism. Amusingly, another survey—this time by the American

Journal of Pain in 2001—found that the typical man not only considered himself better able to withstand painful medical procedures than the typical woman, but also than the typical man. This bravado frequently leads men to disdain the use of anesthetics when undergoing medical procedures, as when the *International Journal of Men's Health* found that most Australian men undergoing a TRUS-Bx—or trans-rectal ultrasound prostate biopsy (during which needles are punched through the rectal wall to obtain tissue samples)—refused painkillers, even though the pain grew so intense that some almost passed out.[32] This sounds impressive, but how does it compare to the medical treatments ancient men suffered, presumably in silence?

You guessed it: terribly. Next to ancestral male patients, we're about as brave as Scooby-Doo visiting the doggie dentist.

Ancient painkillers, for example, were not only completely ineffective, they were also themselves an ordeal. Woodcarvings from the Necropolis of Saggara, dated to 2500 BCE, show that Egyptian surgery patients had the nerves and arteries near their incision tightly compressed to provide a local-anaesthetic effect. This painful technique provides some relief, but not much: attempts by British surgeon James Moore to revive it through his invention of a femoral-nerve clamp for leg operations in 1784 had to be abandoned when the clamp turned out to cause more pain than the operation.[33] The Assyrians used the same technique as a general anaesthetic, compressing the patient's carotid arteries (in the neck) so as to starve the brain of oxygen, resulting in unconsciousness (the word carotid is Greek for "arteries of sleep"). Though drastic, this was perhaps mild compared to seventeenth-century ships' surgeons in the British Navy who placed their patient's head in a wooden bowl and thumped it mightily with a carpenter's mallet before operating (although this was more to stop the patient's screams than for anesthetic purposes).

Ancient surgeons did, at some times and in some places, have a few painkilling drugs available. Pedanius Dioscorides, a Greek surgeon in Nero's army, for instance, wrote of using mandrake root, which contains the anesthetic atropine, when operating on soldiers' wounds.[34] Roman surgeons also had some knowledge of stinking nightshade (a natural sedative) and opium as anesthetics. Medieval Arab physicians used a sponge infused with cannabis resin, which was placed over the nose so patients would inhale the fumes. The problem with all of these, however, as noted by the famous Greek physician Galen, was one of dosage: too little was ineffective, too much could kill (stinking nightshade, for instance, is also known by its Anglo-Saxon name *henbane*, which means "chicken killer"). The fact that ancient surgical manuals invariably include instructions to bind and forcibly hold the patient down shows that most ancient operations effectively took place without any pain relief whatsoever.

This didn't stop ancient surgeons from undertaking incredibly brutal procedures, though. Roman surgeons, as well as medieval Arab ones, commonly removed cataracts by piercing the patient's cornea with a hollow needle to break up the cataract and suck it out, without pain relief. Both also performed limb amputations and the removal of tumors without effective anesthetic. Amputations were such a terrifying procedure that Roman surgeons commonly gave patients a final chance, on the table, to back out; if they signaled they still wished to proceed they were seized by several assistants, held down, and had their limb forcibly amputated no matter what they then screamed. The *real* essential ingredient in

Roman surgical pain management was, apparently, courage—raw, simple courage on the part of the patient. The legendary Roman consul Marius, to quote one famous example, actually underwent surgery to cut the varicose veins out of one leg without anesthetic and also without the customary restraints and bindings. The Roman historian, Pliny the Elder, wrote that Marius maintained an unflinching silence throughout this grisly operation, but declined the surgeon's offer to devein his other leg, saying he thought the results not quite worth the pain.[35]

If such fortitude amazes us, imagine the astonishment of the early nineteenth-century European archaeologists who began unearthing skulls dating from the Neolithic (10,000–4000 BCE.) that showed definite signs of trepanation: having holes surgically cut into them and bone removed so as to expose the brain—for magical purposes or to cure headaches, epilepsy, and other ailments. Their amazement was not because trepanation was unknown to them—it was a technique that had been abandoned in pre-antiseptic European medicine due to its almost 100 percent mortality rate. What surprised them was that many of the trepanned Neolithic skulls showed signs of bone healing, indicating, incredibly, that their patients had survived. Some, indeed, had multiple trepanation holes in various stages of healing, implying they lived for years after some operations. Survival rates of this primitive skull surgery are hard to calculate, but current estimates range from 50 to 90 percent. This does not mean the procedure was a mild one, however. The evidence of trepanned skulls shows four basic methods: scraping, where the scalp and skull were gradually scraped away with a sharp-edged stone; grooving or sawing, where a circle or square was repeatedly sawn in with a pointed stone or arrowhead; drilling, where a circle of closely spaced holes was drilled with a bone or stone awl; and chiseling, where a square of intersecting incisions was hammered into the bone (in Polynesia this was done with a shark's tooth and wooden mallet).[36] These excruciating operations generally lasted about an hour, though in some tribes, like the Algerian Kabyles, they took almost twenty days. Incredibly, these brutal procedures seem to have been not at all uncommon. Not only have prehistoric trepanned skulls been found in Africa, Australia, ancient China, the Americas, and the Pacific islands, the operation was also apparently performed on many individuals in each group. On the Polynesian island of Uvea, for example, 100 percent of the adult males were trepanned. On other Polynesian islands children are known to have been almost as frequently trepanned, simply as a preventative health tonic. In almost all cases the operation seems to have been done without anesthetic—the exception being prehistoric Peru, where surgeons dribbled a mixture of saliva and chewed coca leaves onto the patient's scalp prior to operating.

In all likelihood, trepanation was not the only surgical operation that prehistoric males endured without pain relief. Archaeological evidence of such surgery is rare (it usually involves soft tissues, which are not preserved), so our knowledge is limited to recent hunter–gatherer societies. Even here, though, it is clear that patients often endured excruciating procedures without anesthetic. Those Polynesian trepanners, for example, also employed their shark-tooth chisels as scalpels in cutting tuberculous glands out of sufferers' necks and castrating scrotums swollen from elephantiasis (a grotesque thickening of the skin caused by parasitic worms). Then there was the sophisticated but brutal surgery endured by Maasai patients. Being an extremely violent warrior culture, the Maasai developed such skill in wound repair that their society came to include a specialized caste of surgeons. Among the procedures performed without painkillers by these skilled medicos were: eyeball removal, bone resections, tendon lengthening, excision of lymph glands, and deep intestinal operations such as hernia correction and removal of abscesses on the liver and spleen. Perhaps less impressive in terms of surgical skill, though more so in patient bravery, were the amputations performed by Australian Aboriginals on their wounded warriors. The Assistant Colonial Surgeon of Western Australia, Reverend H. Wollaston, for instance, described in the late nineteenth century an Aboriginal amputee he met whose leg:

> . . . had been severed just below the knee and charred by fire, while about [two inches] of calcined bone protruded through the flesh . . . On inquiry the native told him that in a tribal fight a spear had struck his leg and penetrated the bone . . . he and his companions made a fire and dug a hole in the earth sufficiently large to admit his leg . . . The limb was then surrounded with live coals or charcoal, and kept replenished until the leg was literally burnt off.[37]

Incredibly, Wollaston also reports that this man was up and walking two days later, and had traveled, with the aid of a stick, some sixty miles to see him. Admittedly, this method of amputation sounds barbaric, but just one hundred years earlier it had also been European practice to cauterize amputated limb stumps in boiling oil. Similarly, the death rate from European lower-limb amputations frequently exceeded 75 percent—a level even such brutal tribal amputations might find hard to match.[38]

But if the ordeals that ancient and tribal men endured at the hands of their fellow men make modern ones look about as tough as a Indian rug burn, what about ordeals involving wild animals?

Hunting has been the traditional avenue for displays of bravado since Stone Age hunters in Turkey circa 7000 BCE depicted themselves slaying aurochs (an ancient species of aggressive wild cattle) six times the size of any that ever lived before or since.[39] Xenophon, the fourth-century BCE Greek soldier-historian, for example, described hunting as an essential test of courage and preparation for the manly art of war. U.S. President Teddy Roosevelt, himself a famed hunter in the Dakota Badlands, agreed, urging American males in his 1902 work *Hunting the Grisly and Other Sketches* to prove their masculinity against the wild beasts of nature. U.S. Census Bureau statistics show they obeyed: by 1980 over 16 million Americans held valid hunting licenses. Among certain subsets of men, such as Michigan autoworkers, hunting numbers were even higher, sometimes reaching 30 percent of all males aged twenty-five to forty-four. These modern American huntsmen commonly list the thrill of danger and the challenge of overcoming a worthy animal adversary among their motivations. Yet how dangerous is modern hunting really?

How often, to put it another way, does the animal *win*?

Not very, is the short answer. If we define winning as escaping, apparently very few animals manage that: The Fund for Animals reports that hunters kill over 100 million animals annually in North America—with doves, squirrels, pheasants, and deer being the most bagged trophies. If we define winning as inflicting injury or death on the hunter, animals come off even worse: injuries to hunters by animals in the United States are apparently so rare that statistics on them aren't directly collected (they have to be extrapolated from general animal-attack statistics). About the only animals capable of seriously injuring hunters are bears, of which American shooters kill an average twenty-four thousand annually; yet according to the Alaska Science Center, just nine hunters died from bear attacks in Alaska over the twenty-odd years from 1980 to 2002. The main source of danger to American hunters, in fact, has traditionally been other hunters, but even this threat is now greatly diminished— while thirty-five hunters were shot by other huntsmen in Michigan in 1940, this number had dropped to just three by 2005. Pretty mild stuff, clearly, but how does it stack up against the hunting exploits of our prehistoric and tribal ancestors?

By this stage I was almost afraid to ask.

The ferocious hunting habits of the Neandertals, for example, have already been noted (see pp. **12–15**). Recent studies have re-vealed just *why* they hunted huge animals such as mammoths, woolly rhinos, bison, and wild horses—Neandertals were top-level predators with an awesome appetite for meat. In 2005 paleoanthro-pologist Steve Churchill calculated the probable caloric require-ment of Neandertal males: they came in at 4,500–5,000 calories (21,000 kilojoules) per day, or almost three times that of modern Western men (due to the Neandertals' strenuous lifestyle and large physiques).[40] This translates to about 4.5 pounds of meat per male per day, or 1 whole caribou each per month. With those appetites Neandertal males clearly needed something bigger than the occa-sional hamster to snack on.

Giant animals, however, also fought hard, which accounts for that high level of head and neck fractures among Neandertal males (see page **12**). The fact that these injuries must have come from close-quarters confrontations with thrashing horses, mam-moths, and woolly rhinos, though, begs the question: why didn't Neandertal hunters throw their spears from afar (like their mod-ern hunting brethren), rather than attack the animals by hand? The answer seems to be that their hyper-robust bodies may have inhibited their throwing ability. A 1990 University of New Mexico study, for example, found that the sturdy Neandertal scapula, or shoulder blade, probably restricted the rotation of their arms.[41] My personal feeling is that the shortened limbs of Neandertals (see page 12) probably played a part, too. In this case leverage would have operated *against* them, since their shorter arms reduced both their mechanical advantage and throwing velocity. Evidence for this can be seen in a 1999 study of modern cricket fast bowlers, which found that the fastest were invariably those with the longest arms. Every extra four inches at the wrist, in fact, gave a 3.6 yards-per-second increase in ball speed.[42] This, incidentally, was also the reason for the blitzkrieg of West Indian super-quick bowlers who terrorized world cricket in the 1970s and 1980s: not only did greats like Courtney Walsh, Joel Garner, and Colin Croft average 6'3" in height, their African ancestry also gave them disproportionately longer arms. It's the flipside of Allen's law: organisms living in hot (tropical) environments tend to have longer limbs to aid heat loss.

Ironically, the fact that we *Homo sapiens* are descended from tropical Africans is probably the reason our hunters have become such wimps. The first *Homo sapiens* in Europe, around forty thousand years ago, had those same long African arms (though they shortened somewhat over time as they adapted to the cold conditions of Ice Age Europe) and were thus possibly better adapted for throwing spears than Neandertals, and better able to avoid their rampaging prey. With the invention of the spear-thrower (which, by increasing leverage, almost doubles a spear's velocity) around 15,000 BCE, *Homo sapiens* were able to keep even further away. This then began a technological stampede toward progressively longer-range projectile weapons: bows and arrows, blowpipes, muskets,

and, finally, modern high-powered firearms. The crowning dishonor in our rush to distance ourselves from any possible danger
from our prey, however, has to be the Internet. In 2007–08, thirty-
five U.S. states were forced to ban hunters from accessing new Web
sites through which, for a fee, a live trophy animal was lured to a
feeding station in front of a gun that the hunter could aim and fire
remotely via the World Wide Web. Groups opposing this new "sport"
(many of which, to be fair, were pro-hunting bodies) argued that
Web hunting, from hundreds or thousands of miles away, "violated
the ethics of a fair chase."

You don't say?

In direct contrast to our standoffish hunting ways, however,
there are still places in the world where men hunt very dangerous
animals from close quarters indeed. Pygmy peoples of the Central
African rainforests, for example, still hunt aggressive forest elephants by hand with a short, stabbing spear. Author Kevin Duffy, in
his 1984 book *Children of the Forest,* described how a modern Mbuti
Pygmy *tuma,* "great elephant hunter," tracks and kills his giant prey.
First he plasters his face with black paste, believing this will lead the
elephant, if it sees him, to think him a chimpanzee and ignore him.
Then he tracks the elephant through the forest at a furious pace,
sometimes for days. When he finally locates it, the *tuma* creeps up
by utmost stealth (elephants have incredibly acute hearing and sense
of smell) to stand under its belly—the only place where his spear
can plunge in deeply, unimpeded by bone. After a quick thrust, the
hunter has just split seconds to leap clear of the giant's lethal trunk
(blows from elephant trunks killed several zookeepers around the
world in 2007 and 2008). Then he tracks the animal anew, sometimes again for days, until it either dies or weakens enough to be
attacked once more.

◻ got the guts

According to anthropologist Patrick Putnam, after a Pygmy *tuma* elephant hunt even Pygmy boys far too young to hunt were required to prove their bravery, albeit in more unorthodox ways. Putnam pointed out that by the time the *tuma* reached his kill's corpse, it was often bloated with decomposition gases. These were employed to surprising effect, he said, when:

> ...a man other than the elephant hunter cuts a square of skin off the elephant's side...until he comes down to a point where the body wall is very thin...then a small male child, squalling and screaming, is thrust on the elephant's side; he is told to bite, which he does, and the balloon bursts...the ceremony is...especially repugnant to the child, who does not enjoy having the whole rotten insides of the elephant burst in his face.[43]

Sadly, the story may be apocryphal, since Putnam, although a dedicated and preeminent anthropologist, was also a noted eccentric given to occasional eruptions of hot vaporings himself. ◻

An even more incredible feat of close-quarters hunting is the lion killing of the Maasai tribe referred to earlier. According to nineteenth-century British colonial engineer Frederic Shelford, the bravest of the Maasai *olamayio* hunters actually grabbed the lion by its tail and drove his spear through its body from haunches to chest. This is particularly impressive considering that lions are supremely strong: feline muscle is, pound-for-pound, the strongest in the animal world.

The verdict, it seems, is in—from enduring torture and terrifying treatments to facing initiation and hunting ordeals, we moderns are shadows of the men we never were. Of course, the fact that we *don't* bravely face such ordeals doesn't prove we *can't*. For most of us, everyday opportunities to face real peril have almost evaporated (which is partly why teenage males manufacture such foolish ones). The prime reason for this seems to be our affluence. The basic drive behind bravado has always been the male's quest to better himself—in worldly goods, prestige, or the reproductive stakes. In tribal societies, the avenues open to striving males were few, and invariably fraught with enemies and dangers that simply couldn't be avoided. Today, in our rich and diversified economies, opportunities for advancement and escape routes have multiplied dramatically. Tribal New Guinean "trash men"—low-status warriors who lacked wealth, prestige, and family connections—were known to fight with suicidal courage in clan wars, simply because it was their only chance of acquiring social standing. Modern males, if thwarted in their climb up the career ladder, simply move to another job, or even another occupation.

Another cultural contributor to our waning bravery is probably male–male segregation. As that University of Maine study showed, bravado displays are primarily a form of communication among males. Increasingly, though, those males are now isolated from one another—by the nuclear family, workplace specialization, and (paradoxically) improved communication technologies such as video-conferencing. The band of brothers has been dissolved, and our bravado instinct, thus deprived of its audience, is atrophying. It is no coincidence, for example, that modern displays of reckless courage are generally performed by adolescent and postadolescent males. True, this is partly a physical phenomenon attributable to the fifty-times increase in testosterone levels that pubescent males experience, combined with the lag in development of their prefrontal cortices (responsible for planning and goal setting). But it's also probably a product of audience availability. The school, university, or entry-level work environments they inhabit are almost the last places in the modern world where men gather in appreciable numbers. The decline in young males' risk-taking behavior from age twenty-five onward may not, in fact, be just due to falling testosterone, but also to reduced opportunities to form the male–male bonds that bravado is all about.

Yet for all that our cowardice may be culturally governed, doesn't mean it won't eventually write itself into our genes. Experiments in animal breeding, for example, have found that behavior can become genetically encoded in as few as two or three generations, and firmly fixed after ten to twenty. All that would be needed would be a selective mechanism by which bravery genes were dropped from the gene pool and cowardly ones retained. Is there any such selective mechanism? The answer is yes . . . and no. It is unlikely that sexually selective pressures for altruistic bravery will ease, since women demand it so consistently of their mates. (It's also hard to see them changing in this—how could it benefit a female to breed with males who won't protect their brood?) The selective landscape for non-heroic bravery—bravado—however, has been transformed. Not only is its raison d'être disappearing through the isolation of males from one another, it is also becoming lethal. Barred from our ancestral channels for displaying bravado (like facing down wild animals and undergoing ordeals), young men now do so through such frequently fatal means as train surfing and drunk driving. World Health Organization figures from 2007 show that car accidents are now the leading cause of death for men aged fifteen to nineteen worldwide. The fact that far fewer young females die in such crashes shows they are not just accidents—young male bravado is clearly a major cause. This being the case, it will take some pretty stunning advances in road-safety technology to stop bravado being literally smashed out of *Homo masculinus modernus* in a very short time indeed.

"But wait a minute," I hear several outraged readers belatedly protest. "If we modern men are so cowardly, what accounts for the inexorably rising tide of male violence on TV and in newspapers? It takes courage to fight, so wouldn't *that* prove we are just as brave, or foolhardy, as those males who have gone before us?"

Well, yes it would—if it were true. But is it?

Admittedly, in some ways it certainly seems to be. Consider combat sports, for example. Where once the gentlemanly sport of boxing brought fighting violence into our living rooms, now the supposedly deadly, barbaric sport of ultimate fighting does. This fighting style is considered so extreme that even Senator John Mc-Cain, no mean boxer himself, once called it "human cockfighting." Yet how extreme *is* Ultimate Fighting, really? How would the code's fighters fare if we introduced some *real* hard men into their cage: ancient and tribal brawlers like the original Greek Olympian boxers, say, or South America's Yanomami Indian axe-fighters? And heck, since we're making a night of it, why not throw in a solid under-card, too? Let's rope in the ultimate fighting *soldier* as well, the U.S.

Special Forces warrior, to go mano-a-mano with the original "black ops" experts: the medieval Japanese *shinobi,* or ninjas. Throw in, too, for good measure, a rumble between the would-be baddest terrorist on the planet, Osama bin Laden, and a horde of genuine, blood-curdling horrors from the wastelands of the Asian steppe, Genghis Khan and his Mongols, and this is starting to look like a *fight.*

Be warned though, all those queuing for a front-row seat. Don't wear white. Because by the time this is done we can guarantee you won't be.

Battle

O n April 9, 2005, 2.6 million American cable-TV viewers were treated to a fifteen-minute spectacle of blood and carnage: the finale of Spike TV's new reality show *The Ultimate Fighter*. Two young contestants—a Chicago personal trainer called Stephan "The American Psycho" Bonnar, and an ex-policeman from Georgia, Forrest Griffin—entered the cage to trade punches, kicks, and knee-strikes in an all-out brawl that left the face of the winner, Griffin, looking like a promo shot from Stephen King's *Carrie*. Forrest Griffin would go on to a highly successful career in no-holds-barred martial arts (he later knocked out Brazilian fighter, Edson Paredao, in their "Heat Fighting Championship" bout *after* Paredao had fractured Griffin's arm with a torturous "joint lock") and Bonnar scored a fight contract, too, but the real winner was the supposedly brutal new sport of ultimate fighting. Within three years the Ultimate Fighting Championship, or UFC, would displace the National Hockey League championship as the fourth-most popular sports event in the United States, and attain a regular audience of over 4.5 million. The UFC today is a rolled-gold, blood-spattered American success story, and its president, Dana White, credits it all to the impact of that Griffin vs. Bonnar fight.

What makes the story truly remarkable is that just 10 years

earlier the sport looked dead and buried. The original UFC had started in 1993 as a boy's-own fantasy fight club pitting martial artists from different schools against one another to see who would win a real-life, no-rules street fight. But the apparently brutal mismatches that resulted—as when 176-pound Brazilian Jiu-Jitsu fighter, Royce Gracie, battled 250-pound American wrestler, Dan Severn—led U.S. Senator John McCain to campaign successfully for the competition to be banned in 37 U.S. states (though the smaller Gracie, in fact, won that fight). The competition was even dropped from its cable-TV lifeline for almost 5 years. Under Dana White's patient tutelage, however, it managed to rehabilitate itself. By introducing weight divisions, gloves, and rules banning strikes to the eyes, head, and groin, the UFC was eventually able to obtain licenses from almost every American state's governing athletic commission. UFC fights now take place in 39 American states, and have not only returned to cable TV but have also spawned several imitators on major free-to-air networks.

What is the secret of the UFC's phenomenal appeal? Fans of Mixed Martial Arts, or MMA as ultimate-fighting enthusiasts prefer to call it, insist it is the superb athleticism of the combatants. That MMA fighters are extremely fit is undoubtedly true: I myself once watched a 265-pound giant Tongan UFC gladiator, Australian-born Soa "The Hulk" Palelei, train for a super-heavyweight "King of the Cage" title fight, including running speed ladders that would have left many a sprinter gasping in his wake. (Some UFC training is, however, quite unconventional: at one point I heard a strange *thump* and looked up to see Soa, complete with green mohawk and tribal tattoos, smashing a sledgehammer repeatedly into a giant tractor tire.) Yet the UFC's marketing tells a different tale. UFC fights are given apocalyptic names—"Judgement Day," "Nemesis," "Shootout," "The

Uprising," and so on—which hark back to the competition's original tagline: "There Are No Rules!" Such names clearly aim to invoke an inbuilt male love of uninhibited violence. Anyone who doubts that there is such an inbuilt love should read testimony from those English soccer hooligans who say things such as: "I get so much pleasure when I'm having aggro [a fight] that I nearly wet my pants," and "For me fighting is fun. I feel a great emotion when I hear the other guy scream in pain."[1] The genius of the UFC is to cater to this instinctual delight by providing a legalized fantasy spectacle of men pitted against one another in caged fights to the possible death.

Except that . . . nobody ever *actually* dies. Or even (Forrest Griffin notwithstanding) gets particularly injured (see page 71).

I first stumbled across this intriguing little tidbit on that same research visit to Soa Palelei's "King of the Cage" event. Soa's fight had a solid undercard of seven warm-up bouts, ranging from featherweight to the heavyweights just below him, and I managed to sneak into the fighters' rooms and interview every one, beaten or victorious, as they walked, limped, or were dragged in afterward. They were incredibly gracious to talk to me, considering the hammering some had just taken and the craziness of my questions, but the consistent refrain I received was that not one had ever been seriously injured in any MMA fight. Not even the guy I found mashing his purple, welted face into a handful of ice had anything to report—"Nah, mate, this shiner's the worst I've ever had, and even it'll be a memory by Sunday." Considering the carnage I'd been expecting, this was a puzzle, but I thought maybe it was just because these were younger fighters, too green to have been really hammered yet. So I slipped into the heavyweights' rooms to interview Brian Ebersole, a veteran cage fighter with more than fifty light-heavyweight bouts under his belt. Surely there would be tales of horror and maiming somewhere among those? I found Ebersole, whom I'd met earlier at the fight weigh-in, flat on his back, preparing for his fight by meditating (to keep his heart rate down) and smearing his face with Vaseline.

"Hey, man, what's with the Vas?" I asked.

"Protects the face from cuts," he grunted. "The punches just slide off, and it keeps the edge of the glove from tearing your skin, too." (MMA fighters wear lightly padded, fingerless gloves that allow their hands freedom to grapple and choke.)

Aha! Finally, I was getting somewhere. Incredibly, however, Ebersole also claimed his fifty-plus cage fights had left him completely unscarred.

"I've had a couple of sprains, but no breaks to speak of," he shrugged.

"Not even a broken nose?" I pleaded. By this stage I was getting desperate.

Ebersole just laughed. "It usually cops some hits and bleeds a bit," he said, turning so I could see its straight profile. "But this baby's never even been bent, and I can guarantee you it won't be tonight either."

Sure enough, half an hour and three brutal, flailing rounds later, Ebersole returned to the rooms victorious—his face spattered with his own bright, arterial nasal blood, but the nose itself still proudly unbroken.

A review of the medical research quickly confirmed this puzzling find: ultimate fighting really *is* a ridiculously safe form of combat. A 2007 study of competitive-fighting injuries as reported by the emergency departments of 100 American hospitals, for example, found that martial arts resulted in far fewer injuries than either wrestling or boxing.[2] (Competitive basketball, incredibly, has an injury rate *seven times* that of martial arts.) A mere 1 percent of those martial arts injuries were serious enough to require hospitalization. True, other studies have found a more equal rate—such as a 2008 survey of the 635 official MMA fights that took place in Nevada between 2002 and 2007, which found an injury rate of 23.6 injuries per 100 fights, compared to roughly 25 per 100 bouts in boxing[3]—but this disguises the fact that boxing injuries tend to be far more severe than those suffered in the ultimate-fighting cage. The 2007 American emergency-room study found that while almost 90 percent of boxing injuries were to the head and upper body (the most dangerous injury sites), less than 50 percent of martial arts injuries were to these areas. This seems to tally with the results of a 2006 Johns Hopkins Medical School study that found the knockout and concussion rate in MMA fights to be about half those of boxing bouts. This may sound, to some ears, a little strange: why should boxing with gloves lead to *more* head injuries than the bare-knuckle brawling of ultimate fighting? The secret lies in our misunderstanding of what gloves are for—they don't so much protect the punchee's *head* as the puncher's *hand,* allowing him to strike that much harder. Former UFC gladiator Ken Shamrock confirms this, saying:

> When fighting bare-knuckle, if you slam your fist again and again into the head or face of your opponent, all you will do is to fracture your hand. Trust me here. I have done this more than once.[4]

By way of further proof, the first result of the UFC's introduction of light gloves in 1997 saw also an immediate increase in the (admittedly still low) rate of fights ending in knockouts.

It is probably this low incidence of knockouts, coupled with strict rules that lead to early referee intervention, that accounts for the virtually zero mortality rate in modern ultimate fighting. The UFC itself has never had a death in the octagon (the UFC's ring), although boxing over the same period worldwide has seen more than eighty.[5] True, there have been three fatalities in non-UFC MMA competitions, but each of these was in unusual and extenuating circumstances. American MMA fighter Douglas Dedge, for example, who died from brain injuries after a no-holds-barred fight in Ukraine in 1998, seems to have had a pre-existing condition, possibly a skull fracture, that caused doctors to strongly advise him against fighting.[6] Similarly, a Korean fighter called Lee died in an event called "Gimme 5" in 2004, but from a heart attack rather than any injuries. The one confirmed death in an officially licensed bout, that of Texan Sam Vasquez in 2007 by subdural brain hemorrhage, was found to be probably caused by a collision with a cage post rather than strikes to the head (the Texan Medical Advisory Committee later recommended the adoption of standardized post padding). Another probable factor in the UFC's so-far-nonexistent death rate is the use of choking and strangulation techniques borrowed from judo. Though these sound, and look, brutal (the triangle choke, for example, involves strangling the opponent by crushing his neck in the crook of one leg, thereby squeezing his carotid arteries and shutting down his brain's blood supply), they rarely result in injuries other than temporary unconsciousness. A 1998 study in the *Italian Journal of Neuropsychology,* for example, found that long-time judo practitioners showed almost no later loss of brain function, compared to professional boxers, of whom as many as 87 percent did.[7]

Clearly, in terms of sustaining serious injuries, modern no-holds-barred fighting is about as ultimate as sword fighting with cardboard sabers. Yet has mano-a-mano fighting always been this distressingly wussy? What about in days gone by—were deaths and injuries more common in ancient ultimate fighting?

Curiously, there was such a sport in the Western tradition, and it even went by a very similar name. In 648 BCE a no-holds-barred combat sport event called *Pankration* "All Powerful" or "Anything Goes," was introduced to the Greek Olympic Games, eventually becoming so popular that it was turned into the games' finale. The *Pankration* was a brutal striking and grappling fight with no time limits, no weight divisions, and just two rules: no eye gouging and no biting (the Spartans, true to form, permitted even these). Everything else was allowed—breaking limbs, strangulation, fish-hooking (inserting fingers into orifices and ripping), and the wrenching and breaking of fingers and toes. (A Greek vase dated to 520 BCE, for example, clearly shows one *pankratiast* kicking another in the testicles.) A careful reading of Greek literature shows that, as far as *Pankration* was concerned, the "ultimate" tag was, in this case, completely justified: ancient *pankratiasts* really did often pay the ultimate price for entering the arena.

A volume of *Olympian Odes* by the sixth-century BCE Greek poet Pindar, for example, records that "very many [*pankratiasts*] died in the contests."[8] A more specific reference is found in the later works of Philostratus, who records a letter from a trainer to his *pankratiast* pupil's mother, telling her that "if you should hear your son has died, believe it."[9] The great first century Greco-Jewish philosopher Philo agreed, writing that "many times [wrestlers and *pankratiasts*] endured to the death."[10] Philo even cites the amazing tale of two *pankratiasts* who attacked each other so ferociously that both died simultaneously. This is possibly exaggeration, since Philo doesn't claim to have witnessed the fight himself, yet there is one undeniably genuine instance of a *pankratiast* dying just as he secured victory: the case of Arrichion, a three-time victor in the Olympic *Pankration*, who won his third crown by surviving strangulation just long enough to dislocate or break his opponent's ankle (the sources here are unclear) but then died. Judges crowned his corpse the winner. Given that all these references were to deaths that took place at the actual Olympics (which, though famous, were just one of a multitude of Greek games at which the *Pankration* was fought), it seems likely that the mortality rate in ancient Greek ultimate fighting was very high indeed.

Perhaps the final proof of its lethality, though, is the feared *pankratiast* Dioxippus, who in 336 BCE won by default since nobody dared even to get into the arena with him. Clearly, would-be competitors understood that losing to this champion meant not just defeat, but probably death.

Incredibly, however, *Pankration* was not even the most lethal ancient Greek Olympic combat sport. That honor, as in modern times, goes to boxing. One competitor in both *Pankration* and boxing, Kleitomachos of Thebes, for example, asked Olympic officials to hold the boxing *after* the *Pankration,* since he had a greater chance of being wounded or killed in the former than the latter.[11] Once again, the ancient Greek literature confirms his concerns were only too well founded. Four definite references to deaths in Greek athletic boxing have come down to us (the true number was certainly many more), some of them stunningly gruesome. One work by Greek writer and geographer Pausanias, for instance, describes the victory (but then disqualification) in the 496 or 492 BCE Olympic Games of the boxer Cleomedes, who killed his opponent, Iccus, by driving his hand into his stomach and disemboweling him.[12] This sounds incredible, but ancient Greek boxers were, in fact, allowed a variety of lethal, bare-handed chops, slaps, and strikes forbidden to modern fighters. There is also evidence from Asian martial arts that such a feat is possible: tae kwon do masters maintain that a "spear-hand" thrust, followed by savage grasping and tearing at the impact point *can* rip skin and muscle.[13] Another possibility is that Cleomedes penetrated Iccus's chest cavity, which is much more easily ruptured. But perhaps the final proof of Cleomedes' gory feat is the fact that the very same thing happened again a century later (this time at the Nemean Games) when a boxer called Damoxenus killed his opponent, Creugas, in a penalty punchoff after a grueling, day-long struggle, with another disemboweling spear-hand to the gut.[14] The deceased Creugas, like Iccus before him, was posthumously crowned victorious, but this, too, demonstrates how lethal Greek boxing was—Cleomedes and Damoxenus were stripped of their crowns not for killing but for foul blows.

Those who did survive the boxing or *Pankration* seem, moreover, to have frequently suffered severe injuries. Although no skeletons of confirmed ancient boxers and *pankratiasts* have yet been found, clearly broken bones would have been very common among them. Apart from the possible ankle fracture by Arrichion, we also have records of a man called Sostratus who won three Olympic *Pankration* competitions by simply grabbing his opponent's fingers and bending them back until they either broke or the pain became unbearable.[15] This, in the modern UFC, is called small-joint manipulation, and is outlawed due to the crippling injuries it causes (wrist fractures, apparently, are a frequent result). The Greco-Roman father of modern medicine, Galen, writes disparagingly of *pankratiasts* whose eyes have been knocked out. Vase paintings dating back to the sixth century BCE show that despite the ban on gouging, fighters could punch with thumbs and fingers extended. Boxing injuries seem to have been even more catastrophic—so bad that a second-century manual on dream interpretation, the *Oneirocritica*, lists dreams of boxing as bad omens foreshadowing serious bodily harm. The face of a famous first-century BCE bronze statue of a boxer found in Rome bears a broken nose, cauliflower ears, and numerous gaping cuts—the Greeks jokingly called these last "ant tracks." The statue's hands show where such cuts came from: Greek boxers wore sharp leather thongs wrapped around their knuckles, not to protect their opponent's head, but to damage it. (The facial wounds that resulted were so severe that one ancient Greek boxer apparently failed to inherit his dead father's estate because he no longer resembled his own portrait enough to prove his identity.) Even these cruel instruments, however, were nothing compared to the barbaric refinements that the Romans introduced into boxing. Their gloves, the infamous *caestus* (also known as "limb-breakers"), featured projecting metal spikes, lumps of lead sewn into them, and jutting metal plates with serrated, saw-like edges. Fights using these must have caused almost as many violent injuries as those suffered in straight-out gladiatorial contests.

Given the nonexistent mortality rate of modern ultimate fighting, it seems positively cruel to compare it with *actual* Roman gladiatorial death fights—truly the ultimate in ultimate fighting. There's also the fact that gladiators, unlike UFC fighters, used weapons. Yet boasts by UFC competitors of their willingness to die in the octagon make at least one comparison fair: how does their supposed readiness to face death compare to that of the Roman gladiators? Clearly, for a start, their follow-through doesn't quite measure up to their hype. UFC star Ken Shamrock, for example, once vowed at a UFC fight to "get my respect or die" (he presumably got his respect, since he is alive and fighting at the time of writing). Then there is Aleksander Emelianenko, an expert in the Russian combat sport of Sambo and likewise still alive, who once told an interviewer he was ready to fight ". . . on foot or on horseback. With maces or poleaxes. To first blood or to death." Such vows sound impressive, until you compare them to the *sacramentum gladiatorum*, the sacred oath by which Roman gladiators agreed to be *uri, vinciri, verberari, ferroque necari patior,* or "burnt, bound with chains, beaten and put to death by sword."[16] What's more, the gladiators really *did* follow through. Even low estimates of gladiatorial mortality rates, taken from the least bloodthirsty periods of the empire's history, put their chances of dying in the arena at one in every nine appearances. Nor were these quick, simple deaths in the heat of combat. If defeated and given the crowd's shouted order *IUGULA!* ("lance him through"), the defeated gladiator was expected to kneel, clasp his opponent's thigh, and offer his neck as the victor drove a sword into it or cut his throat. He was also required to maintain a stoic silence, neither screaming nor begging for mercy. Nor did his travails end here. If he somehow managed to hang onto life through this treatment he was then dragged away, through the "Gate of Death" by the *libitinarii* ("funeral men"), and then killed with a blow to the temple by a hammer-wielding servant playing the part of Dis Pater, the Roman god of the underworld. (A second century gladiators' cemetery recently excavated in Ephesus, Turkey, shows that 15 percent of gladiators received these blows.[17])

Equally lethal hammers were employed in contests in prehistoric Australia, again by men demonstrating a readiness to die far exceeding that of modern UFC champions. A survey of ninety-four skulls of prehistoric Australian Aboriginal men held by the Adelaide Museum in South Australia, for example, showed fifty-four to have severe fractures from strikes by knobkerries, or fighting clubs.[18] Re-markably, these probably came from the brutal dispute-resolution process first recorded by nineteenth-century anthropologist John Fraser, in which Aboriginal men took turns to kneel and receive a blow to the head, the loser being the first to die or otherwise become incapacitated. It is unclear exactly what the death rate was in these fights, but it must have been high. (As an interesting aside, this cultural practice, according to paleoanthropologist Peter Brown, may also have left its stamp on the skeletal form of modern Aboriginal people: they have the most robust skulls of any living *Homo sapiens*—possibly due to this selective pressure.)

Clearly, then, we modern males have mouths far bigger than our hearts—at least where fighting and dying are concerned. But what about the sheer love of the fight itself? Are we really the hot-headed, bare-knuckled brawlers, ready to fight at the drop of a hat, we're so often cracked up to be? Some media reports would have it so. English newspapers, for example, often describe the weekend streets of London as charnel houses of bloody, booze-fueled brawl-ing. Some statistics, certainly, bear this out—violent incidents on streets and in hotels rose from 39 percent of all UK violence to 49 percent between 1996 and 2004.[19] A 2006 study by the University of London, similarly, found that one in eight young men admitted having indulged in some form of recreational violence in the past year, and a five-year survey of fifty-eight British hospital emer-gency wards found an average 0.75 percent of the male population presented annually with injuries from assaults or other violence.[20]

These figures do seem to indicate an impressive level of aggres-sion, but how does this aggression compare to the drunken brawling of earlier cultures? An exact comparison might seem impossible, since most such cultures have long since vanished, yet there is, surprisingly, one study that *does* allow a close evaluation. In the 1960s and 1970s anthropologist Mac Marshall conducted a study of male alcohol abuse and violence in the Truk group of the Micronesian Caroline Islands. Trukese culture was still heavily traditional at the time of Marshall's arrival, partly due to the intense aggression of the islands' men, who had long kept colonization at bay (Truk was known to ancient mariners as "dread Hogoleu"). Marshall described a violent drinking culture that set aside "battleground" areas in almost every village for drunken weekend brawling.[21] Young men would strut these "battlegrounds" issuing high-pitched war cries, giving swinging kung-fu kicks (Bruce Lee had been quickly adopted as a warrior role model by the modern aggressive Trukese), and generally seeking opportunities for violence. Clan loyalties meant that the inevitable fights quickly became all-in brawls involving multiple armed participants. While he gives no direct statistics, Marshall implies participation in these brawls far exceeded the one-in-eight ratio of young British males listed above. Similarly, Marshall does not calculate injury and death rates, but the Trukese fondness for fearsome homemade weaponry (such as *nanchaku* made from steel pipes) coupled with their disregard of injury (Trukese warriors often deliberately sliced their own arms open to show their bravery to enemies) suggests far more than 0.75 percent of the islands' men acquire wounds severe enough for hospitalization in any given year—or indeed, on any given weekend.

■ city of fight

To the modern traveler Venice is a city of high culture: the "Queen of the Adriatic," the "City of Light." Particularly charming are its beautiful stone bridges such as the "Bridge of Sighs"— the covered limestone walkway from which criminals were given their last sight of the medieval city before they were thrown into the dungeon. Yet few know that these same bridges were once the scene of brutal mass *pugni* "fistfights" in which thousands of men from the city's two main factions, the *Castellani* and *Nicolotti*, beat, stabbed, and drowned one another for fun. From 1369 to 1710 CE, great mobs of fishermen, arsenal workers, porters, and tanners held *battagliole sui ponti*, "little wars on the bridges," for possession of the tiny stone arches that marked the boundaries of each faction's territory. Such wars usually began with scores of *mostre*, or individual fistfights, in which champions such as *Magnomorti*, "Eats the Dead," *Zuzzateste*, "Sucker of Heads," and *Tre Riose de Cul*, "Three Ashole Roses" or i.e. "Three Farts," fought to bloody their opponent's face or throw him into the canal. Such brutal fist fests usually failed to satisfy the bloodlust of the tens of thousands of onlookers though, leading them to take matters into their own hands by pelting the combatants with roof tiles and rushing onto the bridges with fists, sticks, and daggers flailing. As ferocious as these fights were, the *pugni* were an improvement on the earlier *guerre di canne*, in which fighters charged each other en masse with slaves of cane sharpened and hardened by repeated dipping in boiling oil (fighters also wore specially designed armor and helmets). The *battagliole sui ponti* only began to decline in the 1650s, when the loss of their best fighters to the war with the Turks led the *Castellani* faction to suffer repeated defeats. The coup de grace came in 1705, when the brawlers proved so unwilling to desist from their recreational violence that they wouldn't even save the church of San Girolamo from burning down. The city's secretive governing body, the Council of Ten, didn't see the joke and shut the *pugni* down five years later.

Even the prehistoric Trukese, however, probably couldn't match the aggression of another group of big-drinking brawlers—the premodern Irish. The Victorian-era boyos' fondness for recreational violence was simply mind-boggling. Of the 1,932 homicides reported to police between 1866 and 1892, for example, 41 percent were from brawling for fun.[22] At roughly 35 deaths per year (and no doubt countless injuries) this might seem unbelievably high, but for two factors. First, the Irish didn't fight bare-handed, but with lethal stick weapons such as the lead-filled, knobbed, blackthornwood shillelagh—a cross between a walking stick and a long croquet mallet.[23] Second, they also didn't fight alone, but in massive gangs, sometimes of hundreds or even thousands, known as factions. These armed hordes might form on the flimsiest of excuses: Limerick, for example, was the battleground of the "Three-Year-Olds" and "Four-Year-Olds," who took opposing sides in a 30-year debate over the age of a calf. Equally absurd were the pretexts used to get a stick fight going—Irish author William Carleton describes challengers strutting before opposing factions at county fairs (a frequent venue for faction fights) swinging their shillelaghs and shouting, "Ram's horns! Who dares say anything's crookeder than ram's horns?" or, "Black's the white of my eye. Who dares say black's not the white of my eye?" The fact that these were consensual fights, engaged in purely for fun, is shown by the refusal of Irish courts to convict those who killed in faction fights— only 8 percent ever received prison sentences of more than 2 years.

In the small wars of the arena and the street, then, we modern males obviously would have been judged unfit even for the reserves. But what about in *real* wars? How does the savagery of modern combat compare with that of ancient war? Again, media reports often give the impression that we modern, war-mongering males simply blow our ancient counterparts away. In 2006, for example, newspaper and TV outlets worldwide reported that the 2003 invasion of Iraq had officially become the most destructive war in America's history, based on casualty estimates from a Johns Hopkins Bloomberg School of Public Health study published in *The Lancet* that same year.[24] That study estimated 654,965 Iraqi civilians and combatants had perished as a result of coalition military activities in Iraq between March 2003 and July 2006—an overall death rate of 2.5 percent for those forty months, or 0.79 percent annually. (Meaning, basically, that almost 1 person in 100 died from military violence every year.) Several commentators pointed out that this appalling statistic represents almost double the percentage population loss of the United States in the American Civil War, making the second Gulf War the most violent in U.S. history.[25] While *The Lancet* study's figure is contentious, it seems fair to take it as a baseline for comparison.[26] Such carnage, after all, seems only too believable in light of the devastating advances in the destructive power of modern weapons.

Remarkably, however, these concerns turn out to be simple reruns of arguments that have consumed every generation before us. Members of America's "Greatest Generation" (those born in the first quarter of the twentieth century) for example, often proudly declare World War II, which they fought and won, the most devastating in world history. In terms of percentage of population lost, however, this is not strictly true. Just 3 percent of the world's 1938 population died in World War II—approximately 0.5 percent per year. This pales in comparison to the population loss suffered by Germany in the early seventeenth century due to the Thirty Years War, which may have reached 30 percent, or an average 1 percent of population per year.

The tendency to overestimate current catastrophe seems, in fact, to be a simple resurfacing of the old "Golden Age" concept first introduced by the Greek poet Hesiod, who wrote of an "Age of Gold" when men lived forever in perfect peace—vastly different to the degenerate Greeks of his day, who lived in a violent "Age of Iron." Another way of putting it is that the atrocities each generation experiences directly burn far brighter in its memory than those it merely reads about. Though naïve, this is perhaps forgivable, considering exactly the same mistake was made by scientific anthropologists for most of the last century. Archaeologist Lawrence Keeley, in his book *War Before Civilization*, describes the mistaken notion of a "pacified past" that so blinkered twentieth-century archaeologists that they described finds of ruined Neolithic forts—walled with palisades and littered with the flint arrowheads of their attackers— as "symbolic" enclosures (the frequent scatterings of broken human bone were described as possible funeral by-products). In fact, as Keeley's own research shows, the idea that prehistoric males were pacifists couldn't be more wrong.

His survey of annual death rates from war among twenty-three prehistoric societies around the world, for instance, reveals an average annual mortality rate of 0.56 percent.[27] This already seems appallingly close to The Lancet study's figures, yet several statistical quirks indicate prehistoric casualty rates were often higher. First, 0.56 percent is an average rate—at least five of Keeley's societies considerably exceed The Lancet study's rate.[28] The second quirk is that many of those groups that Keeley records as having a lower rate than wartime Iraq often maintained their rate for decades. Keeley describes two New Guinean societies, the Mae Enga and the Tauade, who averaged an annual death rate of 0.32 percent for over fifty years. Given that, at the time of writing, the casualty rate in Iraq is falling dramatically, it seems highly possible the peak casualty rate in the second Gulf War will be confined to the five years between 2003 and 2008. If so, it might take just another five years for Iraq's annual war mortality rate to equal that of the Mae Enga and Tauade. Within another five (fifteen years in total) it might well fall to half. Even faced with the devastating power of U.S. cluster-bomb artillery shells and four-thousand-round-per-minute mini-guns, modern Iraqis might well have statistically better odds than the average ancient hunter–gatherer did of escaping death through military violence.

Why *was* prehistoric warfare so lethal? One reason is the almost complete absence of prisoners of war. Keeley was unable to find more than a handful of prehistoric societies that took defeated warriors captive—the exceptions being those such as the Iroquois, who waged war specifically to assimilate prisoners, and the Meru herders of Kenya, who might ransom them for cattle. Most, however, killed prisoners outright. If they did save them, temporarily, it was usually for later torture, sacrifice, or trophy taking (such as in the case of the Colombian Cauca Valley chief who proudly showed Spanish explorers his collection of four hundred smoke-dried corpses of his victims, all arranged in gruesome poses with weapons).[29] The usual aim of prehistoric warfare was simple annihilation—of the warrior himself and, sometimes, his entire social unit. Keeley reports, for example, that the subarctic Kutchin frequently sought to exterminate whole villages of their adversaries, the Mackenzie Eskimo, sadistically leaving just one male, "The Survivor," alive to spread word of the massacre. Sometimes defeated warriors even faced the ultimate annihilation—they were eaten. Contrary to the belief that "culinary" cannibalism (eating human flesh for food, rather than ritual) was unheard of in prehistoric societies, eating the loser was clearly a major motivation for war among some groups. The return of a war party with *bakolo*—dead prisoners for eating—in Fiji, for instance, was a cause for wild celebration and feasting using specially carved "cannibal forks." Anthropologist Robert Carneiro, reporting the case of one Fijian chief, Ra Undreundre, who "buried" over nine hundred of his enemies in his stomach, estimates that almost 100 percent of war dead in Fiji became food.[30] English missionary Alfred Nesbitt Brown, similarly, described early nineteenth-century Maori war parties singing, on their way to the slaughter, of "how sweet the flesh of the enemy would taste."[31] Ethnographer Elsdon Best, likewise, confirmed that Maori war parties literally lived off their enemies, describing a procession he saw in which twenty female captives bore baskets heavy with the flesh of their murdered clansmen.

on the wings
of eagles

Viking warriors didn't just kick a man when he was down, they hacked him. Warriors unlucky enough to be bested by a ninth-century Scandinavian swordsman might find a fate worse than death awaited them: human sacrifice via the gruesome "Blood Eagle Rite." Ancient Viking poetry gives us the history of this horrific ordeal. *Ragnars Saga* ("Hairy-Breeks's Tale") records that the English king of Northumbria, Aella, had the image of an eagle carved on his back at sword-point by the great Danish Viking Ivarr. Other sources also have the sadistic Ivarr pouring salt into the wound. A later epic poem, *Pattr af Ragnar's Sonum*, says that Aella's spine was slashed, his ribcage ripped open and his still-breathing lungs pulled out to simulate an eagle's wings. According to later sagas, other victims of the Blood Eagle included King Haraldr Harfagri of Norway, King Maelgualai of Ireland, and even King Edmund of England. Unfortunately, though, scholars have since pointed out that the supposed ritual may be a simple mistranslation of the original poet's reference to the eagles that perched on Aella's back and consumed his corpse. Still, whether dismembered by surgical broadsword or left for bird food, Aella's fate shouts one message loud and clear: Ivarr, like any other Viking warrior, was best avoided. ■

Another reason for the high mortality rate of prehistoric war was the surprising effectiveness of primitive weaponry. Numerous authors have testified to the impressive speed and precision of the ancient Turko-Mongol composite bow. Unlike the slow and feeble early Western musket, the bow shot 10 projectiles per minute to ranges of over 550 yards (a stone monument found in Siberia records that in the 1220s Genghis Khan's nephew, Yesüngge, hit a target there from 586 yards away using a composite bow).[32] Yet even supposedly primitive bows could be devastatingly lethal. The simple flint arrowheads used throughout the prehistoric world, for example, had ragged, tearing edges sharper than modern steel. Keeley reports that in prehistoric North America these basic arrowheads were so deadly, and so commonly used, that up to 40 percent of all deaths were caused by them. Prehistoric warriors also took fiendishly inventive measures to increase killing power. Many groups barbed their arrowheads to make them difficult to remove, and deliberately weakened their shaft attachments so they would break off in the wound. The aggressive Mae Enga achieved the same effect by capping theirs with hollow cassowary claws, which would likewise be left in the body to fester. Numerous groups tipped their arrows with poisons, such as the *muriju* plant sap of the Kenyan *Giriama* (which could stop an elephant's heart in hours) or the snake venom of the ancient Sarmatians. More fiendish again was the use of microbial poisons to cause blood poisoning. Shoshone Indians, for example, buried sheep intestines filled with blood, left them to rot, and then dug them up and smeared the septic ooze on their war arrows. New Guinean groups daubed theirs with grease or human excrement, or wrapped them in orchid fibers. These devices meant the projectile didn't have to kill instantly; it could destroy enemies later through septicemia. Even such derided weapons as the primitive sling were, in reality, viciously effective. Ancient literary sources record that the Roman army (which used slingers as auxiliaries) only recruited those who could hit a target at 200 yards. Enemies greatly feared these whizzing projectiles which, unlike arrows and spears, couldn't be seen and avoided. Though sling stones rarely killed outright, they stunned even armored victims sufficiently that they could then be dispatched with club or spear (or, as in prehistoric Tahiti, with daggers made from a stingray's tail).

Yet another reason for the high mortality rate of prehistoric warfare was the failure to distinguish between soldiers and civilians. Any modern Western air force that conducts a bombing raid faces a severe grilling in the press if civilians are harmed. Yet numerous historical accounts confirm that in ancient times it wasn't just defeated warriors who were slaughtered after a lost battle—everyone was. Victories often turned into annihilating rampages through the losers' territory. Anthropologist of the Pacific Islands, Douglas Oliver, reports that after eighteenth-century Tahitian battles it was common to see "infants . . . transfixed to their mothers, or pierced through the head and strung on cords . . . [and] women . . . disembowelled and derisively displayed."[33] So many were killed in these rampages that the losers' territory apparently often stank of death for weeks. Keeley, similarly, records archaeological evidence from a mass grave at Crow Creek in South Dakota, dated to circa 1325 CE, which shows that over five hundred men, women, and children (60 percent of the population) were massacred there. Only the very young women were spared, probably for incorporation into the victors' tribe.

Even in those societies that *did* recognize a distinction between civilian and military, ancient warfare was an extraordinarily lethal business. Authors Richard Gabriel and Karen Metz calculate that defeated soldiers in ancient Sumerian, Assyrian, Egyptian, Greek, and Roman armies had an average 37.7 percent chance of dying on the battlefield.[34] (Death rates among victorious armies, at an average 5.5 percent, were much lower because the greatest slaughter always occurred when the losing side broke and ran.) Losses in some battles were truly catastrophic, as in the famous battle at Cannae, where the Romans lost seventy thousand men, or 95 percent of their engaged force. How does this compare to modern soldiering? Gabriel and Metz report that the death rate for American soldiers in twentieth-century wars averages 23–24 percent (with a dip to 14 percent during the Korean War due to the introduction of body armor). Interestingly, applying their method of analysis to the Iraq War gives a very similar death rate of 28.77 percent of American combat troops (at the time of writing). Though this is already a third lower than the death rate of ancient soldiers, it doesn't sound dramatically less dangerous. There is, however, a secret buried in Gabriel and Metz's approach—it drastically *overestimates* the death rate of modern soldiers by factoring in the modern military "teeth-to-tail" ratio. This is the ratio of fighting soldiers to support soldiers, which in the modern U.S. army is roughly 1:11. Gabriel and Metz confine their survey to those modern soldiers who actually fight, but in ancient armies *every* soldier fought (their teeth-to-tail ratio was almost 1:1). A modern soldier's comparative chance of dying in battle should, therefore, really be divided by eleven. That gives us about 2.62 percent chance of death in battle for American soldiers in Iraq—a far cry from the terrifying odds faced by ancient Eurasian warriors. It is even further from those faced by Tahitian soldiers fighting at sea in canoes: the Dutch explorer, Moerenhout, wrote that no Tahitian naval battle ever ended with less than 75 percent casualties, even on the victors' side.[35]

Ancient battle was also far more terrifying than its modern counterpart because of its immediacy. Ancient soldiers slashed, stabbed, and clubbed each other from mere inches away, unlike modern combatants, who may be miles distant. The presence of so many thousands of men—all screaming, slaughtering, bleeding, and dying—undoubtedly made ancient battlefields a true vision of hell. At Cannae, for example, the surrounded Romans endured four hours of bloodbath horror as Hannibal's Carthaginians crowded them in so tight they couldn't lift their weapons, then butchered them with sword and spear. The Roman historian Livy records that after the battle several dead Romans were found to have dug holes and buried their own faces in the dirt—to escape their terror through self-suffocation. There is also a special horror to the maiming injuries ancient soldiers faced, particularly from swords. Livy reports that the Greeks were appalled to see the slashed flesh, hacked limbs, and split skulls suffered by their dead countrymen after defeat at the battle of Cynoscephalae—the first time they had fought brutal Roman swordsmen. Nor were the horrifying projectile injuries of modern war entirely absent. The Jewish historian Josephus records some of the gruesome wounds dealt out by Roman ballista (or catapults): one Jewish soldier decapitated by a stray ballista stone, and a pregnant woman whose fetus was smashed from her womb and flung one hundred yards by another. Even the absence of such technology, however, did not restrict the truly horrific injuries primitive warriors might have to face. Champion fighters among those savage Tahitians, for instance, commonly clubbed their opponents completely flat, then cut a neck hole in their flattened corpses and wore them as grotesque ponchos!

Clearly, a very high level of bravery and aggression was needed to face these brutal trials. Would modern soldiers have been up to the job? Again, sadly, the answer is probably not. The famed U.S. Army combat historian Samuel "Slam" Marshall wrote in his World War II classic *Men Against Fire* that on average just 15 percent of American troops actually shot their weapons at the enemy, even when they themselves were under fire. Marshall put this down to the inherent nonaggressiveness of the American soldier and his consequent reluctance to take enemy life. An American officer who fought in the first Gulf War, Captain John Eisenhauer, confirmed this, stating that *all* his battalion's soldiers had failed to fire on attacking Iraqis—except for those artillery gunners who could do so through a long-distance thermal sight. Subsequent studies to Marshall's support this: the rate of fire of modern soldiers goes up in direct proportion to their distance from the enemy.[36] So pronounced is the problem that the U.S. Army has adopted special training methods—such as pop-up firing ranges that create a game-like atmosphere—to raise the fire rate. Amusingly, the current U.S. Army proudly trumpets a 90 percent success rate from these measures—meaning 90 percent of their soldiers now actually fire the weapons it is their duty to wield.

One reason modern soldiers get away with such slackness is the speed of modern projectiles. Who, after all, can tell who fired any particular bullet among hundreds traveling at 933 yards per second? Tribal bowmen, on the other hand, had no such luxury: under the intimate gaze of their fighting brothers, they had no choice but to fight—and to win or die.

Although most, it seems, were so naturally aggressive they hardly needed the encouragement.

There is still one place in the world where the extraordinary belligerence of prehistoric tribesmen can be directly observed. In 1981 the crew of a Panamanian freighter, the *Primrose*, experienced it first-hand. Run aground one night in treacherous seas on a reef in the Bay of Bengal, the *Primrose*'s captain was relieved to see, come morning, that his ship had fetched up a mere few hundred yards from Sentinel Island, a lonely outpost of the isolated Andaman Islands. He shouldn't have been. Just two days later he was forced to send an urgent message to the Indian Navy requesting an immediate airdrop of firearms for protection against a horde of tribesmen who had spent the day showering his freighter with arrows, and who were now, ominously, building canoes to bring their murderous fire even closer. The attacks eventually grew so severe that the *Primrose*'s crew had to be rescued by helicopter from the besieged freighter's deck. Twenty-five years later, in 2006, two Indian fishermen were not so lucky; they were murdered by arrow fire under the horrified gaze of their colleagues after drifting too close to Sentinel Island (their bodies have never been recovered).

All these unfortunate seafarers had, unbeknown to them, stumbled upon an island of super-aggressive tribesmen whose reputation for violence stretches back to Marco Polo and beyond. One Arabic text from 851 CE said of the Andamanese that they:

> . . . eat men alive. They are black with woolly hair, and in their eyes and countenance there is something quite frightful . . . they go naked and have no boats. If they had they would devour all who passed near them. Sometimes [with] ships that are wind-bound . . . in such cases the crew sometimes fall into the hands of the [natives], and most of them are massacred.[37]

British colonialists in the nineteenth century had their own confirmation of this, with attacks like those on the *Proserpine*, relentlessly assaulted by the Andamanese as it searched for the shipwrecked *Emily,* which had itself been attacked earlier. Holding the natives off with cannon shot, the search party found just one set of remains: "the corpse of the second officer [who] had been murdered and his corpse badly mangled, the top of his skull removed with a blunt saw-like instrument."[38] So aggressive are the Andamanese, even today, that they remain, effectively, the last uncontacted people on earth.

Incredibly, hostile societies such as the Andamanese even contain certain warriors *so* aggressive that their own side avoids them, too. In the Andaman Islands these hotheads, known as *tarendseks,* are widely loathed due to their habit of running amok and killing their own (such as the *tarendsek* recorded as murdering two of his tribe's children simply because they disturbed his sleep). Among New Guinean Baruya tribesmen, similarly, berserk warriors known as *aoulattas* brave the enemy's arrows and advance alone to smash those enemies' skulls with their *keuleukas* (ancestral stone clubs), but likewise terrorize their own community with random murders.[39] The prime examples of such super-aggressive warriors were, of course, the Viking berserkers. These ferocious fighters terrorized friend and foe alike in the Scandinavian world between the ninth and eleventh centuries CE. Disdaining armor, berserkers plunged into battle wearing simple wolf or bear skins (possibly even nothing at all) smiting and tearing enemies with unsurpassed fury. Contemporaries witnessed them howling like beasts and frenziedly biting their shields (one berserker apparently tore out an enemy's jugular with his teeth). The key to the berserkers' aggression was the *berserkergang,* the trancelike fury they entered, which apparently made them impervious to death and injury. Though used to devastating effect as shock troops by several early Norwegian kings, berserkers also exacted a heavy toll on their own people. Under King Eirik Bloodaxe in the eleventh century, for example, berserkers were outlawed due to their habit of challenging rich men to *holmganga*, the death duel, then slaying them and confiscating their property (and wives: berserkers were also noted rapists). Despite attempts to attribute the *berserkergang* to the drinking of psychoactive substances such as wine spiced with the bog myrtle plant, it appears the wild men's frothing fury really was a simple case of hyper-aggressiveness, possibly genetic in origin.

■Beating the chest

The ferocious Yanomami Indians of the Brazilian and Venezuelan Amazon don't have to go far for a fight—just as far as the nearest Yanomami man. So often do Yanomami men fight that they have developed a five-stage system of aggressive brawling, starting with the chest-pounding duel. In this ritual, combatants stand stock-still while their opponent adjusts their arms and chest for maximum vulnerability, takes a run-up, then smashes his fist into the man's left pectoral muscle, right over the heart. The victim must withstand four or five of these blows, which raise painful and bloody bruises, to earn the right to retaliate—the winner being whoever doesn't collapse or step away. If chest fighting doesn't solve the dispute, combatants escalate things to a side-slapping duel, where open hands are swung at maximum velocity into the vulnerable spot between the opponent's ribs and pelvis—a blow that frequently results in unconsciousness. The next step is a club fight, where fighters take turns cracking each other over the skull with heavy wooden staves; most Yanomami men tonsure the top of their heads to display their proud scars from this ordeal. If that doesn't help, they might then step it up a notch to an axe fight using the blunt edge of their stone axes—though this is so often lethal they might as well just use the sharp side. If the opponents still aren't sick of fighting (which is often the case), the combat will then turn really serious: bows will come out, along with six-foot arrows tipped with lethal curare poison. Ouch!

Such fighting spirit is clearly lacking in modern soldiers, but so are other martial qualities. A quick scan of historical literature shows that modern grunts are seriously short on strength and endurance, too. The U.S. Army, for example, proudly highlights its physical fitness standards—infantry recruits are expected to be able to run 12 miles in 4 hours by the end of basic training. Yet this is couch-potato stuff. Members of the Yuan Dynasty's Imperial Guard in ancient China had to run 56 miles in 4 hours for their fitness test.[40] Alexander the Great's Macedonians, similarly, ran between 36 and 52 miles a day, for 11 days straight, in their pursuit of the defeated Persian king, Darius. The most leisurely pace of Roman armies, likewise, was 18 miles per day, but they often covered much more distance. In 207 BCE, for instance, the Consul Claudius Nero marched a Roman legion 310 miles in 6 days, at the rate of almost 50 miles per day, to meet and defeat Hannibal's brother, Hasdrubal.[41] This represents a dogtrot of 6 miles per hour, or about half the speed of modern Olympic marathon gold medallists—day after day after day. What's more, marathon runners wear only light clothes, but Roman legionaries marched in full armor and carried extensive baggage. These days the U.S. Army, and even the Marines, limit every soldier's load to a third of the average American recruit's bodyweight which at an average 153 pounds works out to an approximate 50-pound load. Based on this rule, Nero's soldiers, who weighed an average 145 pounds, should have carried just over 47 pounds for their ultra marathon; they actually carried up to 100 (*two*-thirds of their bodyweight).[42] Other warriors, unburdened by such staggering loads, ranged even further, and faster. Shaka Zulu's *impis*, for example, commonly ran over 50 miles a day when on campaign. One war leader of the East African Ruga-Ruga, Mirambo ("Heaps of Corpses"), was similarly once recorded as running sixteen miles to attack a village, conquering it, and then running 30 miles to assault another.[43]

◼ Adidas Army

Former Australian Army physical trainer, Captain David Sanders, has no time for grizzled old soldiers claiming things were tougher in their day. "Infantry training in the Aussie Army today is just like it always was—tough as nails," he insists. "Route marches are just as hard, drills are just as tough, and sergeant-majors are the same as they always were—total bastards." If anything, Sanders reckons, soldiers in the new millennium are getting better, because now (as opposed to the long post-Vietnam lull) they actually *fight*. There is one area in which he will admit modern soldiers fall short, however. "From the eighties onward we started seeing a lot of injuries like shin splints and stress fractures in the lower leg bones," he muses. The reason? "In the old days kids used to walk around barefoot or in hard-soled leather shoes. It made their bones hard. From the eighties on they started wearing runners, so they all grew up with bones like chicken drumsticks."

There was a reason ancient and primitive soldiers were so much fitter than slothful modern grunts: training. To make his soldiers fit, Shaka took them on grueling patrols ranging hundreds of miles—barefoot. When some complained of injury from "Devil's Thorns"—long spines sharp enough to puncture tires—Shaka made them stamp for hours on a parade ground scattered with the thorns, killing any man who failed to dance. Wu dynasty soldiers in sixth-century BCE China trained with eighty-mile runs, without a break, wearing full armor and weaponry. Roman legionary recruits, similarly, trained by marching twenty-four miles in five hours, carrying their full armor and pack weight of up to one hundred pounds. They also sometimes constructed and tore down a complete legionary camp—a procedure which took three hours—three times in one day. The only modern soldiers who even come close to this are the elite and Special Forces units. U.S. Rangers, for example, undertake sixteen-mile training runs in four-and-a-half hours, wearing a forty-pound pack. Soldiers graduating from the U.S. Special Operations Command's assessment program, the SFAS, likewise do training runs of eighteen miles in four-and-three-quarter hours, wearing a pack weighing fifty pounds. This is commendable, of course, but it just damns our ordinary soldiers even further—physically at least, every peasant grunt in the Roman army was a match for modern elite Special Forces.

Nor do we have a monopoly on actual Special Forces, either. A whole entertainment industry has grown up praising the virtues of modern special-operations soldiers: their physical toughness, lethality, bravery, and ability to operate in enemy environments. Yet, one thousand years ago, for example, the Middle East was stalked by a sect of shadow warriors who made Delta Force look like boy scouts on jamboree. These were the *fida'is* ("those who lay down their lives"): the secret agents of the heretical Assassin sect of the Shia Muslims. From the eleventh to the thirteenth centuries CE these fanatical warriors terrorized the orthodox Muslim world by secretly infiltrating the retinues of high officials and suddenly murdering them in brutal and highly public fashion. Among their numerous victims were a Prime Minister of Persia and the Crusader King of Jerusalem, Conrad (whom they assassinated while in the disguise of Christian monks). Even the mighty Muslim warrior Saladin suffered so many attempts on his life from *fida'is* that he began sleeping in a specially constructed wooden tower. A report from a fourteenth-century Crusader priest, Bocardus, records the general awe in which the *fida'is*'s infiltration skills were held:

> . . . the Assassins, who are to be cursed and fled . . . are thirsty
> for human blood . . . by imitating the gestures, garments, lan-

guages, customs, and acts of various nations . . . thus, hid-
den in sheep's clothing, they suffer death as soon as they are
recognized . . . I cannot show how to recognize them by their
customs or any other signs, for in these things they are un-
known . . . [44]

So practiced in the dark arts of secret war were the *fida'is* that orthodox Muslim rulers never quite knew when their most trusted
retainers might turn out to be Assassins. Sharaf al-Mulk, the Prime
Minister of the Khwarezmian Empire (modern Iran), for example,
was appalled to discover in 1227 CE that no fewer than five *fida'is*
had secretly infiltrated both his stable and his office of heralds. So
terrified was he that others would remain undiscovered, he paid
the Assassins' religious leader 50,000 dinars' blood money when
the Sultan made him burn those five alive.

Even the *fida'is* Assassins, however, couldn't match the secret
skills of the archetypal ancient special-operations soldiers: the ninja.
These silent warriors were the scourge of Japan's aristocracy between the fifteenth and seventeenth centuries, when their stealthy
way of war frequently defeated the aristocrats' samurai protectors.
Ninja, or *shinobi* as they were more commonly called in medieval
Japan, came from secret *ninjutsu* training schools in the wild Iga
and Koga provinces. These schools had their origin in the wander-
ings of a defeated twelfth-century samurai, Daisuke, who met up
with the Chinese warrior–monk Kain Doshi, himself a refugee from
the collapsing Tang Dynasty in China, in the Iga Mountains. The
military doctrine that emerged from Daisuke's training at Kain
Doshi's feet emphasized deception, suppleness, speed, and surprise.
Shinobi assassins (for assassins they usually were) used similar tactics
to the Shia *fida'is,* disguising themselves as wandering Buddhist

monks, washerwomen, or even itinerant puppeteers to get close to their targets. Their weaponry far outstripped the favored dagger of the *fida'is*, however. In addition to their fearsome unarmed combat techniques (which eventually gave rise to karate), and their shortened samurai swords, *shinobi* killers might carry powdered sand and pepper to blind their enemies. Their mouths might spit needles. Their hands and feet might feature *tekken*, banded metal claws that served equally well to climb a castle wall, catch a sword blow, or stab an opponent. Tucked into their belt might be the fearsome *shinobi gama*, a long chain flung at victims to immobilize them so they could be hacked to death with the razor-sharp sickle at its end. *Shinobi* also employed a bewildering array of climbing and mobility devices, including hooked ropes and collapsible climbing poles, and wooden flotation shoes that allowed them to cross moats. So murderous did *shinobi* activity become that some aristocrats found their only defense was to construct elaborate "ninja-proof" houses. One such was the famous Nijō Castle in Kyoto, which featured a "nightingale" floor whose specially sprung floorboards "sang" whenever a would-be assassin visited in the dead of night. Yet even these drastic measures failed to stop some *shinobi* killers. A ninja called Ishikawa Goemon, for example, is said to have penetrated the castle of the famous aristocrat Nobunaga and dripped poison down a thread into his mouth as he slept. Nobunaga, however, survived this attempt and sent his own *shinobi* to murder his rival, Kenshin—which the *shinobi* reportedly did by concealing himself in Kenshin's lavatory sewage pit for several days until the chance came to kill the nobleman with a spear thrust to the anus.[45]

Without taking anything away from our many brave and dedicated modern special-ops soldiers, such feats make our bumbling search for Osama bin Laden look like a page straight out of *Where's Waldo?*

Mention of bin Laden seems appropriate here, for his name is often cited by those who claim that another aggressive activity of *Homo masculinus modernus,* terrorism, has reached new, unparalleled heights of destruction. One post-9/11 academic work on terror, for example, pointed out that the 2,974 casualties in the September 11, 2001, attacks constituted an almost forty-fold increase in casualties over the 76 terrorist bombings recorded between 1950 and 2000.[46] Yet the existence of the Shia Assassins—the historical terrorists *par excellence*—shows that terrorism was not unknown in the ancient world. Sun Tzu, the famous seventh-century BCE Chinese military strategist, even coined a proverb summarizing the primary aim of political terror: "To kill one and frighten ten thousand." While there are obvious difficulties in comparing terrorism across vastly different times and cultures (not least because of different killing technologies), al Qaeda and bin Laden have themselves given us two standards by which to measure. Al Qaeda jihadists boast that their attacks will induce surrender of the West through morale-shattering, spectacular, mass-casualty attacks. We are thus entitled to ask how well they have succeeded on two fronts: their number of casualties, and their achievement of those strategic goals. More importantly, for this book at least, we can also ask how well their efforts in both of these compare to those of ancient terrorists.

With which historical terrorists should al Qaeda be compared? Perhaps the best fit would be the medieval Mongols. This north-Asian tribe of ferocious horsemen was, like al Qaeda, an ethnically based group that aimed to forge a universal empire. The Mongols also, again like al Qaeda, employed explicit terrorism in that quest.

The main difference between the two is how phenomenally successful, by comparison, the Mongols were. (Successful, in this case, does not necessarily mean admirable.) Under their ferocious leader, Genghis Khan, the Mongol tribe, which numbered at most 850,000 people in 1260 CE, went on to control a Eurasian empire of over 100 million souls. In fact, the latter number would have been even higher if the Mongols hadn't killed so many, often slaughtering the entire population of cities they conquered. At Merv in Turkmenistan, for example (the largest city in the world at that time), Genghis Khan's son Tolui killed every single inhabitant except a handful of artisans, whom he enslaved. Exact figures are unclear (estimates range from 400,000 to 1.3 million), but this was clearly an incredible feat of extermination, considering it all had to be done by hand and took five days (Tolui apparently assigned 300 to 400 victims to each Mongol warrior for decapitation). The same fate befell Iran's Nishapur (whose citizens had unwisely killed Genghis's son-in-law, Tokuchar), where separate pyramids of men's, women's, and children's skulls were piled up outside the city walls.[47] (This atrocity was, unbelievably, exceeded by the later Turkish conqueror Timur, who constructed a tower of *living* victims, each cemented in place, after his conquest of the city of Sebsewar.) The Mongols were so thorough that they often returned to such cities days later to kill any refugees who had managed to avoid the first massacre. It was by means such as this that the Mongols killed somewhere between 30 and 60 million people over the 90-year period of their major conquests. Al Qaeda and its affiliates, by comparison, succeeded in killing 14,602 people worldwide in 2005 (the rate has since dropped).[48] Multiplied by 90 years, even this high figure would result in 1,314,180 casualties, considerably less than the Mongols.

Then there is the question of aims. Al Qaeda's strategic aim has demonstrably failed, resulting, in fact, in a ferocious *renewal* of the Western will to fight—to wit, the war on terror. Mongol terrorism, by contrast, was devastatingly effective. Several ancient sources record the paralyzing effect Mongol atrocities had on future victims, frequently leading whole cities to surrender without a fight. Arab historian Ibn al-Athir, to quote one, wrote:

> *Stories have been related to me . . . which the hearer can scarcely credit, as to the terror of them [the Mongols] . . . so that it is said a single one of them would enter a village . . . wherein were many people, and would continue to slay them one after the other, none daring to stretch forth his hand . . . I have heard that one of them took a man captive but had not any weapon wherewith to kill him; and he said to his prisoner, "Lay your head on the ground and do not move"; and he did so and the Tartar went and fetched his sword and slew him therewith.*[49]

Without making light of the evil that modern Islamic jihadists have inflicted on the world, comparisons like these make it plain that Osama bin Laden wouldn't have even made *noyan* ("captain") in the army of Genghis Khan.

Fortunately, this means most of us in the Western world will never suffer terrorist violence. Instead, any lethal violence we *do* suffer will probably be individual, criminally motivated homicide. This type of violence is universally a male domain: U.S. Bureau of Justice Statistics figures for 2005 show that men committed 88 percent of murders in the United States, and were victims in 74.9 percent. Despite the marked decline in homicide rates in the United States over the past fifteen years (total murders in the United States were 24,526 in 1993, and only 16,692 in 2005), we often assume aggressive male homicide is a disease peculiar to modern life. Yet how accurate is this? Consider gang violence, for example. In 1996, the Los Angeles County Gang Information Bureau estimated the county's gang population at 150,000 members; that same year the number of gang members killed in intergang violence was just 803, making for an annual rate of 0.53 percent. This is considerably below the average death rate from violence recorded by archeologist Lawrence Keeley for prehistoric societies. Even the baddest-assed Crip from the meanest street of South-Central L.A., it seems, stands less chance of being capped than an ancient or tribal male did of being shanked with a flint, bronze, or sharpened bone blade.

Clearly, very few modern males really have the fight stuff. So why then do we aspire to it? Why have so many young American males taken up training for MMA, or ultimate fighting, that the U.S. Army now runs a championship tournament out of Fort Benning simply to cash in and swing recruits its way? The simple answer is: it's written in our genes. However feeble we are now, modern-male bodies still bear the physical stamp of the fighters we once were. Consider, for example, our sexual dimorphism: the degree to which male *Homo sapiens*'s bodies differ from those of female *Homo sapiens*. Men are, on average, 9 percent taller than women worldwide. They also weigh 20 percent more, with much of the gain attributable to that 50 percent increase in upper-body muscle that men have over women (see page 13). As in most mammal species that show a sex-based difference in size, there is a simple reason for this: fighting.[50] The evidence of our bodies, therefore, is that male-on-male violence has been a part of our lineage for a very long time. Several other features of the male physique also seem to be adaptations to fighting. True, the fact that men have a 30 percent greater aerobic capacity than women could just as easily be an adaptation to hunting as to mano-a-mano combat. It is hard, though, to see the fact that men's blood carries higher levels of coagulation factors such as thrombin and vitamin K (which promote wound healing and reduce pain sensitivity) as anything other than an adaptation to those times when two ancient male hominins decided there was nothing for it but to take it outside and let their fists do the talking.

Then there is the emotional machinery we have inherited. Many a woman has shaken her head at the tendency of her man to react with extreme aggression and violence to seemingly trivial insults. On the surface, of course, she's right: a study of male-on-male homicide in Victoria, Australia, found that a large number were confrontational killings arising from insignificant slights to the aggressor's "honor" such as jostling or staring.[51] It's easy to write this off as male stupidity, but the truth seems to be that this short fuse is actually hardwired into the male brain—and for good reason. More than one anthropologist has pointed out that it is only the threat of massively disproportionate violence in response to minor infringements that guarantees social order among men in tribal societies, which have no central government to dispense justice. Only through a balance of terror can every man's drive to deceive and take advantage of his fellows be deterred. Thus, as in any system of mutually assured devastation, a tribal male who tries to opt out by refusing to fight to the death at the drop of a headdress will soon find himself losing out to his more aggressive brothers.

But what, exactly, can he lose? What, in other words, is he fighting for?

The short answer, as any evolutionary psychologist (or bartender, for that matter) can tell you, is: women. The struggle to transmit genes to the next generation can be, for tribal males, a brutal, winner-takes-all contest well worth fighting and dying for. (Females, in contrast, suffer no such pressure—almost every fertile tribal woman is virtually guaranteed to have children, providing she stays alive.) True, some masculine über-violence is clearly aimed simply at personal, rather than reproductive, survival. A survey of homicides among ancient Scottish and Icelandic Vikings, for example, shows that victims' families were almost seven times less likely to attempt a revenge killing if the murderer was known to be a dangerous berserker. But this itself could be looked at as a reproductive strategy—another study found berserkers also fathered significantly more children than other Viking warriors.

Again, the secret sexual drivers of male-on-male violence can probably be more clearly studied in our closest relatives, the chimps. One survey of a chimp troop in Tanzania, for instance, revealed that the three top males only ever fought when their surrounding females were in season. The reproductive consequences of these fights were also striking: the sexual share of the alpha male, Kasonta, plummeted from 85.66 percent of matings to just 12.99 percent when he was overthrown by the beta male, Sobonga. (Interestingly, just as in the case of de Waal's chimp, Yeroen (see page 42), the next-best place to be, after alpha, was the gamma, or third, position. Kamenafu, the weaker gamma chimp who played Kasonta and Sobonga off against one another, was at one stage able to sneak in 51.4 percent of the sexual encounters as the price of his support.) Even the violence of male chimps against other troops of males, which is far more lethal than their intragroup fighting, seems to have a sexual function. This is somewhat obscured by the fact that male chimps on war patrol also attack foreign females, unless they are in season, but a study by the Jane Goodall Institute's Center for Primate Studies found that aggressive troops of males, by extending their ranges and increasing food availability, boosted both the reproductive rates of their resident females and their own number of sexual contacts with them.

Are the reproductive consequences of male violence as positive in *Homo sapiens*? The terrifying Mongols, once more, give us devastating proof that they are. It was their Khan, Genghis, after all, who said, "Man's greatest joy is to slay his enemy, plunder his riches, ride his steeds, see the tears of his loved ones, and embrace his women." The evidence, too, is that Genghis was not backward in embracing his embracing opportunities: a 2003 genetic research project on men living in the lands of the former Mongol empire found 8 percent of them carry identical Y-chromosomes—since Y-chromosomes are passed from father to son unchanged, this means sixteen million Eurasian men are direct descendants of Genghis and his close male relatives! On a smaller scale, many a Greek and Roman soldier emulated these feats in the inevitable rape orgies that followed conquest of an enemy city (Agamemnon, in the *Iliad*, tells his Greek troops, "let there be no scramble to get home, then, till every man of you has slept with a Trojan wife"). The reproductive pay-off of male violence is also explicit among the headhunting cultures of pre-colonial Borneo, in which a man was not allowed to marry until he had taken a head (and might then present it as his bridal gift).

A frequent criticism of the sexually driven theory of male violence has, however, been that no evidence exists of specific genes for aggression. In fact, though, this is no longer true. In the early 1990s scientists discovered that male mice carrying mutations in a gene sequence called MAOA displayed excessive circulating neurotransmitters, such as serotonin, in their brains, resulting in extreme aggression. The same mutation was soon also identified in humans—first in the males of one particular Dutch family who all displayed similarly high levels of impulsive aggression.[52] A later back-up study on antisocial children found that the gene variant was, in fact, reasonably widespread, and could be used to predict whether abused children would go on to develop aggressive, antisocial personality disorders.[53] Interestingly, a 2000 research project then found high levels of this genetic complex in Macaque monkeys, too: the most widespread genus of primates worldwide after humans.[54] It seems a remarkable coincidence, as the authors pointed out, that the two primates with the highest levels of this aggressive "warrior gene" have been the most successful of all ape and monkey colonizers.

This doesn't, of course, prove that all male aggression is controlled by this particular gene. It does, however, show a mechanism by which aggression can be, and probably is, regulated by natural selection.

That being the case, what is the evolutionary significance of the decline in the fighting ability of modern males, as documented here? Has there been a genetic change to the fighting heart of *Homo masculinus modernus*? So far, I think, probably not. The fact that modern men no longer go toe-to-toe in revenge-driven death matches has more to do with the fact that we have surrendered our right to take bloody revenge to the state, which now punishes our enemies for us (or indeed, us for them, depending on the degree to which we give in to our instinctual aggression). This cultural change has, however, upended the selective landscape. As in all matters BRAWN and BRAVADO, our BATTLE instincts are more likely to *eliminate* us from the gene pool these days than to have us sweep its reproductive stakes. Does that mean we have doomed *Homo masculinus modernus* to an ever-feebler future? Will hotheaded young duelists, instead of firing at ten paces, start bitch-slapping one another over matters of mortal honor—retiring to the nearest hospital at the first sign of a broken nail? A long-term experiment in breeding silver foxes at Novosibirsk in Siberia seems to indicate yes: researchers there were able to breed heritable aggression completely out of their foxes within forty years.[55]

Yet several things may save modern males from this fate. Our increasing ability to tailor drug treatments to specific genetic conditions, for example, will probably allow those human males who bear the MAOA mutation to regulate their brain serotonin levels, thereby saving them (and their genes) from the potentially fatal consequences of their impulsive aggression. Then there is the awkward yet incontrovertible fact—so distressing to those fathers whose teenage daughters fall head-over-heels for sociopathic, wife-beater-in-waiting young punks—that women are somewhat sexually attracted to aggression in men. A 1987 study of female university students, for example, found that almost all rated dominant males (who employed aggression as a strategy in achieving their dominance) as significantly more attractive than non-dominant men (even though the women also expressed strong distaste for the aggression itself).[56] But we don't need to just take the word of these obscure eggheads and their love-struck human lab rats for it. No less an authority than Tony Soprano, the TV mafioso, confirmed it by reproaching his wife, Carmela, for her hypocrisy in claiming she didn't care that he had just lost a fight to underling Bobby, reminding her of their young days:

> *You were there, in the crowd in the parking lot that night at*
> *Pizza World when I took Dominic Tedesco. I didn't even*

know your name, but I remember our eyes met. And you were
blown away.[57]

With female mate preferences like these in operation it is unlikely that male aggression will disappear from the gene pool any time soon. Then there are the surprising ways in which pathological aggression can be turned to both the individual's and society's advantage in the modern world. Several studies have found, perhaps unsurprisingly, that criminal bombers exhibit physiological characteristics in common with psychopaths, among them pathologically low heart rates (indicating very high thresholds for response to stress). More surprising is that so, too, do the most successful bomb-disposal experts.[58] No studies of the relative reproductive rates of criminal bombers and bomb-disposal experts have, as far as I know, been done, but this does at least add one more piece of evidence that male aggression in the modern world—and the qualities associated with it (in this case, an extraordinarily pathologically steady hand) need not be a one-way ticket to genetic oblivion.

Another way, of course, that we modern men can turn what aggression we still have into chick-pulling, gene-propagating success is through sports. Many sociologists, in fact, claim the reason we males have become so docile is that all our violence now goes into that form of ritualized combat. Some even insist the rise of sport explains the civilizing process of the past two hundred years. It's an intriguing theory, but considering the degree of violence and aggression we've witnessed in our forebears, it would seem to require modern male sport to be better, faster, stronger, and harder than sports in history ever were. Is there any evidence that they are?

Hmm. I've got a bad feeling about this.

Balls

On February 16, 2004, those spectators crammed into Vancouver's hockey stadium, "The Garage," witnessed one of the most violent incidents to ever blight the sport of ice hockey when power forward Todd Bertuzzi stunned opponent Steve Moore with a roundhouse sucker-punch then drove him headfirst into the ice. When Moore left that ice ten minutes later, it was on a stretcher and for the last time: his three fractured vertebrae terminated his career as brutally as Moore himself had concussed Bertuzzi's captain, Markus Näslund, weeks earlier with a shoulder-charge. The incident focused attention, yet again, on violence in the Canadian and U.S. National Hockey League, or NHL—the only professional sporting league to have rules *permitting* fighting (combatants are not ejected, but simply required to drop sticks and gloves and slug it out bare-knuckled). Loud calls from school boards and medical bodies to ban brawling in the league followed, to no avail. Just three years later, Philadelphia Flyers "enforcer" (a semi-official team position whose duties include physically attacking opponents) Todd Fedoruk was laid flat by his New York Rangers counterpart, Colton Orr. Fedoruk, whose skull had already been reconstructed that season with titanium plates, was likewise stretchered off (though unlike Moore he was later able to return). Nothing had changed, nor has it since.

There is a simple reason for the NHL's foot-dragging on the issue of violence, though: the fans. As the league well knows, many spectators attend hockey games specifically *for* the fights. A 2003 study published in the *American Journal of Economics and Sociology* proved this by demonstrating that the number of fights per NHL game is the best predictor of ticket sales—far outstripping even the number of goals or wins. While the connection is notable in Canada, it is particularly marked for games played in the United States.[1]

Another thrilling spectacle of American sporting violence is the National Football League, or NFL. Here, though, the violence arises not from on-field fights but from the brutal nature of the sport itself. Game stats tell the story—by the third-to-last week in the 2008 season, 1 in 15 NHL players had been forced out through injury. In any given year these injuries might include: fractured skulls and other bones, concussions, snapped collarbones, torn rotator cuffs, shoulder dislocations, fused vertebrae, and shredded tendons and ligaments. Most of these injuries come from high-energy collisions with other players: one physicist calculated that a pair of 245-pound NFL linemen crashing into each other at 18 miles per hour would generate enough force to shift a 30-ton mass by an inch.[2] Tests on one Detroit linebacker, similarly, showed he was frequently hit by blows measuring 5,780 Gs (astronauts, by contrast, experience about 10 Gs during blast-off). The long-term effects of this abuse are why three-quarters of former NFL players report permanent disabilities from their playing careers.[3] Some don't even make it to old age—118 American university football players died playing the game in the 21 years from 1977 to 1998.[4] The cause of these heavy hits and their resulting injuries isn't hard to find: it's the increasing size of the players. One anthropologist, for example, calculated that the average height and weight of university football players increased by 2.6 inches and 35 pounds between 1899 and 1970. Since then the trend has gone stratospheric—the average player weight increased by another 24 pounds between 1985 and 2008, and the league now includes more than 500 linemen who top out at over 300 pounds.

It is gladiatorial contests such as hockey and football that give modern sport its reputation for rising violence. At a superficial level, this seems to confirm the idea that brutal athletic contests are both the reservoir of modern-male aggression and the reason it is disappearing from other areas of masculine life. Yet is it really true that sport wasn't as aggressive in the ancient past? As it happens, a direct comparison is possible, since football and hockey happen to be two of the oldest sports played on Earth. Some form of these two games (sometimes both) has been played almost everywhere for thousands of years (John Davis, the first English explorer to search for the Northwest Passage through the Arctic ice, was amazed on his 1586 expedition to be challenged to a game of football by the Inuit tribesmen he encountered). If modern sport really does act to civilize by soaking up excess male aggression, it should follow that football and hockey in ancient times were *less* violent and strenuous than their modern counterparts.

The bad news, though (for proponents of the theory, at any rate), is that ancient and prehistoric footballers and puckmen actually played their games long, hard, and incredibly brutally.

Hockey in Europe, for example, seems to have been a violent game from its very inception. One of the earliest types of hockey played there was Irish hurling, a stick-and-ball sport still played today. The very first recorded hurling match, between the Fir Bolg and Tuatha Dé Danann tribes in 1272 BCE, saw stick-blows rained upon the losing

Tuatha Dé Danann "till their bones were broken and bruised and they fell outstretched on the turf."[5] To consummate their victory, the Fir Bolg players promptly slew the Tuatha Dé Danann team. Observations by the English man of letters John Dunton in seventeenth-century Dublin show that Irish hurling hadn't grown much gentler in the intervening three thousand years—he reported that players rarely left the field without "the broken heads or shins in which they glory so much."[6] Other forms of stick games, such as the Icelandic game of *knattleikr,* seem to have been even more murderous. One Viking saga records a *knattleikr* game in which "before dusk, six of the Strand players lay dead, though none on the Botn side." Egil's Saga, similarly, describes the young Egil's axe-killing of an opponent on the *knattleikr* pitch in revenge for rough treatment during play—seven others died in the subsequent pitch invasion.[7] Incredibly, given this level of aggression, some *knattleikr* games reportedly lasted fourteen days.

◼ sods and clods

Quite apart from the deadly Old Icelandic game of *knattleikr,* Viking sport, it seems, was not for the faint-hearted. Horses, for example, provided excellent recreation for ancient Scandinavian sportsmen—but not in races, in *fights.* In the popular sport of horse fighting, Viking men goaded their stallions into attacking an opponent's steed, usually as a prelude to the humans' direct exchange of blows. In one famous horse fight, a Viking named Odd had his ribs broken by the deliberately misaimed prodding of the staff of his enemy, Grettir. Brawling seems to have also accompanied the uniquely Viking sport of "turf throwing." This was something like a snowball fight, only with clods of earth thrown so hard that they often knocked their targets off their feet, unconscious. In one case, recorded in Eyrbyggja's Saga, the downing of one man with a well-placed clod resulted in a gang brawl between his teammates and the men of Eyrr, most of whom ended up joining him, injured, on the ground. Turf throwing probably holds the title of the most brutal catching sport in all history, at least until the invention of high-school dodgeball. ■

Ancient hockey-like games in the New World were, apparently, no less violent. One Choctaw/Creek Indian lacrosse game witnessed by American settlers in the early 1790s, for instance, resulted in over five hundred deaths, mostly in the post-match fighting.[8] These casualty figures might seem unbelievably high, were it not for the fact that Native American lacrosse games often (according to colonial-era American painter George Catlin) involved five hundred players a side and were played on a field almost two miles in length. Baron de Lahontan, the seventeenth-century French commander of Fort St. Joseph in the Huron tribe's country, similarly remarked that lacrosse there was "so violent that they [the Hurons] tear their skins and break their legs very often."[9] Other sources state that blows from lacrosse sticks and hard stone or wooden balls left large blood clots and hematomas that had to be lanced by medicine men using

a special deer-horn sucking cup. Such injuries seem only too understandable, given that almost every foul in modern hockey and
lacrosse—tackling, wrestling, tripping, charging, and striking—was
permitted in Native American lacrosse. Some tribes, for instance,
specialized in tackling by the hair. The Cayuga, similarly, liked to
lift opponents off the ground with their sticks and dump them (a move
that partly explains the frequency of shattered collarbones noted by
early European observers). Cherokee players favored straight-out
choking of their opponents, though this brutal strategy was, admittedly, often pursued simply to make opponents disgorge balls they
had hidden in their mouths (a legitimate move in Native American
lacrosse). Fighting, as in modern ice hockey, was explicitly encouraged by rules such as the one allowing strikes with the stick, providing it was held two-handed. Native American lacrosse was still a
violent sport as late as 1845, when a game involving the Choctaw
Tallulah Indians resulted in three deaths (caused by deliberately
stampeding horses onto the field) and injuries so severe some players were unable to leave the ground until they had recovered *nine
days* later.

Returning to Europe, football in the medieval West may well
have been played by much smaller players than today's NFL players, but its violence would clearly have sent our hulking lineback-
ers scurrying for the safety of the injury list. Called various names
across Europe—*la soule* in France, Shrovetide football in Middle
England, camping in Norfolk and East Anglia, and *cnappan* in Wales—
the game resembled modern football in that it was commonly played
with an inflatable ball (though often, in this case, an inflatable pig's
bladder sewn into a bull's scrotum; it was also sometimes sheathed
in tin to stop losing teams knifing it). That, though, is where the

resemblance ends. Medieval football involved teams of several hundred, since it called for one village's menfolk to drive the ball through an opposing village's territory into the town square or church, which served as goal. Play was a riotous affair, with fists, cudgels, and even horses employed freely. Chronicles of the time testify to the violence of the sport. One sixteenth-century scholar, Sir Thomas Elyot, described "foote balle" as a game "wherin is nothinge but beastly furie and exstreme violence; wherof procedeth hurte, and consequently rancour and malice do remaine with them that be wounded."[10] An anonymous sixteenth-century tract in Old Scots, similarly, claimed that bruises, broken bones, blows, and crippling in old age were among "the bewties of fute ball."[11] Such injuries seem, once more, eminently understandable given the only rules in medieval football were apparently those prohibiting murder and the use of weapons.

Not, it seems, that they succeeded in eliminating either.

In 1280 CE, and again in 1312 CE, for instance, two players died in collisions with opponents wearing sheathed knives (one of the killers being a football-playing priest). But medieval soccer could be lethal even without such weaponry. A Middlesex coroner's inquest in 1581 CE, to illustrate, recorded the case of Nicholas Martyn and Richard Turvey, who both simultaneously "struck Roger Ludford . . . under the breast, giving him a mortal blow and concussion of which he died within a quarter of an hour."[12] In 1303 CE an Oxford University student, similarly, found his brother dead after a football game played in the High Street with some Irish students; this time the cause of death was not reported. This lethal violence was not confined to the distant past, either: author William Dutt reports that a match held on Diss Common between Norfolk and Suffolk in the mid-eighteenth century resulted in nine deaths. Perhaps the ultimate proof of the rambunctious but popular violence of medieval football, though, was how often English monarchs and government officials sought, unsuccessfully, to ban it: thirty times between 1314 CE and 1667 CE.

Obviously, modern hockey and football would have struck these ancient players as being about as risky as hopscotch. This is clearly difficult enough for "sport as civilizing reservoir of aggression" believers, but the theory's problems are, I'm afraid, just beginning. A more extensive look at ancient sports, both historic and prehistoric, reveals most were so explicitly violent they'd have made even a modern illegal-dog-fight organizer blush.

▢man bites dog

Modern sports like horse and greyhound racing are often labeled freak shows of exploitative violence toward animals, but they couldn't hold a candle to medieval and Victorian-era English pit sports. These basically involved anything violent that could be done to any creature in an earthen pit dug into some tavern basement or village green. Sometimes, indeed, the pit could even be dispensed with, as when the village folk of Stamford beat a bull to death in a field for sport in 1836. More normally, however, a badger might be thrown into the pit to be torn apart by fighting dogs; bears with their paws cut off might be treated the same.

Fighting cocks fitted with metal spurs might eviscerate each other for the enjoyment of the crowd, while dogs specially bred for viciousness and tenacity (the original pit bulls) would similarly maul each other to death.

An even more popular pit sport involving dogs was "ratting," in which a terrier was thrown into a pit filled with rats and had to kill as many as he could within a given time. A record was set in 1848 by Tiny—a terrier himself so close to a rat in size that he wore a woman's bracelet for a collar—who dispatched three hundred rodents in just fifty-four minutes.

Such canine blood sports continued merrily until 1866, when an outcry erupted over a fight between a bulldog called Physic and a human dwarf named Brummy, held in the town of Hanley. Though Brummy won, the cruelty of the encounter was the last straw for outraged public opinion, as this report from the *Daily Telegraph* of the time shows:

> By the time Round 10 was concluded the bulldog's head was swelled much beyond its accustomed size; it had lost two teeth and one of its eyes was entirely shut up; while as for the dwarf, his fists, as well as his arms, were reeking [with blood] . . . in Round 11 the bulldog came on fresh and foaming . . . but . . . the dwarf dealt him a tremendous blow under the chin, and with such effect that the dog was dashed against the wall, where, despite all its master could do to revive it, it continued to lie.[13]

Hanley miners, incidentally, were reportedly so furious at the extinction of their favorite sport that they were still threatening the paper's reporter, James Greenwood, with physical violence thirty years later. ■

Many ancient athletic events were, for one thing, intimately connected to war. Some, indeed, *were* war—such as the tournaments of the later European Middle Ages. The name conjures images of gallant knights splintering softwood lances harmlessly against one another's armor in chivalrous charges (though the death of Henry II, King of France, in 1559 CE from a splintered lance in the eye shows jousting could be lethal). Yet jousting was actually a later, pale imitation of the real twelfth and thirteenth-century tourneys, which were brutal, bruising affairs of masses of armored men hammering each other, sometimes to death. In these melees, tourney entrants formed opposing teams, charged each other using war lances, flinging themselves on unhorsed knights with daggers, and hacked at opponents with broadswords, axes, and maces. Given the numbers involved, melees were often hard to distinguish from real war. Baldwin of Hainault, for example, took three thousand foot soldiers to one tournament for protection from his enemy, the Duke of Brabant.[14] Casualties similarly confused the issue—when sixty knights died in the melee at a 1240 CE tournament in the German town of Neuss, spectators could have been forgiven for wondering how the event differed from real combat.[15]

Even those ancient sports that weren't actual war often served as training for it. Many Greeks, for example, believed that their athletic culture was the reason they had triumphed over the vast armies of the Persian kings Darius and Xerxes. As ever, of course, the most extreme examples come from the Spartan Greeks. The two main sporting events of the Spartan state were strange, violent rituals aimed at toughening their boys for life as citizen-soldiers. The first, the *agon karterias* ("endurance contest"), was a public whipping match in which graduating boys competed to see who could withstand a brutal (and sometimes fatal) flogging at the altar of the goddess Artemis Orthia—the winner earned the title of *bomonikes* ("altar winner"). The second, the *Platanistas* competition, was a vicious gang fight in which two opposing mobs of boys were isolated on an artificial island in a plane-tree grove and made to brawl until one team was forced off. The Greek writer and geographer Pausanias wrote that participants "fight with their hands and by jumping up to kick. They bite and gouge out eyes. They fight man to man this way, but they also attack as a group violently and push one another into the water."[16] Since Spartan soldiers did things like this even to their own countrymen, it is no surprise other peoples considered them dangerous madmen best avoided.

Some ancient sports, such as dueling, by contrast, had their origins in one-on-one violence. The medieval Vikings, in this case, provide the most egregious examples. One was the Swedish "sport" of *bältesspänning* (knife-wrestling). This event, which only died out in rural Sweden in the eighteenth century, featured two contestants, tied to each other by a single large belt, writhing and stabbing at one another with daggers. Combatants' wives also apparently attended, usually clutching large sheets with which to bind their husband's bleeding wounds. The only safety measure seems to have been the competitors' occasional agreement to wrap their blades with strips of cloth to shorten their tip-length.[17] *Bältesspänning's* dueling origins are self-evident, and so, too, are those of *glima* (belt-wrestling), which is now the national sport of modern Iceland. *Glima* also uses belts, though in this case each opponent wears one around his stomach and two around his thighs, which his opponent grips and uses to throw him. While modern *glima* doesn't use knives, its ancient version used something just as lethal: a waist-high, tapered rock onto which wrestlers tried to throw their opponent so as to break their back.[18] Apparently such matches were used to resolve (obviously permanently) personal disputes.

Other ancient sports, in contrast, owed their violent nature to their origin in religious ritual. One clear example is the rubber-ball game of ancient Central American civilizations such as the Olmecs, Aztecs, and Maya. This game, which bears a passing similarity to modern basketball, is worth describing in detail not just because it shows how intertwined prehistoric sport and religion were; it also illustrates, when compared to its modern counterpart, just how feeble present-day sports really have become.

The rubber-ball game that Cortés and his conquistadors saw in sixteenth-century Central America was played from as far south as Honduras to as far north as Arizona. Matches were held on stone courts roughly the same area as modern basketball courts, and even featured stone hoops through which players could shoot game-winning goals. Since these hoops were only fractionally bigger than the ball, however, only one in every two hundred or so shots probably scored. The Meso-American ball game was not only more difficult than basketball, however; it was also far more dangerous. Native Americans played the game with solid rubber balls that could weigh up to twenty pounds (fifteen times the weight of a modern regulation basketball) and generated enormous speed and force on the stone court. So hard did these balls strike that they could only be safely hit using a player's thigh, hip, or buttocks. A strike anywhere else often killed the player, as noted by the Spanish monk and historian Diego Durán:

> Some of these men were taken out dead . . . [because] the ball on the rebound hit them in the mouth or the stomach or the intestines, so that they fell to the floor instantly. Some died of that blow on the spot.[19]

Even when players hit the ball correctly (which they did with an accuracy and dexterity that amazed the Spaniards) the resulting injuries were often horrific:

> With this bouncing . . . they suffered terrible injuries on their knees and thighs so that the haunches of those who made use of these tricks were frequently so bruised . . . [they] had to be opened with a small blade, whereupon the blood which had clotted there because of the blows of the ball squeezed out.

Aztec, Mayan, and Olmec ball-game players did, admittedly, wear some protective gear, but this simply proves how phenomenally athletic they were in comparison to modern basketballers. The leather hip-guards, and even the heavy "handstone" gloves they sometimes wore, are uncontroversial, but the ancient sixty-pound stone girdles that are occasionally unearthed at ball-court sites have been dismissed as too heavy for any human to wear. Yet this is probably unjust. Cortés himself, after all, was so impressed by the muscularity of the Central American ball-players that he took a team of them back to Spain in 1528 to play before the court of Charles V.

A painting of the event by Christoph Weiditz confirms Cortés's impression: the painter shows the stout bodies of the native ball players rippling with muscle. I personally think they'd have noticed the weight of those stone girdles about as much as they would sweatbands.

Perhaps most terrifying, however, was the prospect players faced of being sacrificed. All Central American civilizations regarded their ball games as more than just sport; each match was a reenactment of the mythical battle between the gods and the underworld. Archaeological evidence shows that these reenactments often ended in the sacrifice of one or more players. One stone mural adorning a ball court at El Tajin shows a player having his heart ripped out by priests. A stone column at one Mexican archaeological site, Aparicio, shows another being decapitated. The famous ball court at Chichen Itza, the largest in the world at 540 by 220 feet, not only has murals depicting balls containing human skulls, it also features a massive skull rack—a somewhat grisly wall of fame. Incredibly, it is not clear whether those sacrificed in these games were the winners or the losers (offering one's body in sacrifice was considered an honor in Mayan society).

The civilization theory of sport thus seems about as dead as any unfortunate Huron lacrosse player, Welsh medieval *cnappan* footballer, or Aztec sacrificial ball-gamer. Modern sport is less violent, intense, and aggressive than in days of old (and very old), not more. But why? It's tempting—in fact, inescapable—to put it down to increasing wussiness among modern sportsmen, despite their boasts and our willingness to believe them. But something else is going on here, too. What stands out about ancient sports is how entwined with other ends they were, be those ends military, religious, or conflict-resolution related. The famous sociologist of sport Norbert Elias claims, in fact, that this distance from original aims is what defines modern, "real" sport.[20] Present-day athleticism elevates that which used to be a minor part of sport—the contest—to its whole raison d'être. Hunting, for example, used to be about the pleasure of personally killing (and, usually, eating) an animal, while modern fox hunting (in those places of the world where it is still legal) is about simply chasing one—the killing being delegated to the hunters' hounds. Aztec ball games used to be about scoring goals to obtain the favor of the gods; modern basketball is just about how many you can score. This being the case, we're entitled to ask how well we compete compared with ancient sportsmen.

How well, in other words, do we perform in the contest?

Early twentieth-century anthropologists would have thought it ridiculous to even ask. They figured the question had already been answered: at the 1904 Olympic Games in St. Louis, Missouri. By happy coincidence, those Olympics coincided with the St. Louis World Fair, which featured a massive anthropological exhibit of real, live "savages" from all across the world—Japanese Ainu, Philippine Igorots, Eskimos, South American "Giant Patagonian" tribesmen, African Pygmies, and many, many others—who had been specially shipped to the city for the event. The man in charge of this breathtaking folly, disgraced former Smithsonian Institute anthropologist Dr. W. J. McGee, hit upon an incredible idea: why not combine the two and determine once and for all the true sporting capabilities of "primitive" athletes? Thus was born "Anthropology Days," two days of athletic events testing the tribesmen's sporting prowess in Olympic events such as high jump, 100-yard dash, shot put, and javelin. The results, as the official history of the World Fair records, were dismal:

> The world had heard of the marvelous qualities of the Indian as a runner . . . [the] remarkable athletic feats of the Filipinos, and of the great agility and muscular strength of the giant Patagonians. All these traditions were dashed . . . the representatives of the savage and uncivilized tribes proved themselves inferior athletes, and greatly overrated . . . An African Pygmy [in the 100-yard dash] made a record that can be beaten by a 12-year-old American school boy. The giant Patagonians' . . . best [shot put] performance was so ridiculously poor that it astonished all who witnessed it.[21]

These poor performances, though, clearly had more to do with unfamiliarity, lack of practice, and often a simple refusal to take the events seriously (the Pygmies made great sport in the dash by climbing all over the man with the starting gun). Unbiased observers thought the non-Western athletes had been unfairly judged. One such was Baron Pierre de Coubertin, the French founder of the modern Olympic movement. To his eternal credit, de Coubertin was appalled by the St. Louis spectacle, calling it "an outrageous charade." He thought the athleticism of uncivilized peoples was, in reality, every bit the equal of civilized peoples, predicting that "black men, red men, and yellow men [would one day] learn to run, jump, and throw, and leave the white men behind them."[22]

This statement, though both brave and insightful, didn't go far enough. For, as the evidence of archaeology and colonial historians once more shows, the athletic abilities of prehistoric and tribal sportsmen often far outstripped that of their modern, "civilized" brethren.

Those fossilized footsteps proving prehistoric Australian Aboriginal men could probably outrun modern Olympian sprinters, for example, have already been noted (see page 22). Unequivocal fossil evidence like this, though, is very rare. In its absence our only real alternative lies in historical records, yet these, too, can be problematic. The ancient Greeks, whose Olympian obsession with athletics has left us records of 794 winners from their 1,221 years of games (786 BCE to 435 CE) might be expected to help, but they had neither the time-keeping technology nor the interest to record sprinting speeds (Greek sprinters seem to have cared only about whom they beat on the day, not their speed compared to a record). Measurable reports really only began in the colonial era, when literate Europeans came into contact with tribal peoples. One famous account from the nineteenth-century Western Australian frontier, for instance, describes an Australian Aboriginal man who outran a pursuing police horse at Forty Mile Beach. Since an average horse gallops at 25 to 30 miles per hour, this report is both impressive and plausible, given the Willandra Lakes footprint evidence (see page 22). What's more, several other reports describe ancient and tribal men performing similar feats. Spanish conquistadors in the seventeenth century, for instance, complained of fugitive Native Americans who left their mounted pursuers in their dust.[23] Later, Mexican ranchers took to hiring local Indian runners to run down escaped horses.

∎The one-legged man is king

The ability of prehistoric Australian Aboriginal men to shame modern Olympic sprinters has already been noted (see page 22). Those same fossilized footprints also show, though, that disabled Aboriginal athletes would have humiliated modern Paralympians, too.

Archaeologist Stephen Webb reports that when his team found the fossilized trackways they were puzzled by those of the individual labelled "T4," which featured 22 right footprints but no left prints. They also included several circular impressions that looked like the imprints of the end of a blunt stick. The footprints were spaced so far apart that it was thought they couldn't possibly belong to a hopping man, who would have had to have been traveling at over 13 miles per hour to make them. The group settled on the explanation that T4's other foot had been in a canoe he had been pushing through the shallow lake with his stick—until they spoke to several traditional Pintubi people from outback Australia. Not only are the Pintubi accomplished trackers, it so happened that they themselves had grown up with a famed one-legged hunter. They were thus able to show Webb how T4 had achieved his phenomenal hopping speed: by building up momentum with the aid of his stick, then casting it off and hopping unassisted. Admittedly, modern Paralympians achieve much higher speeds than T4 did, but only with the high-tech assistance of spring blades and other aids. They also don't hop. A better indication of T4's feat is to compare his speed to the modern *Guinness Book of Records'* 1-mile hop record-holder's speed of 1.3 miles per hour.

One possible objection to the superiority of prehistoric athletes is that Jesse Owens, the modern (1930s) track star, did exactly the same thing, racing and beating horses over one hundred yards several times. Owens later admitted, however, that he won by choosing skittish horses that were startled by the gun, giving him a crucial head start. A more serious objection is the mighty performance of marathon runner Huw Lobb, who in 2004 definitely *did* outrun a horse in the annual "Man vs. Horse" race in Llanwrtyd Wells, in Wales, for the first time in the event's twenty-five-year history. That race, though, was over twenty-two miles—and therein lies the rub. For it is a peculiar fact that we humans, so feeble in almost every other respect compared to our animal cousins, are stellar endurance athletes. Not only did ancient athletes often run down horses over longer distances (such as the Olympic champion Lasthenes, who did so in a twenty-two-mile race from Coroneia to Thebes in the fifth century BCE), prehistoric hunters frequently performed similar feats simply as part of their daily lives.

Biomechanical tests have confirmed that the remarkable endurance of human runners stems from both our bipedalism and our superior heat-loss mechanism (sweating). Running upright means we can vary the rhythm of our breathing, whereas quadrupeds such as horses have to breathe according to a pattern dictated by the compression of their lungs from their front legs. Sweating heavily also allows us to escape the constraint that stops fast animals such as cheetahs running more than a half-mile at a time: lethal overheating. I had first-hand confirmation of this from an Australian Aboriginal friend in the remote Pilbara region. Brendan Bobby, an initiated man of the Kurrama mob, once told me, laughing, how he and his mates hunt kangaroos in the scorching desert heat—by running them down in a six-cylinder pickup truck: "That 'roo, if you scare him up on a hot day when he's lying in the shade, he'll run out a few hundred yards, then stop and hop right back to the shade! Too hot for him; if he goes too far he'll die." Unfortunately for the 'roo, his days are numbered anyway, with Brendan and his mates dishing out death by roadkill.

Colonial-era accounts confirm that Brendan's ancestors have been taking advantage of this behavior for millennia, though using their own legs rather than Ford utility vehicles. Australian Aboriginal men in Western Australia practiced endurance hunting—running their prey down until it collapsed through exhaustion and, often, died without the need of a blow or spear. The bushmen of South Africa did (and still do) the same with antelopes, chasing them for up to twenty-five miles until they crumple. This is clearly fantastic training for athletic running, since another group of antelope chasers, the Tarahumara Indians of Mexico, are on record as some of the best athletes in the modern world. The phenomenal endurance of the Tarahumara, though often remarked on by conquistadors and early anthropologists, was only brought to the modern world's attention in 1963. In that year a party of American endurance athletes had to be rescued by local Tarahumaran men after failing, through exhaustion, to complete their "river run" through the

forbidding Barranca del Cobre canyon. One grateful but awed survivor described his Tarahumaran rescuers thus:

> Each one of us [the Americans] carried a canteen, but nothing
> else. For five miles we climbed that trail, which seemed de-
> signed only for goats. At one point, as we toiled upwards, the
> Indians passed us, each carrying a 60-pound pack of our gear.
> Suddenly, I realized it was their third trip of the day.

How did the Tarahumara develop these phenomenal athletic abilities? One study estimates their athletes can perform over 17,000
calories of work effort in 24 hours, whereas the average Tour de
France competitor expends just 8,000 to 10,000 (a calorie is not just
a unit of energy that we take in through food, but also a unit of
energy we can expend through work. Cycling uses about 1,000
calories per hour, and so does the Tarahumara's running. The difference is that the Tarahumara often run right through the day and
night.) Partly it's geography. The Tarahumara live in hamlets so
widely separated that communication between them requires running vast distances. But they also seem simply to enjoy running.
Several early anthropologists describe the Tarahumaran sport of
"kick-ball" racing, where teams of men run up to 190 miles through
wild, craggy terrain in 24 to 48 hours (running by torchlight at
night), all the while kicking a crude wooden ball before them.[24]
This sounds impressive, but not necessarily superior to the performance of modern ultramarathoners. The current world distance
record for a 24-hour run, for example, is 188.6 miles, set by Yiannis
Kouros, the "Running God," in 1997. Yet this record was achieved
on a flat, rubberized track, whereas Tarahumaran runs take place
in rough country. There are also, what's more, records of other

Indian athletes exceeding this speed and distance. John Bourke, the nineteenth-century American soldier and ethnologist, was told of a Mojave runner who ran from Fort Mojave to the Mojave reservation and back—a distance of 200 miles—in less than 24 hours, again through harsh country.[25] American historian William H. Prescott, similarly, wrote of Aztec *titlantil* ("courier runners") who also covered 200 miles a day, through mountainous country, to bring messages to the emperor in the Aztec capital Tenochtitlan. Even further back in history, the mighty Sumerian king Shulgi is reputed to have run 218 miles from Nippur to Ur and back again in 24 hours (though this time in two 12-hour stints) circa 2075 BCE.[26]

Endurance-wise, it seems, ancient and tribal runners may well have left our modern athletes gasping in their wake.

Jumping, too, was an athletic activity in which prehistoric and tribal men probably raised the bar to heights we modern men are unable to reach. In BRAWN (see page 18) we discovered that our near cousin, the bonobo chimpanzee, can jump three times the height an average human male can. Archaeological evidence of early human leaping ability, though, is practically nonexistent. There are, admittedly, some Greek records of phenomenal long-jump performances (like that of Phayllos, who cleared the jumping pit and broke his leg with a leap of 55 feet in the fifth century BCE; the modern record is 29.36 feet), but confusion about measurements (it isn't clear if this was a single, or multiple, jump event) makes these impossible to confirm. Some medieval knights, similarly, could vault as high as 5'3" to mount their steeds while wearing 88 pounds of armor, but this, too, is difficult to translate into a useful comparison. In fact, the earliest incontrovertible evidence of tribal men's superior jumping abilities comes from colonial era photographs of the Tutsi peoples of Rwanda. The German anthropologist Adolf Friedrich, Duke of Mecklenburg, was astonished to discover, in the course of his 1907 anthropological survey of Rwanda, that the majority of the tribal men he met there were able to jump heights over 6'4" and frequently did so. This was due to Tutsi tradition of *gusimbuka-urukiramende*, an initiation ritual in which young men had to jump their own height to progress to manhood. Many, however, did far better than that, apparently jumping heights up to 8'3". As proof, Friedrich sent back to Europe a series of photographs showing Tutsi men jumping over him and a companion. There they provoked general astonishment and despairing questions from at least one prominent German physician, who asked, "What then will be left of our records?"

His concerns, it turns out, were well founded. Even today, the world highjump record remains at the relatively feeble 8' set by Cuban high jumper Javier Sotomayor in 1993. Even worse, Sotomayor's jump was made using the modern Fosbury flop—a technique invented by athlete Dick Fosbury in which the jumper launches himself back-first over the bar—which adds approximately 10 percent to the jump's height. If Mecklenburg's Tutsi jumpers had used that, they may well have jumped an unreachable (by modern standards) 9'1".[27]

Spear throwing, too, appears to be a sport in which tribal men, predictably, exceled, though again reliable measurements are hard to verify. The current world record for javelin is the 107.7 yards thrown by Jan Železný of the Czech Republic in 1996. Anthropologist J. Edge-Partington, on the other hand, reported that Australian Aboriginal men of the Dalleburra tribe in the early nineteenth century could throw their hardwood spears, without the aid of a spear-thrower (which increases range through lever-age), 120 yards or more. The British author, Lieutenant Colonel F. A. M. Webster—himself a national-championship-winning jav-elin thrower—similarly reported in the early 1900s that Turkana men of East Africa regularly out-threw him by yards in competi-tions using their traditional spears (though he always triumphed with a regulation javelin). The evidence from the ancient Olym-pics, though, is once again uncertain. Depending on the transla-tion, we have records of Greek javelin throws measuring either 110 to 164 yards. While even the lower measurement beats to-day's record, there are two complications. First, Greek javelins were probably lighter than modern Olympic javelins, and thus easier to throw. Second, Greek athletes used a special leather thong, the *amentum,* which increased range by 10 to 25 percent by imparting spin and giving extra leverage. Sadly, we can't therefore say for sure just how good the ancient Greek Olympian javelin throwers were. The situation is exactly the same with ancient Olympian discus throwers, where the varying weights of Greek stone and brass *diskoi* (some weighed four times as much as modern dis-cuses) make performances impossible to compare.

One projectile contest about which we *can* be certain, however, is archery. Modern Olympic archers use high-tech, carbon-fiber recurve bows with sights and stabilizing weights, yet their shots are still shorter, slower, and less accurate than those of ancient ar-chers. To take the gold in the individual men's archery event at the 2008 Olympics, Ukrainian Viktor Ruban shot 12 arrows at the rate of one every 40 seconds at a target 77 yards away, landing just 5 in the 2-inch bullseye (7 others landed in the 4-inch outer bullseye). Ancient Mongol archers, however, despite their "primitive" wood-and-horn bows, often bettered this from greater distances, at faster speeds and on horseback to boot. Even leaving aside the ability of Genghis Khan's nephew, Yesüngge, to hit a target from 586 yards away (see, page **91**), a Mongol historical text, *The Blue Sutra,* records that several of Genghis Khan's warriors hit a tiny red flag at 164 yards in a competition before an enemy khan. One, in fact, set himself a real challenge and brought down a flying duck with a single arrow through its neck. Mongol archers could loose 12 aimed arrows a minute (one every 5 seconds, compared to the modern standard of one every 40 seconds) and usually did so from horseback, timing their shots to fire between steps, when their horses' hooves were off the ground. The official history of another nomadic Asian people, the Khitan, similarly states that Khitan soldiers held competitions to cut a 1-inch thick willow branch with a single arrow at full gallop. Other ancient archers also outstripped modern Olympic archers' performances. Henry VIII, for example, in a contest with the French king at the "Field of Cloth of Gold" tournament in 1520 CE, sent several arrows into his target's bullseye from 240 yards away. A Spanish chronicler in 1606 likewise testified that Carib Indian archers of the Antilles Islands could consistently hit an English half-crown coin at 100 paces.

It isn't just in the Western world that modern archers fall short, either. In 1987 a fifth-degree black belt in the art of *kyūdō* (Japanese archery), Ashikawa Yuichi, was humiliated in his attempt to recreate the traditional Japanese bow sport of *tōshiya,* "clearing arrows." This sport, which began in medieval Japan in 1606, required competitors to shoot arrows down the 130-yard corridor of Kyoto's Rengeō-in Temple, hitting the far wall without touching the side walls, floor, or roof on the way. Successful efforts were called "clearing arrows," and archers competed to see how many each could score out of 100 or 1,000 attempts. Yuichi, despite his high level of skill and months of additional training, managed just 9 tōshiya from 100 attempts.[28] Though probably the best any modern Japanese archer could do, this was ridiculous in light of the record set by fifteen-year-old Kokura Gishichi in 1830: 94 tōshiya in the 100-arrow event and 978 in the 1,000 arrow. To add insult to injury, Yuichi's slow and careful shooting would have been scorned by early tōshiya competitors. In 1686 CE Wasa Daihachiro, for example, shot 8,133 clearing arrows out of a total 13,053 over the course of 24 hours—a rate of 1 arrow every 6 seconds.[29]

Other sporting contests in which ancient competitors shame their modern counterparts are those involving animals. The U.S. Professional Bull Riders tour, for instance, where top riders fight to stay atop ferocious, bucking bulls for eight seconds, proudly calls itself "the toughest sport on earth." Yet a study by the Canadian Professional Rodeo Sport Medicine Team found that serious injuries, in Canadian professional bull-riding events at least, were rare—occurring in just 1.5 percent of rides.[30] Now consider an equivalent ancient sport: the "bull-leaping" ritual of the Minoan civilization on the island of Crete from 2700 to 1450 BCE. Frescoes unearthed there depict aristocratic youths grasping charging bulls by the horns and somersaulting over their backs (some paintings, alternatively, show them diving over the bull's horns to perform handstands on its back). We don't have to rely on imagination for a picture of how dangerous this was: some frescoes also show unsuccessful leapers entangled, possibly fatally, in the beast's horns. We have no figures, of course, but it seems a safe bet the injury rate exceeded 1.5 percent. Polo, similarly, is often considered a particularly tough modern equestrian sport. Yet compared to its ancient Afghan counterpart, *Buzkashi* ("goat grabbing"), it seems positively sissy. *Buzkashi* matches, which are still played today, involve hundreds of mounted competitors (each carrying a whip for attacking opponents) battling one another for possession of a calf's carcass—which usually disintegrates during play. The action is brutal, with players charging, whipping, and unseating one another in their attempt to drag the carcass clear. Games rage for days and range for miles. Injuries include fractured skulls, concussions, broken limbs, cracked ribs, punctured lungs, and severe bruising—and even the occasional fatality. It's a safe bet action like that would send most modern polo players scurrying back to their clubhouse for a restorative pink gin or three.

medieval cheerleaders?

Medieval fairs may have lacked many of the accompaniments of modern sports events: mascots, stadium seating, and jumbo-vision screens. They did, however, have cheerleaders—in a manner of speaking. Fair organizers often injected sex appeal into proceedings with a half-time prostitute race. Between the archery contests, jousting, and gander pulling (a horrific sport in which a greased goose's head was ripped from its body), organizers often scheduled a race of the town's "fallen" women, either among themselves or against their supposedly more virtuous sisters. History doesn't record what drew these athletic jezebels to enter such competitions, but the motivation of the mostly male spectators seems clear: one ogling onlooker records appreciatively that the women ran "with skirt tuckt very high."[31]

It seems puzzling, given this apparent feebleness in the contest compared to our ancient brethren, that any modern competitor should be tagged "super." Yet the trend toward record medal hauls, such as Michael Phelps's eight gold at the 2008 Olympics, has led some commentators to label ours the "age of the superathlete." These, supposedly, are those superior competitors who win multiple events in the one Olympics, such as Jesse Owens in 1936, Mark Spitz in 1972, and Carl Lewis in 1984. Yet even here modern competitors fall short of ancestral male sportsmen. Not one modern superathlete, for example, has repeated his feat consistently over successive Olympics (though Lewis, to be fair, came close with fewer wins in 1988 and 1992). None of them, what's more, has won all their events on the one day (even Michael Phelps's maximum was two events on the one day). Yet ancient Greek Olympians did this so frequently that authorities kept a special list of *triastes* ("those who won three events on the one day"). Leonidas of Rhodes won this title at four successive Olympics in the twelve years between 164 and 152 BCE, taking out the *stadion* ("220-yard sprint"), the *diaulos* ("440-yard sprint") and the *hoplitodromos* ("440-yard race run in heavy armour, helmet, and shield") at each one. Carl Lewis, by comparison, was only able to win one event, the long jump, in every one of his four Olympic appearances. Hermogenes of Xanthos nearly equaled Leonidas's feat, winning eight victories in the *stadion, diaulos,* and *hoplitodromos* in three Olympic appearances, and Astylos of Syracuse was just behind him, with seven. The stamina needed to win these three demanding races on one day must have been incredible. The ability to then back up and perform the same feat in Olympics after Olympics was nothing short of superhuman.

Some Greek Olympians, moreover, had even longer careers than Leonidas—and ones *far* longer than those of their modern counterparts. The champion Spartan wrestler Hipposthenes, for example, scored victories in six consecutive Olympic wrestling competitions in the twenty-four years between 632 and 608 BCE. The hulking Milo of Kroton (he was reputed to eat more than twenty-two pounds of meat and twenty-two pounds of bread at every meal) did the same one hundred years later. (Only one modern wrestler, Adolf Lindfors in 1920, has ever won gold at an Olympics when over the age of forty, and even Lindfors only won at a single Olympics.) What makes this longevity even more incredible is that Greek wrestling was a brutal sport only marginally less lethal than boxing and the *Pankration* (see, pages **77–80**). Greek athletes also sometimes competed at much higher intensity than modern athletes—running, throwing, or fighting two or three times a week. Their modern counterparts typically compete in just a handful of events per year. The champion boxer Theogenes of Thasos, to quote one example, fought fourteen-hundred bouts over twenty-two years. Muhammad Ali, by comparison, fought just sixty-one in his twenty-one-year career. (Theogenes, what's more, apparently never lost a bout; "The Greatest," by contrast, dropped five.) Crowning laurels for stamina, however, must go to the fifth century CE chariot racer Porphyrius. Not only was Porphyrius known to occasionally race fifty times in one day, he continued racing for forty years until his retirement in his sixties. Porphyrius, similarly, won almost every race he entered—he even frequently performed the *diversium:* winning a race, then swapping chariots with his defeated rival and winning again. Again, what makes Porphyrius's career so remarkable is the danger he faced: chariot races were notorious for their *naufragium* ("shipwreck") crashes. The Greek poet Pindar, for example, describes one race in which forty-one chariots started but just one finished.

Performance-wise, it seems, our superathletes no more deserve the title than they do (some argue) the multimillion-dollar endorsements that follow. Yet others insist that it is precisely these rewards that *make* a male superathlete—the money, the lifestyle, the women, and the fanatical worship from millions of fans. Surely no ancient athlete could compete in this cult of the super sportsman? Call it schadenfreude, but the good news for all envious couch potatoes is that modern superathletes don't, in fact, compare favorably. Whether financially, sexually, or in terms of public adoration, ancient sportsmen often make their modern counterparts look like impoverished minor league wannabes hustling change for a big date.

Golfer Tiger Woods, to start at the top, is thought to have set a new standard for modern superathletes, earning, as he did, U.S. $112 million in 2007.[32] One of the ways he was able to do this was through his U.S. $2.5 million appearance fees. This is certainly steep, but it might surprise the struggling tour promoters who had to fork it over to know that they actually got off lightly. In ancient Greek games (of which there were many besides the Olympics, since every important Greek city staged its own), appearance fees were sometimes double that (in relative terms). One inscription, for instance, records that a top athlete at one city's games received 30,000 drachma just for turning up—the equivalent of a soldier's wage for 100 years. Given that the average modern American soldier's annual wage is approximately U.S. $45,000, this makes for a relative value of U.S. $4.5 million. Then there were the prizes, which could be substantial indeed (giving the lie, incidentally, to the modern Olympics' hypocritical pretensions of amateurism). At the Panathenaic games, for example, even winners of the lowest events received 100 *amphorae* "nine-gallon clay jars" of olive oil, the combined value of which was equivalent to the wage of a skilled worker for 3 years—roughly U.S. $225,000 in modern money. Winners also received free food for life at their home city's expense, probably worth about U.S. $245,000 today.[33] It was through rewards like these that Greek and Roman athletes were able to become some of the wealthiest men in the ancient world. The star second-century charioteer Diocles, for example, competed for purses worth up to an astronomical 60,000 sesterces at a time— equivalent to 60 times a soldier's annual pay, or U.S. $2.7 million today. Given that he raced 4,257 times—and won on 1,462 of those occasions—it is no surprise Diocles accumulated a fortune of 35,823,120 sesterces, or U.S. $1.62 billion over his 20-year career. Admittedly, Tiger Woods *might* go on to equal this feat, yet we have to remember that Diocles was not even the Roman world's most successful charioteer; he's just the only one for whom we have figures. One dreads to think what the winnings of Porphyrius— who raced twice as long, much more frequently, and invariably won—would have been.

Another frequent boast of modern superathletes (the more ungentlemanly ones, at any rate) is the number of women they've slept with. Wilt Chamberlain, NBA basketball center for the Lakers and Harlem Globetrotters, to quote the most outrageous, famously claimed twenty thousand conquests. Though Chamberlain probably *was* exaggerating, it's undeniably true that male athletic success is seriously sexy for women. One anthropologist who lived with the Mehinaku Indians of Brazil, whose men hold frequent public wrestling competitions, in the 1960s and 1970s wrote that village women coyly "made themselves available" for champions who triumphed in the wrestling square.[34] Yet have modern superathletes really reached a high-water mark in sexual conquests? It's difficult to make exact comparisons, but we do have some evidence that ancient athletes were no slouches in the romance department. Gladiators, for example, seem to have carried enormous sex appeal for Roman maids and matrons, if the following graffito descriptions from walls at Pompeii are anything to go by:

> Crescens, the net fighter, is master of the girls [and] lord of the maidens, giving them their nightly medicine.
> Celadus, the Thracian, is the girls' hero who makes them all sigh.[35]

Even the poet Martial wrote of a phenomenally successful gladiator called Hermes, who was "the care and suffering of women."[36] Nor were the conquests of these ring heroes invariably lower-class groupies. Literary and archaeological evidence shows that gladiators often commanded the affections of very high-class Roman women. The satirist Juvenal wrote pointedly of a senator's wife, Hippia, who forsook her family and social position to shack up with a gladiator, Sergius, whose "face was really disfigured: . . . [with] an enormous lump right on his nose, and the nasty condition of a constantly [dribbling] eye."[37] It was the steel, Juvenal complained, that they were in love with. Rumors abounded that powerful Roman men—even the Emperor Commodus—were actually the illegitimate sons of gladiators. An archaeological find from Pompeii, what's more, may confirm that this wasn't just talk—the skeleton of a very high-class woman (judging from her gold and emerald jewelry) was found entwined in a gladiator's arms in the barracks there. Dallying with senators' wives and emperors' mothers would, to put it in perspective, be like first ladies Michelle Obama and Laura Bush shacking up with two tag-team wrestlers from the WWF. So while we can't say for certain just how many women ancient athletes had assignations with, they clearly sometimes went right to the top when they did.

The adulation of millions of fans is also considered a mark of the modern superathlete. Yet some ancient athletes were *actually* worshipped, not just hero-worshipped. Theogenes, to give one example, had a statue erected for him and became a god in his native city of Thasos. Citizens prayed to him to preserve crops, prevent disease, and rid the city of plague. A later inscription on a shrine shows his cult was still going strong five hundred years later and had spread far beyond his home city.[38] Porphyrius the charioteer would probably have been made a god, too, if the empire had not become Christian by his time. As it was he received every honor short of it, having no fewer than seven statues of gold, silver, and bronze erected to glorify him, the first two before he had even grown a beard. This was unheard of, since such statues had to be approved by the emperor and weren't normally authorized until the charioteer had retired. Michael Jordan, by comparison, had to wait until 2009—six years after his retirement—for induction into the Basketball Hall of Fame.

These two ancient athletes also show that another supposed mark of modern superathletes—bad behavior—has all been done before. Dennis Rodman may have ignited the airwaves in the early twenty-first century with cross-dressing, suicide attempts, and domestic violence incidents, but Theogenes and Porphyrius were *serious* bad boys. The Greek historian Plutarch, for instance, states that Theogenes was prone to challenging every guest at his banquets to fistfights. He was also once fined two talents (U.S. $250,000) for abruptly withdrawing from an event at the Olympics—a serious offense. This massive fine, and the fact that Theogenes was able to pay it, again emphasizes how wealthy Greek athletes were. Even Theogenes' behavior, though, paled beside Porphyrius's outrages. The famous charioteer once led a rioting mob on a burning and murdering rampage through the Jewish quarter of the city of Antioch, resulting in a mini massacre, and later, in 532 CE, played a part in the infamous *Nika* "victory" riots in Constantinople in which thirty thousand people died (see below). Next to that, even the 2007 dogfighting conviction of NFL football player Michael Vick seems mild.

◼ fans

The new millennium has often been described as an era of unprecedented spectator violence, particularly soccer hooliganism. As of 2008, for example, 185 Argentinean soccer fans have died from violence and hooliganism in soccer stadiums, with even more killed in related off-field attacks. Though tragic, this carnage is still just a shadow of ancient spectator violence. Roman sports crowds were not only so brutal they would have scared even English soccer hooligans, they also showed greater fanaticism than the most diehard of modern fans. This was partly because ancient crowds at some events were, incredibly, even larger than modern mobs. The hippodrome at Constantinople, for instance, seated 250,000 spectators for the chariot races. The biggest sporting event in the twentieth century, by comparison, the 1950 FIFA World Cup in Brazil, saw just 199,500 fans squeeze into the Estadio do Maracana to see Uruguay defeat Brazil.

These Roman fans were so committed that they sometimes followed their sporting idols into death, as in the case of the distraught supporter of the "Reds" chariot team, who suicided by jumping onto the funeral pyre of his favorite driver. Ancient fans could also have shown modern hooligans a thing or two about rioting. European soccer fans might overturn cars and smash windows at every UEFA Cup final, but rampaging fans in Constantinople actually burned the entire hippodrome down *on four separate occasions* between 491 CE and 532 CE. Nor did Roman fans lack organized hooligan gangs equivalent to the infamous "crews" of English soccer. Supporters of the "Blue" and "Green" factions at Constantinople, for example, wore flamboyant, billowing robes that would have put any English thug's uniform to shame, and styled their facial hair so bizarrely it would have made modern skinheads look conservative. It was these gangs that almost toppled the Emperor Justinian in the week-long *Nika* riots of 532 CE—more than thirty thousand people were butchered before the government managed to put the rowdies down. ■

In just about every respect, then, our athletic performance would probably relegate us modern males to the prehistoric benches. But isn't it nonetheless true that we are, at least, the best sports in history? Haven't modern athletes set new highs in terms of fair play and sportsmanship—defined by one sports ethicist as the ability to "take loss or defeat without complaint or victory without gloating and . . . [treat] . . . opponents with fairness, generosity and courtesy"?[39] Has any modern sporting team captain, though, ever seen one of his players killed but then still agreed that the murderer was, indeed, the game's MVP? Yet that's exactly what a troop of Scottish knights at a jousting tournament in 1341 CE did. Given the honor of naming the tournament prize winner, they chose the knight who had killed their countryman, William Ramsey, with a lance through the head.[40] One could argue, of course, that European knights are a poor comparison, since their code of chivalry partly gave rise to the modern ethos of fair play. Yet other, non-Western, athletes historically showed sportsmanship that frequently amazed colonial-era Europeans. Swiss anthropologist Curt Nimuendajú was astonished to witness the aftermath of a 1940s Timbira Indian "log-race," a grueling relay event in which teams of men struggled to run a ten-mile course carrying a two-hundred-pound wooden log, describing it thus:

> And now we come to the feature that remains incomprehensible . . . The victor and the others who have desperately exerted themselves to the bitter end receive not a word of praise, nor are the losers and outstripped runners subject to the least censure . . . Not a trace of jealousy or animosity is visible between the teams . . . Who turns out to be the victor makes as little difference as who has eaten most at a banquet.[41]

Another European observer of around the same era likewise noted that although young wrestlers and stick fighters of the African Nuba tribe spent months in harsh training, come fight day so little attention was paid to the champions that "there are essentially no victors and defeated."[42] Anthropologist Raymond Firth, similarly, commented on the remarkably sporting behavior of winning teams in the Polynesian Tikopian contest of stick throwing, writing: "It is the custom for the winners to gather a large number of green coconuts which are distributed among the losers. Both sides then sit down together to drink, eat and refresh themselves."[43]

It is sometimes said, on the other hand, that what really marks modern competitive sport is its *lack* of sportsmanship. According to this theory, the commercial pressure to provide a spectacle, combined with our accelerating obsession with winning and records, has led to a retreat from the glorious sportsmanship we inherited from the ancient Greek Olympians. Once again, however, we're really just the wannabe bad boys of the sports world. The ancient Greeks, to begin with, would have laughed at the notion, first voiced by the National Sportsmanship Brotherhood of America in 1926, that what matters is not "that you won or lost—but how you played the game."[44] Greek Olympians were so hypercompetitive they didn't even record second or third places—all that mattered was who won. The poet Pindar, for instance, scorned second-place getters at the games, writing that theirs would be "a hateful homecoming [in] disgrace and secrecy . . . they slink along back alleyways, shunning enemy eyes and nursing pain, the bite of defeat."[45] Greek athletes were so preoccupied with winning that they were also quite prepared to die in the pursuit of victory, as evidenced by an inscription found at Olympia honoring a boxer, Agathos Daimon, who "died, boxing in the Stadium, having prayed to Zeus for either the crown or death."[46] Other ancient athletes went to further extremes, killing *other* people to win, as in the case of the Aztec priest-king Axayacatl, who had his men murder another city's ruler, Xochimilco, when the latter got the advantage in a one-on-one match of the rubber-ball game that resembles basketball.[47] Trobriand Islands men, according to the great anthropologist Bronislaw Malinowski, were even less chivalrous (if not quite as deadly)—not only did they force their women to enter a hopelessly uneven tug-of-war contest with them, and then, when the women inevitably lost, rub it in with a sneering and howling display; they also flung themselves upon their defeated womenfolk and had public and repeated sex with them.[48]

The high (or possibly low) point of bad sportsmanship, though, must be cheating. The succession of Olympic doping scandals in the 1990s and beyond have led some to claim that modern sport has entered an age of cheats. Yet even the most cursory study of ancient sport shows it was ever thus. True, Greek Olympians didn't have the fantastic medicine chest of drugs we do, but it wasn't from want of trying. Not only were Greek athletes suckers for any fad diet that might give them an advantage—figs, soft cheese, poppy seeds, mushrooms, pigs fed on berries, and so on—they also happily downed whatever supposed performance enhancers their technology *did* allow them (one favorite being *gloios* ("gum"), the mixed sweat, olive oil, and sand scraped off winning athletes' bodies).[49] Other ancient athletes also indulged. Native American lacrosse players, for example, smeared themselves with liquid mixed from wolves' tracks and crawfish burrows.[50] They also tried to secretly douse their opponents' legs with the juice of a rabbit's stewed left leg to lame them (the idea coming from the rabbit's curious habit of leaving just three tracks in the snow).

If such concoctions failed to help, however, ancient sportsmen were only too ready to cheat outright. One European observer stated dryly that Samoan games of stick throwing were only honest because every single participant cheated, thereby canceling out his neighbor's underhanded efforts. Greek Olympic athletes proved just as willing, bribery being their favored method. One Athenian pentathlete, Calippus, bribed every one of his competitors in 332 CE, duly winning the five-leg pentathlon. Demonicus of Elis, similarly, bribed the father of another competitor in the boys' wrestling to let his (Demonicus's) son win. We know this because both individuals were caught by the *hellenodikai* ("judges of the Greeks") who forced them, by way of a fine, to pay for several statues (called *zanes*) of Zeus bearing the inscription: "An Olympic Victory is to be won not by money but by swiftness of foot or strength of body." So many athletes were caught bribing that the *hellanodikai* were able to line the walkway to the Olympic stadium with these *zanes* in an attempt to shame other would-be cheaters. The evidence, though, shows that not all *were* so shamed. One lad who agreed to throw his wrestling match at the Isthmian games for 3,000 drachmas, for example, was so incensed that the victor refused to pay that he dragged him before the judges at the local temple and swore an oath on Poseidon that his opponent had bribed him fair and square.[51] A little less forward, though far more malevolent, were those athletes who resorted to black magic to win. Around one thousand five hundred *tabula defixio* ("curse tablets") have been found in ancient Greek and Roman arenas bearing appeals to devils and demons to intervene in the contest. At the hippodrome in Carthage, for instance, a concealed lead tablet was found carefully smoothed and nailed to the arena floor, inscribed with the words, "I beseech you O! demon and demand of you that you torture and kill the horses of the Greens and the Whites and that you cause the drivers Clarus, Felix, and Primulus to have fatal accidents."[52] True, these sound quaint to our ears, but given that chariot-race deaths were frequent, and that the people invoking the curses believed them utterly, it's clear that ancient athletes were ready to take cheating to levels at which even Tonya Harding's husband would have balked.

Why *are* modern contests so pale an imitation of ancestral sport? Why *do* we, apparently, run slower, jump lower, and shoot and throw more feebly than our tribal and prehistoric forebears did? Is it because we are, in some way, physically lesser than they were? Many sports historians, for example, originally believed that the Rwandan Tutsis were only able to jump so high because of their towering height compared to Europeans. Yet Tutsi men, it turns out, aren't taller than modern Europeans; generally they're shorter.[53] True, at an average height of 5'7", they *did* tower over Europeans of the early 1900s, when those sports historians were writing, but Europeans and Americans have since grown to an average 5'8"—and yet our high-jump record still lags behind the Tutsi jumpers', meaning it can't be a simple matter of height disadvantage.

Once again, I believe, the explanation is ontogenetic. Tutsi boys practiced *gusimbuka-urukiramende* (see page 137) all the time, since it was the only way they could pass initiation and enter full manhood. Modern high-jumpers, in contrast, though no doubt highly motivated, don't face the prospect of not being allowed to drive, vote, or drink if they fail to clear the bar. Tutsi men, just like those ancient Greek rowers, also passed tough childhoods as shepherds, in which they frequently had to run, jump, dodge, and even fight off lions. I'm also willing to stick my neck out and say that ontogeny probably explains the superiority of ancient archers, too. An average Olympic archer today, for example, trains forty hours a week on the range[54]— though certainly demonstrating commitment, this is nothing compared to Genghis Khan's Mongols. Not only did Mongol archers probably train eighty hours a week, they also did so from early childhood, as Franciscan friar John Carpini, who visited the Khan's court in 1247 CE, confirmed:

> The men do not make anything at all, with the exception of arrows . . . they hunt and practice archery, for they are all, big and little, excellent archers, and their children begin as soon as they are two or three years old to ride and . . . are given bows to suit their stature and are taught to shoot.[55]

Later sources show that ancient Turkish archers practiced gripping and drawing heavy bows for years before they were even allowed to fire them. When finally judged ready, they then trained by firing 1,000 arrows a day. It was probably because of this strenuous training that Turkish archers were able to use much heavier bows than modern archers—some Ottoman Turkish bows, preserved in museums, take over 220 pounds of force to draw, or four times that of modern Olympic bows.[56]

■training

t might be thought that the super performances of our ancestral athletes demanded super preparation. Yet their match-day preparation often seems to have been at best useless and at worst positively harmful. Most athletes, indeed, probably succeeded despite rather than because of it. Ancient Chinese martial arts masters, for example, undoubtedly had logic on their side when they smashed their shins into logs repeatedly to toughen them, but the number of fractures and muscle hemorrhages must have also been enormous. Greek Olympic athletes, similarly, showed some sense in their *tetrad* system of training, which alternated endurance running, weight-lifting, ball exercises, and sand running in a four-day cycle of hard and soft exercise. Yet the recommendation of some Greek authors that aspiring athletes wrestle with animals, including bulls and lions, seems more questionable. Cherokee ball-game players, on the other hand, mauled *themselves* in preparation for each match. By the time they had finished their pre-game "scratching" ordeal, in which each player was gashed bloodily three hundred times with a claw-like blade, they must have looked like they'd tangled with a horde of massive carnivores. Nor did Native American athletes go in for any nonsense about carb-loading: sound preparation for an Iroquois lacrosse match involved swallowing a disgusting emetic to make each player vomit. Still, there was some consolation to be had from this wild and woolly amateurism. The famous Greek doctor Hippocrates, for instance, had a simple remedy for an athlete's aching muscles: he should "get drunk on wine once or twice."

One word, I think, sums up the various causes of ancient athletic superiority: engagement. Ancient athletes were so much better at sport because they were so much more deeply engaged with it. Often they *lived* it. That's also the reason, I believe, that ancient sport was frequently more dangerous and violent—usually so much more was at stake than it is today. An ancient Greek *pankratiast* couldn't settle for second-place honors; there were none. He had to fight on, if need be to the death. An Aztec ball-gamer couldn't play soft; to do so would be to dishonor the gods. This is the real truth of the "sport as a civilizing influence" theory: it has things backward. Modern sport is not the repository of aggression that has allowed other aspects of life to become more civilized: sport itself has been tamed and pacified as part of the civilizing process. This is largely the result, as Norbert Elias said, of the divorcing of sport from its original aims in ritual, war, hunting, and dueling. The flipside of this, however, is that modern sport is played with less passion, lower intensity, and vastly reduced drama. One reason for the high death rate in Roman chariot races, for example, was the charioteers' habit of wrapping their reins around their waist. Since getting entangled in wreckage and dragged by frightened horses was a major killer of drivers, this was a serious statement of intention to "go down with the ship." This is why charioteers attracted fanatical crowds the size of which LeBron James could only dream, why they made money beyond the fantasies of mere modern super-golfers, and why they earned the awe of kings and nobles: they literally put their lives on the line every time they raced.

What modern sportsman, in this era of the "blood rule" and hair-trigger litigation, would dare do the same?

In any case, the situation for *Homo masculinus modernus* is clearly getting serious. If sport isn't our game then where *do* we modern males excel? What achievements *can* we use to salve our pride, impress our women, and ensure the propagation of our half of the species? Given our physical failings, might we, like Cyrano de Bergerac, make good such deficiencies through the power of our honeyed words? The eloquent poet of Rostand's play did, after all, win Roxane's heart, despite his oversized schnoz. There is even some scientific support for the notion: several studies have found women rate verbal creativity more highly than looks or even wealth in the sexual-attractiveness stakes.

That being the case, perhaps we can breathe easier. We are, after all, more literate, better educated, and more creative than any men in history . . . aren't we?

To take one example, some literary theorists claim that modern hip-hop and rap represents the height of male poetic wordplay, superior to even classical poets such as Homer and Virgil. Rappers, they insist, improvise complex and witty lyrical barbs, *on the spot,* in the course of their live "battle raps"—a far cry from the years Virgil took to write Rome's national poem, the *Aeneid.* To pursue a "beef," or fight, with a rival, rappers must also write and release "diss [disrespecting] tracks" within days to respond to their enemy. What's more they are also some of the best-paid entertainers in history: Curtis Jackson, aka 50 Cent, raked in U.S. $150 million in 2008 alone, placing him on top of Forbes's "Hip-Hop Cash Kings" list.

So far, so reassuring, but how do these claims fare under proper scientific study? Do modern rappers *really* blow ancient bards away with their incredible feats of memory, improvisation, creativity, and wordplay? Courtesy of the next chapter, BARDS, ladies and gentlemen, we are pleased to announce a once-in-a-lifetime chance to find out. Sit back in ringside comfort then as, for one night only, the insults fly, grown men cry, and poetic reputations are deflated, berated, eliminated, and fustigated in this, the ultimate rappers' beef: Homer vs. 50 Cent.

It should be a hell of a show.

Bards

first, let's meet the contenders. In the red corner we have 50 Cent, a multi-award-winning rapper from New York whose albums have sold more than 22 million copies. Orphaned at eight and dealing crack on the streets of Queens by the age of twelve, Curtis Jackson is a poster boy for the violent world of "gangsta" hip-hop music. In 2000 he was even shot nine times by a rival gangster; his voice still carries a trademark slur from the bullet that hit his jaw. Jackson got his break, musically speaking, when he released the single "How to Rob," which gave a comic but violent rundown of how he would rob a series of famous artists and entertainers. He went on to combine his thuggish but undeniable street cred with melodious rap beats and riffs on the hugely successful albums *Get Rich or Die Trying* and *The Massacre*. 50 Cent then parlayed these musical successes into a multimillion-dollar empire of clothing labels, beverages, films, and even mining interests.

So much for the man, but what of his art? What *is* rap, and why is it sometimes considered the pinnacle of male poetic creativity?[1] Some critics, of course, dispute that it is, citing the undeniable obscenity, cruelty, boastfulness, and violence of many rap lyrics. Yet scratch a little deeper and another picture emerges. These crudities are often wittily and skillfully employed, as when New York rapper Supernatural won the crowd's admiration in a live, "freestyle" (improvised) battle with rival rapper MC Juice (who had earlier defeated Eminem) using these lines:

> Know it for a fact, nigger, you're totally wack, you never could ever start to f#$! with Supernat. I could switch ya, one time, brother feel the mixture, I'm gonna come over, rip down this nigger's picture.

Considering they were made up on the fly, these multi-syllabic, rhymed insults and threats are impressive. Not only do they fit their words into a fixed rhythm (what poets call a meter), they also organize each couplet around a finishing rhyme, with a secondary layer of internal rhymes: "never could ever" and "switch ya . . . mixture . . . picture." These complex internal rhymes are, in fact, rap's signature, and a skilled practitioner can pack multiple examples into a verse, as in Public Enemy's line: "Their pens and pads I snatch 'cause I've **had it**/I'm not an **addict,** fiending for **static**/I see their tape recorder and I **grab it**/No, you can't have it back, silly **rabbit**." Rap battles are also, surprisingly, a deeply traditional art form. Insult competitions like the Supernatural/MC Juice battle hark back to the verbal jousts of slave days known as "Playin' the Dozens," in which rival African males competed to win over a crowd using back-and-forth insults of the "Yo' mama so fat she wear a tent for a dress" variety. The high esteem in which verbally skilled males are held in African-American communities may, in fact, date back a thousand years to the *griots* ("wandering poets") of West Africa.

But if this gives us a snapshot of 50 Cent, what of the blue corner—the ancient Greek poet Homer? Why pick this literary fossil whose poetry is written in a long-dead dialect and of whom most people only know through his fat, dimwitted cartoon doppelgänger, the father of Bart Simpson? It is because of Homer's (the poet's, that is) central role in Western literature. Due to his two epic poems, the *Iliad* and the *Odyssey,* both of which tell the story of the ancient Greeks' war against the Trojans, Homer is considered the founder of European writing. But hang on, isn't pitting the written works of this father of Western literature against the spoken compositions of rappers comparing apples to literary oranges? Actually, it isn't. Leaving aside the fact that most rap lyrics, even apparently improvised ones, *are* written (see below), it turns out that Homer's poetry, too, was originally spoken rather than put down on paper (or, more properly, papyrus).

Literary theorists had long been puzzled by certain recurring set phrases in Homer's poems, such as "rosy-fingered dawn" and "the wine-dark sea." In the 1930s linguists Milman Parry and Albert Lord demonstrated that these were a memory aid used in traditional *spoken* epic poetry across the world—Homer, it seems, didn't write his poetry, he rapped it! It's highly possible, in fact, that Homer, the greatest poet in Western literature, *couldn't* write, since the Greek alphabet wasn't invented until circa 800 BCE, around the time Homer was composing. The fact that we now have written versions of both the *Iliad* and *Odyssey,* however, has led to the "transcription hypothesis": the theory that both poems were transcribed by some scribe directly from Homer's, or one of his disciples', oral performance.

Again, so much for the man, but what of his art? What type of poems were Homer's oral epics? Like modern rappers, Homer would have delivered his lines to musical accompaniment, though probably a lyre rather than a turntable, beat box, and drum kit. His poetry, like rap, also depended on rhythm, though in Homer's case this was the strict meter known as the dactylic hexameter—an arrangement of six dactyls, or long syllables followed by two shorts. Unlike rap, however, ancient Greek poetry didn't rhyme. It also relied far more on narrative than rap does. Much of this narrative was actually true history, as the excavations of archaeologist Heinrich Schliemann, who found the ruins of Troy in the 1870s, showed. Homeric poetry was also vastly different in motivation and style to modern rap. Where modern rappers compete for social position through boastful insults, ancient Greek poetry recounted the deeds of the Greeks' glorious ancestors, and even their enemies, in order to pay homage to them. This essential difference is clearly shown by Homer's noble treatment of the Greeks' adversaries—not once does he call the Trojans "fools," "wack," "biyatches," or any other favored rap putdown.

Comparing the two art forms is, of course, fraught with difficulty. Value judgments about poetry are notoriously subjective. Given rappers' boasts about their prowess in the fields of memory and improvisation, though, we do have some objective measures with which to compare. Let's bring it on, then, by launching directly into round one: memory.

Modern rappers are, admittedly, considered to be excellent mnemonists, or memory experts. They have to be: their songs, focused on wordplay, are much heavier on lyrics than regular pop numbers. Interestingly, this is probably why rappers often make a better transition than other singers into film careers. Rapper Busta Rhymes, for instance, states that his method for learning lines for his movie appearances is to rap them. But how many lines does the average rapper, in our case 50 Cent, actually have to remember? To get an idea I sampled 5 of Jackson's songs: "In da

Hood," "Thug Love," "Back Down," "What's up Gangsta?" and "Candy Shop." These average about 60 lines each. To date Jackson seems to have written around 100 songs; let's be generous and assume he can remember each one of them perfectly. (An incident at the 2007 Black Entertainment Television awards, during which 50 Cent was caught lip-synching, shows he may not always need to.) That makes a total of 6,000 lines. Now consider our ancient Greek poet, Homer. Just 1 of his poems, the *Iliad*, comprises an astonishing 15,693 lines of text. If you add the *Odyssey*, that takes his total to 27,803 lines of memorized verse. This is bad enough, but we have to remember, too, that these works are just those that have come down to us. Homer probably had more in his repertoire. Indeed, the evidence of linguists Lord and Parry shows he might have had *many* more. As part of their study of oral epic poetry, Lord and Parry researched the *guslar* tradition of Serbia and Montenegro. Medieval *guslars* were poets who performed epic tales of the Slavs' struggle for independence against the Turkish Ottoman Empire. Remarkably, the tradition continued into the early twentieth century, and the two scholars were able to meet and interview some of the last *guslars*. One of those, an illiterate butcher named Avdo Mededović, proved capable of recalling an astonishing 58 epic tales.[2] The 13 that Lord and Parry had time to record totaled 78,555 lines of verse, meaning Mededović's complete repertoire probably comprised 350,476 lines of poetry. If Homer had anything like Mededović's recall, his lyrical memory would have been fifty times that of 50 Cent.

Mededović's feats, incidentally, also tell us something about the endurance of modern rappers compared to traditional epic poets. British rapper Ruffstylz claims to hold the world record for the longest freestyle rap at ten hours and thirty-four minutes.

This was set in 2003 under official Guinness World Record rules, which allow a fifteen minute break every four hours and as many short breaks (less than thirty seconds) as the rapper wants. By comparison, Lord estimates a full recital of the *Iliad* would take about twenty-four hours nonstop. Modern academic opinion generally holds that these performances wouldn't have been given in one sitting, but again, I think that's judging by our own lax standards. In an illiterate age with very limited recreational options, visits from traveling bards would have been rare and exciting events, and I wouldn't be at all surprised if ancient spectators eagerly sat through an entire reading in one hit. In any case, Mededović's phenomenal performances prove what traditional bards were capable of, blowing Ruffstylz away in the process—one song of Mededović's that Lord recorded, for example, filled up one hundred LP albums, or sixteen hours' solid recital time.[3]

Memory-wise, then, it seems modern rappers would have had trouble recalling Homer's laundry list. By now, though, 50 Cent would probably cry foul—his *real* skill, and one old fossils like Homer lacked, he would argue, is improvisation. Jackson and his fellow rappers are experts at "spitting" on-the-spot lyrics, as their freestyling shows . . . or does it? Leaving aside the fact that many rappers cheat by pre-writing lyrics, one philological (a fancy word for literary) study of rap also found that freestylers use numerous tricks such as pre-written generic rhymes and stock phrases to help their flow. "Brooklyn" for example, is often paired with "took and" or "tooken"; "Illin" often takes the partner "chillin." Then there are the stock phrases. Even the aforementioned Supernatural, widely considered the best freestyle rapper in the world, was found, in one 254-line freestyle, to use repeated phrases such as, "I'll tell you what" (11 times), "far as I can see" (3 times) and "it don't make a dif" (5 times).[4] Without dissing rappers' impressive verbal skills, these tricks clearly reduce enormously the difficulty of rhyming on the spot.

More remarkably, however, it turns out that Homer's poetry wasn't just memorized, either: it, too, was substantially improvised. We know this because of those memory aids that Parry and Lord found scattered through Homer's works. The linguists identified two classes of these: formulas and themes. Formulas are those set phrases, such as "the wine-dark sea," which, because of their syllabic structure, could slot into the end of a couplet and maintain the strict meter of Greek poetry. Themes are longer passages of text that described a key scene—a battle, a feast, the assembling of an army—that were repeated at key points, often in the same words. These show, Parry and Lord said, that Homer didn't just remember the *Iliad* and the *Odyssey,* he improvised them anew in every performance. This is a remarkable feat, by anybody's standards. It's also humbling to realize that the preserved copies of the *Iliad* and *Odyssey* we have today are simply snapshots of a one-time performance that happened to be transcribed.[5]

Once again, the Slavic *guslars* give us a sample of this remarkable process in action. To test how quickly their "modern" Montenegrin *guslar,* Mededović, could learn a new song, Parry and Lord had him listen to an unfamiliar epic called *Bećiragić Meho* sung by another *guslar.* The fact that Mededović was able to turn around and sing the 2,294-line song after just one hearing is incredible enough; even more remarkable is that his version, while still faithful to the narrative, was now 6,313 lines long. Mededović had lengthened it by three times, on the fly, with an improvised "rap" filling in detail about the characters, their actions, and motivations. What modern rapper could possibly duplicate this feat? Other historical poetic traditions also feature phenomenal improvisation skills. On the island of Malta, for example, men have long fought poetic duels called *spirtu pront* in which 2 singers compete to denigrate each other with improvised lyrics sung to music. Given that *spirtu pront* singers often sing an average of 5 hours a day for 50 years, ideally without repeating themselves, it's clear they had, and have, improvisation skills probably even exceeding those of Homer and the *guslars*.[6]

◻primetime poets

I n the 1990s author Martin Amis published a witty and incisive short story, "Career Move," that imagined a role reversal in which poets reaped fame and fortune while Hollywood screenwriters scrabbled to wring measly dollars from their action-filled, blockbuster scripts. It might astonish those struggling poets who smiled wryly at this conceit to learn that there *is* a place in the world where an ancient poetic art, still surviving, really is that popular: the Basque country of northern Spain.

In 2005 more than thirteen thousand ticket holders crammed into the *Bertsolari Txapelketa*, the national poetry championship of the Basque people, in the city of Barakaldo.[7] Another one hundred thousand watched the seven-hour event live on TV. The championship was the culmination of a grueling, four-year round of elimination contests, many almost as well attended. In the Basque art of *Bertsolaritza*, dueling poets are given a topic and twenty seconds in which to create an eight to twelve-line rhyming poem that fits both a specific meter and a melody chosen from a stock of three thousand traditional songs. It is a supreme feat of improvisation and gamesmanship—for contestants must also then battle one another directly, twisting their opponent's words into a clever putdown that will win the crowd's and judges' applause. It is the deeply traditional nature of *Bertsolaritza*, whose origins can be traced back at least as far as the fifteenth century, and its role as a symbol of Basque nationalism, that accounts for its sell-out appeal.[8]

I think we can all agree that our bout has ended prematurely with a second-round knockout. 50 Cent, the pretender, is flat on the canvas with his trainer dabbing his face and yelling for the doctor. Homer, the contender, meanwhile, is riding off in the promoter's limo to party with supermodels and take a call from the president. But if rappers have been shown up as totally wack in the virtuoso stakes, might they still not have a claim to fame in how *bad* their rap is? After all, rap—particularly gangsta rap—is widely acknowledged to be the most violent, obscene, and irreverent art form to ever grace (or disgrace) the airwaves, isn't it?

Sorry. Even violence-wise, it seems, modern rappers would have made ancient audiences yawn.

This seems hard to believe, since gangsta rap lyrics are so notoriously violent they have sparked a number of public campaigns to censor them, not least by the Parents Music Resource Center run by Tipper Gore, wife of the former U.S. Vice President (though Gore was even more incensed by heavy metal). Nor were her concerns unfounded—one study found that in a sample of 490 rap songs, 41 featured a murder and 66 described an assault or rape.[9] The language used to describe these crimes was also often exceedingly brutal, as when rappers Too Much Trouble sang of one imaginary victim that they would: "Beat her head with the phone until her skull caved in." Tough (if cowardly) stuff, granted, but it pales in comparison to the body count of Homer's *Iliad*. In that epic 105 victims lose their lives, proportionally (comparing by number of lines) *four times* the rapper's death list. Nor was Homer short on blood and gore in his lyrics, to wit:

> *Then Idomeneus smote Erymas upon the mouth with a thrust of the pitiless bronze, and clean through passed the spear of bronze beneath the brain, and clave asunder the white bones; and his teeth were shaken out, and both his eyes were filled with blood; and up through mouth and nostrils he spurted blood as he gaped, and a black cloud of death enfolded him . . .*
>
> *The bronze helmet did not stop the spear, but the point of bronze broke clean through the bone, and all his brain was spattered about inside it.[10]*

In such graphic detail were these injuries described that one modern neurosurgeon was able to use them to make accurate diagnoses of specific neurotraumas among the Greek and Trojan soldiers.

Rap does, however, have a better claim for the obscenity of its lyrics. Decency prohibits the extensive listing of examples, but suffice it to say many gangsta rap songs use the word "motherf*cker" at least once; "bitch" and "ho" also feature prominently. One academic survey of sixteen Snoop Dogg songs, similarly, found half of them featured explicit descriptions of rape.[11] Homer, it's true, has nothing to equal this, though the *Iliad* does start with the kidnap and semi-rape of the beautiful Helen. What erotic references the epic does have are of the euphemistic "melting hearts" and "veiled desire" variety. Yet other Greek authors were not above including explicit obscenity in their works. In one of his plays the famed comic playwright Aristophanes, for example, takes great delight in calling Cleon, the Athenian general and politician, a "wretch and b*ttf*cker in matters of state."[12] He also gleefully fantasizes about a rival poet getting hit in the face by a dog turd. Perhaps the height of Aristophanes' obscenity, however, is his description of a prominent Athenian citizen, Ariphrades, whom he accuses of inventing cunnilingus, saying:

> *[Ariphrades] defiles his tongue, with shameful pleasures, licking up foul secretions in the brothels, and staining his beard as he stirs up the nether-lips. What's more, he writes poetry like Polymnestos, and hangs out with Oionichos!*

The last two were, it seems, by far the worst transgressions.

▪latin limericks

Smutty limericks are often thought of as a peculiarly modern art form. This is partially true—although limericks were first created by Edward Lear in the 1840s—it was in the twentieth century that they assumed their current mandatory obscenity. Yet it might surprise those who decry the lewdness of such stall-wall scrawls to know that several Roman classical poets also wrote positively filthy little ditties. Renaissance translators, for example, were horrified to discover that their hero, the poet Virgil, hadn't only written the *Aeneid* and the *Eclogues*: he had also apparently penned a scandalous collection called the *Priapea*, poems dedicated to the Roman phallic god Priapus.[13]

Priapus was considered the god of orchards and fertility, so wooden statues of him were often set up in gardens. But he was also the god of male genitalia, meaning those statues frequently featured an absurdly large wooden penis. This gargantuan member often doubled as a club with which gardeners would beat off would-be-thieves, yet Priapus himself could use it to inflict dire punishments, as the god's threat in one of Virgil's *Priapea* poems makes clear:

> But when I thrust up thee [robber] my great, thick
> pole, stretched without wrinkle will be thine a**hole.

Priapus, according to Virgil, even maintained a sliding scale of penetrative punishments (sorry), differentiated according to the age and gender of the thief:

> Whoever the robber may be, each has something to
> offer me, the woman her c**t, the man his gob; if a boy
> his a** will do the job.

Despite the similarity of tone the *Priapea* poems are, though, far superior in poetic technique to limericks. One author, indeed, states that the collection "displays the full perfection of metrical art." In the end, though, it is the sameness of comic sensibility that binds the two forms together. What else can we do, for instance, but laugh at Priapus's shameful final confession, in poem 51, that all his threats have failed miserably. Despite the inferior quality of its fruit it is *his* orchard, rather than his neighbor's, that the thieves continually plunder—it's his "punishment" that they crave!

To digress briefly, Aristophanes' comedy also provides a fitting case study for another modern conceit: that our comedians are more obscene and reliant on shock value than ever before in history. On the face of it, this seems eminently reasonable. Didn't Eddie Murphy, after all, top off one legendary performance by commanding his audience, as well as an imaginary Bill Cosby, to fellate him—in considerably cruder terms than that? And didn't British comedienne Jo Brand confess to once using the F word ninety-three times in one show? Add in the fact that the 1990s also saw the development of "male genital origami" as a form of comedy and it certainly seems modern comics will do anything for a laugh. Yet, as ever, compared to their ancient counterparts, they're

just try-hards. Male actors in Greek comedies, by way of comparison, wore huge, dangling red leather phalluses for giggles. One
leading ancient Greek playwright even wrote a play featuring the
Persian king's supposed eight-month struggle to pass a turd, and
some actors simulated defecation on stage to titillate the audience.[14]
Even these excesses, though, were pale imitations of the antics
of some tribal comics. Many of the Plains Indian tribes of North
America in the eighteenth and nineteenth centuries, to illustrate,
featured "contrary" clowning societies whose members did everything backward for comic effect. They spoke backward, walked
backward, and played outlandish tricks such as plunging their
hands into boiling water and complaining it was cold. Zuni Indian
Koyemci clowns acted even more bizarrely—biting the heads off
mice, tearing dogs apart and feasting on their entrails, and empty-
ing bowls of urine over their heads, to the appreciative laughter
of their kinsmen. They also *drank* urine, sucking down great
draughts and smacking their lips at how delicious it was, and ate
both dog and human excrement, all for a laugh.[15] Famed anthropologist Adolph Bandelier wrote that he even saw Zuni clowns
masturbating and sodomizing one another in their attempts to
raise a chuckle.

Decency once again prohibits me from stating exactly which
body part the above examples show Eddie Murphy has failed to put
where his mouth is. But you get the idea.

■puppetry of the polynesian penis

Comedians Dave Friend and Simon Morley really started something when their "Puppetry of the Penis" show debuted in the 1998 Melbourne (Australia) International Comedy Festival. The act—in which Friend and Morley stretched, twisted, and folded their genitalia into fantastic shapes such as "The Pelican," "The Atomic Mushroom," and "The Mollusc"—was regarded as hilariously original, and soon found a legion of imitators around the world. Yet Friend and Morley were, in reality, too late to claim an original creation—about 350 years too late. Captain William Bligh, of mutiny-on-the-*Bounty* fame, was disgusted to receive a very similar performance on his first visit to Tahiti, in which one man:

> ... had his penis swelled and distorted out into an erection by a severe twine ligature ... applied so tight that the penis was apparently almost cut through. The second brought his stones to the head of his penis and with a small cloth bandage he wrapped them round and round, up towards the belly, stretching them at the same time very violently until they were near a foot in length ... the stones and the head being like three small balls at the extremity. The third person ... seizing his

Returning to rap, isn't it still true, though, that the hip-hop art form can lay claim to one last unique element: that of the contest? Though Homer, the Slavic *guslars,* and other ancient poets might have been quicker, smarter, funnier, stronger in memory, more creative, and more violent in their lyrics, isn't it still the case that modern rappers are the only poets to risk their reputations, and even sometimes their lives, in mano-a-mano confrontations with rival lyricists? Freestyle rap battles such as that of Supernatural and MC Juice are, after all, undeniably grueling lyrical tests of courage, quick-wittedness, and humor. Rappers also face possibly devastating humiliation if their poetic attempts to win the crowd over fall flat. They can even face violence or death, given the hip-hop institution of "beef"—feuds in which rappers attack each other with songs and, sometimes, blades and bullets. Surely no ancient or tribal poets dueled thus, risking their reputations and lives in the process?

The bad news is that some, in fact, did. And the worse news is that *when* they did, it was more difficult, more violent, and more dangerous than any modern hip-hop MC could possibly imagine.

The *nith* song duel of the arctic Inuit peoples in pre-colonial times, to illustrate, was an intense battle of words, wits, and wills in which men attempted to outsing one another to settle disputes such as wife-stealing or other insults. Since their object was to win over public opinion, performances took place in front of the whole village, the winner being decided by applause. Combatants strove to humiliate rivals with withering insults (accusations of cannibalism and incest being particular favorites) and witty boasts. They were required to suffer, in turn, the pantomime antics of those same opponents, who might stuff their mouths with seal blubber or blocks of wood to muffle their voices. The later consequences of *nith* song combat could also be devastating. As one Inuit duelist noted, *nith* song lyrics were "little, sharp words, like the wooden splinters which I hack off with my axe." In the close-knit conditions of Inuit life the shame of losing often led to suicide, while winning might well lead to murder. Inuit song duels were, in addition, extremely long compared to modern rap battles (which rarely last more than an hour or two). Not only might one *nith* dueling bout last a whole day, tit-for-tat duel cycles often spanned the entire winter season, and might even be kept up for years.[17]

Another lengthy, vicious, and frequently devastating poetic contest was the *haló* song duel of the Anlo-Ewe people in colonial-era Ghana. It, too, had as its goal the winning of public support, though in this case not for resolving disputes but for marshaling fighting power to better pursue them. *Haló* duels, unlike *nith* contests, were fights between villages, and whole communities practiced for months to prepare their lyrical assaults on their neighbors. These practice sessions were usually held in the strictest secrecy, since the lyrics of *haló* songs were so insulting they inevitably provoked premature fighting once their content became known. In just one song recorded by an American anthropologist, for example, one village's women were accused of: sleeping with their brothers, with all the men in their village, and with bulls; pleasuring themselves with sticks in the vagina; and setting bushes alight with their flatulence. The men were accused of: having absurdly rotund scrotums, selling their grandparents into slavery, and looking like monkeys. With verbal fireworks like these, and the inevitable violence they sparked, it is no surprise that the Ghanaian colonial police finally banned the ancient art of *haló* in 1960.[18]

Lest it be thought such lyrical mud-fights were beneath ancient Western poets, the medieval Anglo-Celtic literary tradition of *flyting* deserves a mention here. *Flyting* contests were insult competitions conducted in verse, but their lyrics were anything but poetic. The most famous recorded bout, for example, between poets William Dunbar and Walter Kennedy at the court of James IV of Scotland in the late fifteenth century, has been described as "500 lines of filth."[19] A brief scan of the verses of *The Flyting of Dunbar and Kennedy* shows why. Scatological references abound—at one point Kennedy insists Dunbar's "arse drips with excrement, [to] scrub your bottom tired out ten old women." He also accuses Dunbar's loose bowels of almost sinking a ship. And the clever, convoluted rhymes, triple-rhymes, and alliterations of the piece do not disguise its other ferocious insults—insane werewolf, deformed dwarf, spawn of Satan, horse-fornicator, and so on. Dunbar and Kennedy's poetic duel also employed shockingly violent threats. They happily accused each other of heresy and treason, crimes for which the listening king could have hanged them. Each poet also took great delight in vividly describing the brutal tortures his rival would suffer once his misdeeds became known.

Compared to the violence of this poem, one rapper threatening to cap another with his Glock seems distinctly ho-hum.

So much for violent language in poetic contests, but isn't it still true that rappers have set a new record in *actual* violence between contestants? Their "beefs" are, after all, known to frequently end in assault and even murder. Perhaps the most famous example is that of rapper Tupac Shakur, who was shot and killed in September 1996, some believe on the orders of Notorious B.I.G., a rival rapper with whom Shakur had maintained a longstanding beef (and who was also later shot and killed). Even 50 Cent himself was stabbed by rapper Black Child, an associate of Ja Rule and Murder Inc., in one episode of 50 Cent's beef with them. Yet ancient poetic contests were no stranger to violence between contestants either. Some, indeed, required it. Combatants in the Inuit *nith* song duels, for example, sometimes accompanied their ripostes with a savage head butt or straight-armed blow to the side of the head, which their opponent was required to accept stoically until his turn came to return it. Nor was fatal violence completely absent. True, the official ideology of the duel required combatants to laugh off their defeats and depart in good humor, but Inuit society was also strongly revenge driven: one early twentieth-century anthropologist reported that every man he met at one Copper Eskimo camp had been involved in at least one vengeance murder. It seems unlikely, therefore, that no defeated *nith* singer ever sought to even the score with a later harpooning (the usual method of Inuit murder). Tellingly, *nith* singers rarely included the accusation of murder among their insults—since all of them were killers, the charge lacked sting.

Physical violence was similarly common in the *haló* duels of the Anlo-Ewe people. Anthropologists reported witnessing frequent cases where the victims of the singers' insults broke through the rope separating them from the performers and attacked them with weapons.[20] These assaults usually prompted other audience members to join in, resulting in the inevitable mass arrests with which *haló* duels generally ended. *Haló* violence was even continued into the supernatural realm, with contestants eagerly attempting to injure or kill one another through the casting of spells and curses. Nor has the Western literary tradition been without its share of accompanying brutality. The reason for the violent language of the Scottish *flyting* contests was that the contest had originally been a simple prelude to battle, in which contending heroes would shout boastful abuse at one another. Even later, more refined literary disputes, however, also had their violent elements. Alexander Pope, the eighteenth century English poet, to quote one famous example, was forced to carry a loaded pistol and keep a savage guard dog to deter would-be attackers enraged by his popular satire *The Dunciad*. Given that *The Dunciad* was essentially a four-book "diss track" humiliating every one of Pope's rival poets by calling them servants of the great goddess "Dulness," we can well understand their murderous impulses.

Sadly, it seems we modern males have once more been trounced by our ancient forefathers. The verbal skills of modern rappers really are closer to Homer Simpson's than to the Greek Homer's. But this begs the question—why, then, do we bother? Why *do* rappers invest so much effort in proving their worth at wordplay when their literary skills, compared to pre-civilized standards, are so patently inadequate? The short answer, of course, is that they don't know they are. Only our blissful ignorance of Homer's poetic feats—and those of the Slavic *guslars,* the Maltese *spirtu pront* singers, the Inuit *nith* duelists, and others—allows us to make the ridiculous claims of superior wordsmithing that we do. Even if we *did* know, however, the evidence is it wouldn't make any difference. As with those earnest young fighters who sign up in droves for ultimate-fighting classes, even though not one would make more than an appetizer for an ancient Greek *pankratiast,* our inability to perform doesn't kill our desire to try. Rappers would still battle because the drive to demonstrate verbal skill is actually an essential one to the art of being male. The reason, as ever, is those omnipotent arbiters of male genetic fate—women.

■A muse of manure

A principle stated repeatedly in this book is that the instinctual drive to perform certain actions doesn't necessarily correlate with any actual skill at doing them. Poetically, no man epitomizes this more than William Topaz McGonagall, the anti-poet laureate of Victorian-era Scotland. McGonagall was certainly afire with *some* muse: he published more than two hundred lengthy poems over an extended career, and wrote several autobiographies. Unfortunately, he was completely talentless, and is now known to history as one of the worst poetasters (second-rate poets) to ever mangle the English language.

McGonagall's literary career kicked off with what he called "the most startling incident in my life . . . the time I discovered myself to be a poet, which was in the year 1877." Audiences who heard McGonagall perform were equally startled. The poetaster proved totally unable to scan (hold a poetic meter), as shown by this stanza of his most famous work, *The Tay Bridge Disaster*:

> *Beautiful Railway Bridge of the silv'ry Tay!*
> *Alas! I am very sorry to say,*

That ninety lives have been taken away,

On the last Sabbath day of 1879,

Which will be remember'd for a very long time.[21]

Undeterred, McGonagall took his act on the road, spending the next twenty-five years getting pelted with eggs, flour, rotten vegetables, and dead cats as he read his poetry to clearly unappreciative audiences in pubs, fairs, and circuses.

These assaults didn't even scratch McGonagall's remarkable self-belief, however. He still had the temerity to trek over sixty miles through a thunderstorm to petition Queen Victoria for the post of poet laureate in 1892. In typical McGonagall fashion, however, it turned out Her Majesty wasn't even home.

The crowning humiliation of McGonagall's life, however, was probably the time he was forced to pay for the privilege of appearing as Macbeth in a performance of the Scottish play at Giles Theatre in Dundee (McGonagall also considered himself an actor). McGonagall had the last laugh, though. When the time came for him to die at the hands of MacDuff he refused, bringing the house down with a ridiculously extended combat scene.

Numerous scientific studies have shown that women rate verbal creativity in men very highly. In a survey of thirty-seven different cultures across the world, for instance, women cited intelligence and creativity as their second-most important attribute in a male mate (the first was kindness).[22] More tellingly, creativity rises to first place when women are ovulating. This is important because other studies have shown that the male attributes women find most attractive when their menstrual cycle is at its fertile peak correlate strongly with genetically desirable traits. To put it simply, ovulating women give the most honest insight into the genetic traits they *really* value, since it is then that their offspring get stuck with the consequences of the woman's mating decisions. There is plenty of evidence, too, that men are acutely aware of these female predilections. One intriguing experiment at Arizona State University in 2006 found that males could be provoked to extravagant displays of involuntary verbal creativity when shown photographs of attractive women and told to imagine going out with them. (One dreads to think what lengths they would go to if presented with a real, live muse.) Once again, however, even clearer evidence can be seen on the street in the long lines of young female dancers who line up to audition for sexually explicit rap videos. As hip-hop feminist Joan Morgan points out, "the road and the 'hood are populated with women who would do anything sexually to be with a rapper for an hour, if not a night."[23]

This seems puzzling: why do women demean themselves by trading sexual availability for the chance to worship at some rapper's feet? Why do women rate verbally creative men so highly they are willing to endanger their long-term relationships for the chance of a fling with them (according to the evidence of their preferences at ovulation)? The reason the male voice acts as such a powerful trigger for female sexual behavior is because of the information it conveys about masculine evolutionary fitness. If the stomach is the way to a man's heart and the eyes the window to his soul, then truly is his voice the road to divining his suitability as a mate. Even its pitch and volume carry useful information: a low, robust voice can indicate a powerful body and high testosterone, both attributes preferred by many women. This is strikingly shown by one scientific study demonstrating that baritone opera singers have more lovers than tenors do.[24] (The tenors needn't feel so bad, though, it was ever thus. anthropologists can testify that deep-voiced hunter-gatherer men father more children than their high-pitched brothers.)

■war of words

Both Hitler and Churchill regarded their fiery words as real weapons of war, even though they delivered them from the safety of parliamentary or propaganda pulpits. Some ancient orators, though, literally backed their words with their bodies. Tahitian *rautis* ("exhorters") chose the thick of battle to declaim their ferocious poetry—the better to stir their soldiers to frenzied violence.[25] Naked but for a girdle of leaves, and weaponless save for a stingray-tail dagger (with which they were nonetheless deadly), *rautis* led Tahitian troops into war by thundering out tales of their ancestors' glorious deeds mixed with commands to slaughter the enemy. Though bloodthirsty, these were full of rich poetry, to wit:

> Hang on them like the forked lightning that plays above the
> frothing surf . . .
> Devour them as does the wild dog . . .
> Let the army be an open passage [on the reef] within which is a
> furious shark . . .

Rautis often kept up their efforts for days on end, moving through battlelines by day and camp by night to urge their soldiers on. Some were even known to die of exhaustion. The general dread in which they were held can be seen in the cry of protest common to Tahitian men receiving onerous commands from their wives or others: *tini rauti teia*—"this is equal to a rauti."

An even more reliable guide than the pitch of a man's voice, however, is his verbal skill. This is because the ability to produce quick, complex, intelligent speech is polygenic—it depends on a large number of genes, each equally essential for the finished product. Witty wordplay therefore proves that a man is largely free from any damaging mutations to his genome that might be passed on to his offspring. It is, as in the case of those testosterone-fueled muscles discussed in BRAWN, an honest and unfakeable sexual signal to a prospective mate. It is even possible that this sexual selection for verbal skill is the original cause of the evolution of human language. Some anthropologists theorize that long before meaningful words were created, female proto-humans were rewarding males with sex for the complexity of their repertoire of meaningless hoots and calls.[26]

Modern women, of course, might well feel that male language hasn't grown any more meaningful in the intervening million years or so.

If creative wordplay is a sign of a mutation-free male genome, does that mean modern rappers' second-rate efforts are all down to defective chromosomes? Clearly the answer is no. The polygenic nature of oral poetic creativity means mutant males probably couldn't produce *any* wordplay, however mediocre. Once again it is, I think, an ontogenetic phenomenon. Oral poetry has declined drastically in impact, length, and quality because we modern males get so much less practice at speaking. Ancient hunter-gatherer societies were much more steeped in verbal culture. Anthropologist Lorna Marshall, for instance, described the !Kung Bushmen of Africa's Kalahari desert as:

> . . . *the most loquacious people I know. Conversation in a !Kung werf [camp] is a constant sound like the sound of a brook, and as low and lapping, except for shrieks of laughter.*[27]

Individual conversations might last, she reported, for many hours, or even days. She also found that male Bushmen were far more talkative than women. Modern men and boys, on the other hand, frequently spend those long hours with their noses buried in the voiceless worlds of TV, computer games, and Internet pornography. Nor are the misguided efforts of concerned educators to instead get those noses between the pages of a book any better (except for this one, of course). Writing is, it turns out, a major cause of modern males' decline in verbal poetic skill. It is no coincidence, for example, that the best of the epic poets mentioned here, Homer and the Slavic *guslars,* were illiterate. In the case of the *guslars,* in fact, Lord and Parry were actually able to watch the negative effects of writing in action when a few *guslars* who had received an education began writing, rather than performing, their poetry. The results, the linguists reported, were abysmal: the *guslars'* poetry immediately lost its grandeur and became stilted and pedestrian. The problem was the precision that writing allowed, leading poets to forsake memorable, stirring phrases such as, "Once in the days of old, when Sulejman held empire" in favor of prosaic constructions such as, "In the bloody year of 1914, on the 6th day of the month of August, Austria and Germany were greatly worried."[28] Granted, rap is at least partly an oral art form, but it is composed by literate practitioners (very few rappers are truly illiterate, despite the image-making) in a literate environment. It is no wonder, then, that it falls so far short of Homer and the *guslar* epics.

In any case, the situation for *Homo masculinus modernus* is definitely growing dire. We can't, it seems, rely on our Cyrano-esque skills to woo our women; we haven't got any. Might we not then instead play the part of Christian in Rostand's play—the beautiful but blockheaded cadet whose good looks cause Roxane to fall hopelessly in love with him? Commentators such as author Mark Simpson, who coined the term "metrosexual," say we're already doing so. We modern metrosexual men are, according to these pundits, the most narcissistic, exhibitionist, and beauty-obsessed males in history. A whole industry has sprung up, virtually overnight, to pamper us with lotions, cosmetics, hair-care products, and even plastic surgery. The poster boy of modern metrosexuality is perhaps English footballer David Beckham, who wears more sarongs, nail polish, mascara, and hair product, and shoots more half-naked glam-porn shots, than even his ex-popstar wife, Victoria "Posh Spice" Beckham.

Surely he, and by extension we, have the right to call ourselves the most beautiful men ever? Surely no other males in history have oiled, coiffed, perfumed, and surgically altered themselves as much in that quest for beauty as we have?

There's obviously only one proper, scientific way to find out—a beefcake beauty parade. Remarkably, we don't even have to contrive one. As it happens, there are men alive in Africa today who maintain an ancient tradition of male beauty contests: the Wodaabe nomads of Niger. For hundreds of years their men have shaved, preened, painted, and ornamented themselves to vie for the title of most beautiful man in their annual *gerewol* ceremony. It's a grueling ritual in which tribesmen line up and dance the whole night through for seven days on end, swaying and weaving in time to chanted music, all the while contorting their painted faces to better display their charms to the young female judges. It's possibly the ultimate test of male beauty. So how, I wonder, would the consummate metrosexual, the icon of modern-male beauty, David Beckham, fare if we entered him?

I'll just go call his agent.

beauty

actually, Becks's agent says he'll get back to me.

To tell the truth there seemed to be some confusion—David, I was repeatedly assured, only gives his time to the most major of corporations and charities, neither of which this "science" that I claimed to be representing appeared to be. It didn't bode well, but let's get on anyway, while we're waiting, with introducing this round's contestants.

Who, for example, *are* these metrosexuals that Mark Simpson, and everybody else, is going on about? Simpson says he first stumbled across them at a 1994 "style" exhibition held in London called "It's a Man's World."[1] There, stalking through the stands of Ralph Lauren, Calvin Klein, and Giorgio Armani grooming products, Simpson found a peculiar masculine specimen—metrosexual man. A young male of high income and low commitments, metrosexual man seemed to indulge in some oddly (for the time) feminine pursuits. He bought, and used, moisturizer. He plied his hair with gel, his face with cosmetics, and his brothers with tips on the best shops for hand creams and pedicures. At that time, according to Simpson, metrosexual man usually worked in central London—hence the "metro" half of his handle—but he has since expanded his range worldwide, thanks to the advertising industry and TV shows such as *Queer Eye for the Straight Guy*. We are all, to paraphrase Milton Friedman, metrosexuals now.

But what does that mean exactly? David Coad, a cultural theorist from the University of Valenciennes, France, writes that the conventional definition of male metrosexuality comprises three central characteristics: narcissism, feminization, and eroticization.[2] Metrosexual males, it seems, are narcissists in that they are openly obsessed with their own personal beauty. This leads them to embrace a female culture of pampering to enhance that beauty—feminization. It also encourages metrosexual men to exhibit their bodies as objects of sexual desire—eroticization. This exhibitionism is also probably responsible for the synergetic connection, noted by Simpson, between metrosexuals and another group of muscular men for whom self-exhibition is a way of life: sportsmen.

It is this connection that accounts for the iconic status of David Beckham in the annals of metrosexuality. Actually, Becks was not the first sportsman to bare his body in the service of male narcissism; that honor goes to the non-sporting but highly ripped and athletic rapper-turned-actor Mark Wahlberg, who appeared seminude in ads for Calvin Klein underwear in the early 1990s. Beckham, though, took the icon of buffed, exhibitionistic, erotically charged sportsman and made it his own. Simpson insists that it was Beckham's embrace that allowed metrosexuality to go mainstream—it was only the movement's adoption by a genuine male role model, a real sportsman, that allowed other men to accept it as legitimately masculine. And Beckham is, by anybody's standards, a true sporting champion. Picked up by champion English soccer team, Manchester United, at the age of fourteen, Beckham has twice been been voted soccer's "World Player of the Year" runner-up. He is noted for the phenomenal precision of his kicks and his ability to curve the ball massively in flight to defeat defenders.

Beckham has not, however, allowed these deep talents to interfere with his embrace of everything shallow and superficial. Indeed, he virtually personifies all three defining characteristics of metrosexuality, as outlined by Coad. His narcissism, to give an example, is legendary. One Web site devoted to Beckham's hairstyles, for instance, lists eighty-nine different styles over ten years, eight of them mohawks. Becks seems similarly forward in his embrace of his own feminine side. In one of the *three* autobiographies he has currently written, Becks himself tells his audience, "I'm not scared of my feminine side and I think quite a lot of the things I do come from that. People have pointed that out as if it's a criticism, but it doesn't bother me."[3] "Golden Balls" (as his wife reputedly calls him) doesn't fall short in feminine follow-through, either, as his appearance in a sequined tracksuit at the 2002 Commonwealth Games proves. Beckham is also not ashamed of offering himself up as erotic fodder for the public's lascivious gaze. The frequency of his soft-core appearances on magazine covers led Simpson to observe that Beckham "clearly enjoys getting his tits out for the lads and lasses."

Presumably, Becks will have precious few philosophical grounds for objecting to our attempt to enter him into the Wodaabe *gerewol*. But what exactly is this bizarre beauty contest? The *gerewol* is actually the name of a dance that, along with another called the *yaake*, has been performed at the yearly *gerewol* ceremony of the Wodaabe nomads of Niger for hundreds of years—the festival has taken its name from the dance. Both dances are effectively beauty contests (the word *gerewol* comes from the verb *yera*: "to line up") in which young female judges assess the attractiveness of young Wodaabe males. The dances do, though, differ slightly in focus. The *gerewol* is a straightforward contest of physical beauty; in it male dancers wear the same plain make-up of red ochre mixed with fat, and identical (though admittedly gorgeous) costumes of beads, belts, turbans, jewelry, and ostrich-plume headdresses. The *yaake*, by contrast, is the contest of charm, in which the dancers contort their bodies into elegant poses, and their faces into fantastic expressions combining wide, fluttering, rolling eyes and teeth-baring grins (a man who can roll one eye while simultaneously holding a grin is considered a paragon of beauty). It is also in the *yaake* that contestants are free to paint their faces with the gorgeously feminine cosmetic patterns that have made the *gerewol* festival world famous.

This public reversal of male and female norms of beauty shows why the *gerewol* festival is the perfect test of modern males' metrosexual credentials. Metrosexuals are renowned for applying traditionally feminine notions of beauty to men; the Wodaabe, by contrast, actually invert them. They consider men, not women, to embody human beauty. Consequently, Wodaabe men spend more time than Wodaabe women fussing about their appearance (narcissism); ornament themselves in women's clothing and cosmetics (feminization); and display themselves in sexually provocative contexts (eroticization). So obsessed with male beauty are the Wodaabe that tribesmen may even allow their wives to sleep with a man more handsome than themselves, in order to guarantee the beauty of their sons. Clearly, as far as male sexuality goes, things don't get much more metro than with the Wodaabe. That being the case, let us see then how Becks fares against some real competition.

Actually, *that* may explain why his agent seems reluctant (he still hasn't called, I'm sorry to say). No matter—we'll push on with the contest regardless. To paraphrase the movie-actor emperors of those Hollywood "sword and sandal" flicks (apparently no real Roman emperor ever used the words): Let the games begin.

Tackling the first leg of Coad's metrosexual trifecta, just how narcissistic are modern males? Mark Simpson says enormously so, putting it down to male insecurity over their changing place in the world. Stripped of their traditional breadwinning role, he says, men now seek affirmation by virtue of something much more superficial—their appearance. This sounds reasonable, but what evidence is there that modern metrosexuals, and Beckham in particular, *are* preoccupied with their looks? Plenty, as it happens. One recent survey of modern-male grooming habits, for instance, found that the average man now spends 3.1 hours in front of the mirror per week, almost an hour more than the average woman. Another survey found that over 66 percent of straight men, and more than 80 percent of gay men, had removed their pubic hair at least once to improve their appearance. Beckham's narcissistic credentials, similarly, seem too obvious to even need comment. His own words, once again, will suffice: when quizzed by *Attitude* magazine (a publication for gay men) as to why he was so comfortable with his status as a gay icon, Beckham stated, with disarming frankness, that what mattered to him was being admired, and the more the merrier. It is difficult, indeed, to say which quality of Beckham's this best represents a victory for—his tolerance or his exhibitionism. There is also the not-too-surprising revelation, splashed about by several British tabloids, that Becks spends an average £600 a month on bulk packs of Calvin Klein underwear, never wearing the same pair twice. Given this level of sartorial extravagance, we are probably safe in assuming he spends considerably more than 3.1 hours in front of his mirror every week.

Impressively narcissistic, to be sure, but it might surprise

Beckham and his metrosexual emulators to learn that they still come a distant second to Wodaabe males, who were, and are, more likely to spend 3.1 hours *per day* in front of their mirrors. A pocket mirror is, in fact, the one indispensable accessory of every single Wodaabe man's costume. Anthropologist Mette Bovin, who studied the Wodaabe for 32 years, noted that even though their country is so sparsely populated that a man may walk for days without seeing anyone, the first thing Wodaabe males did on waking was spend several hours in front of their hand mirrors, prettying themselves with make-up and arranging their hair.[4] (Wodaabe men are herders, an occupation that allows a lot of leisure time.) One aid worker who lived with the Wodaabe for a short time similarly reported that their favorite gifts, even more valuable than flashlights and sunglasses, were Polaroid cameras that allowed them to photograph and view themselves instantly.

Nor are the Wodaabe a freakish exception among ancient and tribal cultures. Tuareg nomads of the central Sahara, another surviving ancient culture, also believe that men, rather than women, epitomize beauty.[5] So attractive do Tuareg men consider themselves that they, alone among the world's cultures, veil themselves rather than their women—to protect Tuareg females from the devastating effect of that beauty. Tuareg men, like the Wodaabe, lavish considerable time on their appearance, too, braiding their hair, for example, into elaborate styles—despite the fact that their hair and faces are never seen, since an adult Tuareg male wears his veil even while sleeping. Such narcissistic seclusion may seem extreme, yet it pales, literally, in comparison to those ancient Tahitian men who stayed indoors for their entire lives from boyhood to ensure they achieved the lightness of skin that Tahitian women (and sometimes other men) found so beautiful.[6]

We modern metrosexuals are even outdone in the narcissism stakes by our own foppish forefathers. The mid-eighteenth-century "maccaroni" men, to give one example, showed an extravagance of dress that leaves Beckham looking like a plain Dwayne. Maccaronis were young British gentlemen who came back from their "grand tour" of the continent's cultural landmarks sporting exaggerated versions of the fashions they had seen—rouge and face paint, red-heeled shoes, and tight, embroidered outfits. The true mark of a maccaroni, however, was his enormous wig. These powdered, horsehair monstrosities were so huge that the obligatory *chapeau bras* hat topping them could only be put on by the tip of a sword. Ironically, the inevitable reaction against this extravagance gave rise to the movement that is to us a byword for male narcissism— the dandies. Dandies were young English gentlemen who threw off the wigs, perfume, pumps, and colorful embroidery of the maccaronis, and embraced instead the sober colors and plain-cut clothing of middle-class fashion. Though less flamboyant than their maccaroni forefathers, the dandies were, if anything, even *more* narcissistic. Their leading light and founder, Beau Brummel, famously took three hours to dress, and changed his shirt as many as four times a day. He also insisted on polishing his boots with champagne. Even the motives driving the dandies' narcissism seem to mirror those of modern metrosexuals, as this quote from Thomas Carlyle, the Scottish man of letters, illustrates:

> *A Dandy is . . . a Man whose trade, office and existence consists in the wearing of Clothes. Every faculty of his soul, spirit, purse, and person is heroically consecrated to this one object . . . what is it that the Dandy asks in return? Solely . . . that you would recognise his existence; would admit him to*

be a living object; or even failing this, a visual object, or thing that will reflect rays of light.[7]

Beckham then, and by extension we modern metrosexuals, seems to have lost the first round of the narcissism challenge. Not just *gerewol* dancers, but also Tuaregs, Tahitians, maccaronis, and dandies apparently would have left us coughing in their powdered, pampered, and perfumed wake. It's clearly time, therefore, to bring out the big guns—the airbrushing, cosmetic make-up guns, that is. Doesn't our astonishing invention of male cosmetics (the very phrase was once considered an oxymoron) prove our bona fides as history's supreme narcissists? After all, one recent British consumer survey found that the average English man now spends £111 a year on cosmetics, just £27 less than the average English woman. Leading the charge, as ever, is Beckham, whose nail-polishing antics were put on display in a cover shoot for *GQ* magazine in which he appeared wearing mauve nail varnish. So far ahead of the metrosexual pack is Beckham that he has even crossed the ultimate male make-up frontier: use of eyeliner and mascara.

Shockingly sissified stuff, to be sure, but not enough, sadly, to raise even a single, plucked Wodaabe eyebrow. *They've* been wearing eyeliner for thousands of years—in the form of the famous kohl used by every ancient man from pharaohs to Philistines. Wodaabe kohl is made from ground stibnite, a gray crystal, mixed with soot and animal fat, and applied liberally to both brows and lashes. Kohl is, however, just the first ingredient in the Wodaabe male's make-up palette. The Wodaabe also routinely use that most basic of womanly cosmetics: foundation. Modern metrosexuals, it's true, have started using this, too, but it costs them no more than a little money and a few sniffs from traditionalists to prettify their faces thus. The Wodaabe, on the other hand, must trek over nine hundred miles for their supplies of *makkara*, the saffron-colored powdered clay that makes their faces radiant, pale, and blemish free. Nor would the outlandish ingredients of modern male cosmetics—cucumber facials, chicken-bone-marrow creams, et cetera—be anything new to the Wodaabe. The whitener they use to paint intricate patterns of dots, lines, and crosses over their kohl and *makkara,* called *doobal,* is actually the dried and powdered excrement of the *doobal* bird.[8] Nor did the cosmetic concoctions used by non-Wodaabe ancient and tribal males lack their own bizarre and sometimes hair-raising ingredients. Polynesian men in the Marquesas Islands in precolonial times, for example, achieved those cherished pale skins by applying a mix of coconut oil, turmeric, and the crushed leaves of the *paya* vine to the skin. It temporarily turned the wearer green from head to toe, before peeling off days later to reveal the desired bleached skin.

Other tribal men, too, put Beckham and his metrosexual emulators to shame in their use of beautifying cosmetics. Papuan men of the Mt. Hagen tribe, for example, are known for their gorgeously painted and ornamented faces—these days displayed annually in the grand Mt. Hagen Cultural Show. But Mt. Hagen men, in the old days at least, also painted their faces daily with red, blue, yellow, black, and white clays. Their motives, once again, exactly mirrored those of modern metrosexuals. Sexual attractiveness was prominent, of course, but so was an aim often quoted by modern-day lawyers and investment bankers: business success. Some Papuan men, indeed, combined the two—Trobriand Island men who went on long-distance *kula* trade voyages painted their faces to charm their (male) trading partners into falling in love and giving them a better deal.[9] This might seem like wishful thinking, but a recent economics study did, in fact, find that time spent grooming is one of the strongest predictors of a modern male's salary level.[10]

Some tribal men went even further than either the Wodaabe or the Papuans. Young Nlaka'pamux Indian men of Canadian British Columbia, for instance, changed the patterns and colors on their painted faces three or four times a day. African Nuban males were just as extravagant, seldom appearing in public without whole-body artwork of painted patterns or animal motifs. (Nuban male cosmetic use was not solely motivated by aesthetics, however. It frequently had direct sexual consequences: if a girl was particularly impressed by a Nuban man's make-up at a tribal dance she might throw her legs over his shoulders in a none-too-subtle signal that she desired an assignation.[11])

▪cosmetics for carnivores

All body ornamentation is a form of communication, according to anthropologist Ted Polhemus. What message, then, we might wonder, was intended for those who saw Chief Guangol, a leader of the Oromo people of Ethiopia encountered by explorer James Bruce in the eighteenth century? Bruce wrote that Guangol:

> . . . had long hair plaited and interwoven with the bowels of oxen . . . which hung down in long strings . . . he

had likewise a wreath of guts hung about his neck, and several rounds of the same about his middle . . . below which was a short cotton cloth dipped in butter . . . his body was wet and running down with the same . . . and the day being very hot an insufferable stench of carrion soon made everyone . . . sensible of [his] approach.[12]

I have never come across an explanation for this extraordinary outfit, but I'm willing to hazard a guess. The fierce Oromo warriors over whom Guangol was chief were noted for their cult of feasting on raw meat. Indeed, Bruce wrote that Oromo warriors preferred their meat so rare that at some feasts they cut their steaks out of live, screaming cows. Might it have been that Guangol's rotting clobber was actually intended to display his access to the commodity that made him a successful warrior chief—raw, red meat?

If ancient and tribal metrosexuals, then, make Beckham look like a sissy boy who's broken into his big sister's Revlon case, what about Becks's fabled hairstyles? After all, Golden Balls reportedly gets his mane done at least once a week (though he claims, belying the extravagance of his underwear budget, that he gets these weekly do-overs gratis from a mate). Then there are those eighty-nine hairstyles—surely *they* testify to Beckham's supremacy as hairhorse extraordinaire? Here, admittedly, Beckham does have it over Wodaabe males, who *never* cut their hair. This is not from sloth, however, but from the Wodaabe belief in the beauty of long hair. Rather than cut their locks, Wodaabe men actually tug on them to make them longer. They do, it's true, shave their hairlines high up on their crowns in preparation for *gerewol,* to increase the length (and, therefore, beauty) of their faces. But this still doesn't equal Beckham's revolving door of hairstyles, so it seems Posh's hubby has won this round by default.

Or has he?

While Wodaabe men might be relatively uncreative in their hairdressing, other tribal males had hairdressing repertoires that make Becks's efforts look like pudding-bowl cuts. Mt. Hagen men, for example, style their hair with wigs so enormous they have to be built onto a supportive frame of cane and clay. These monstrosities, which take months to make, comprise tresses of other men's and women's hair and marsupial fur cemented with wax and grease, ornamented with scarab beetles and painted in fantastic colors. (These may seem ridiculously extravagant to us, but Mt. Hageners believe that friendly ghosts live in a man's hair; baldness, therefore is a sign of fortune deserting him.)

Beckham partisans might protest, at this point, that this is still just one hairstyle, however time-intensive, compared to Beckham's procession of curtain-cuts, cornrows, mullets, and mohawks. Some tribal men, however, arranged and rearranged their hair in styles every bit as varied and bizarre as Beckham's. The British Consul to Samoa in the late nineteenth century, William Churchward, for instance, wrote that he saw so many different hairdos on men there that he had given up trying to catalogue them. Instead, he noted just the more bizarre ones—like "the mushroom," where Samoan males clipped their back and sides but left the top to grow into an eighteen-inch crown, which they then dyed dazzling white.[13]

They also dyed their hair shades of blue, red, yellow, and green—sometimes all at once. True, Samoan men did have a more sedate, traditional style, the *fonga,* in which their long hair was tied up in a knot—but even that had twelve different names, depending on where on the head the knot was worn.[14] Samoan men were so preoccupied with their hair, Churchward wrote, that "one can rarely pass through a village without seeing some branch of hairdressing, either cutting, oiling, combing, liming, or shaving." Other Polynesian men also indulged, as evidenced by anthropologist Ralph Linton's writings on the Marquesas Islands, where, he said:

> . . . *some men never cut their hair, others did it up in two horns . . . still others arranged the crown in fantastic ways, [such] as one half shaved, the other long, or the front shaved and the back long, or in a series of shaved strips . . . [and] in time of war finger bones or other trophies of slain enemies were attached.*[15]

Beckham's hairdressing hijinks, it seems, would probably have made Polynesian men simply yawn.

Another supposed hairdressing innovation of modern metrosexuals is hair gel. Beckham, after all, uses lashings of the stuff to create styles such as his legendary "fauxhawk." But this is, as ever, nothing new—prehistoric men were using hair product when Westerners were still covering their syphilitic scalps with ridiculous horsehair periwigs. Churchward's Samoans, to give one example, shaped their hair by massaging a paste of burnt coral and grease into it. The Wodaabe, on the other hand, along with other North African tribesmen, have dressed their hair with rancid butter for hundreds, and possibly thousands, of years. Even northern European men had once been prolific users of lime-based hair product, as this quote by the first century BCE historian Diodorus Siculus illustrates:

> The Gauls are very tall with white skin and blond hair, not only blond by nature but more so by the artificial means they use to lighten their hair. For they continually wash their hair in a lime solution, combing it back from the forehead to the back of the neck. This process makes them resemble Satyrs and Pans since . . . [it] . . . makes the hair thick like a horse's mane.

The spikiness of the hair on "the Dying Gaul" statue in Rome shows how similar to modern hair gel this was in its effect.

Becks's supporters might, though, insist that it is really his *absence* of hair—body hair, that is—that makes Golden Balls a male beauty pioneer. Exact figures on Beckham's waxing activities are not available, but his hairless appearance in several underwear ads certainly suggests he is no stranger to the hot wax and spatula. Beckham is, in fact, anecdotally credited with driving the explosion of male genital depilation worldwide—the infamous "back, sack, and crack." This procedure, in which pubic hair is stripped from a man's scrotum, anus, and buttocks with hot wax, is reputedly the most excruciatingly painful cosmetic procedure a man can suffer, and many cite it as evidence of just how far modern metrosexuals will go in pursuit of narcissistic beauty. But are both these claims really true? Is Beckham truly such a pioneer in the art of shucking right down to his bare skin? And is the "back, sack, and crack" genuinely the most painful method of depilation men have ever undergone?

I think we all know where this is heading.

A quick scan of anthropological literature shows that, in fact, not only were many ancient men preoccupied with trimming their bear-hair, they also invented every supposedly modern way of doing so hundreds, and sometimes thousands, of years before we did. South Australian Aboriginal men in the nineteenth century, for example, initiated their young men with an all-over hair-stripping—using beeswax.[16] Shaving, also, was employed by numerous groups, among them: the Polynesians, who denuded themselves with the aid of sharp shells and sharks' teeth; and the African Nuban men, who shaved themselves all over with iron razors to achieve the blank canvas needed for their extravagant body painting. Roman men had their armpits, beards, chests, backs, and legs tweezered by slave attendants in public bathhouses. Even chemical depilatories were occasionally used by ancient and tribal metrosexuals. German anthropologist Martin Gusinde, for example, wrote that the Papuan Ayum Pygmy men he visited in the 1950s:

> . . . get rid of their beards by rubbing the juice of a certain herb into the areas of beard growth. This loosened the hair roots, enabling them to be plucked singly with the nails of the thumb and middle finger.[17]

But if Beckham clearly has nothing to teach these prehistoric preeners, then, depilation-wise, it also turns out our estimate of the relative agony of our "back, sack, and crack" procedure is way off. Anthropologists' reports of those waxing Australian Aboriginals, for example, make it plain that the procedure was excruciating. That, in fact, was its point: it was an initiation ordeal. Waxing, Australian Aboriginal style, involved the unfortunate youth being held down while an older man plucked his pubic, armpit, and body hairs out, *one by one,* with a lump of wax on his finger—the older men swapping shifts as they tired. Aboriginal boys were, however, only slightly worse off than ancient Greek metrosexual men: *they* stripped their pubic patches by burning them with an oil lamp. If the depilation was applied as a punishment (which it sometimes was for adultery) the procedure was even more severe, being carried out by harsh rubbing with a handful of fiery embers.[18] Roman soldiers used almost as harsh, if not quite as hot, a technique in removing their beards—they *ground* them off with abrasive pumice stone. Then there were the astonishingly dangerous chemical concoctions medieval Turks used to depilate themselves at the baths—arsenic mixed with extremely caustic quicklime and water.[19] Considering quicklime is often used to dissolve human corpses, I think it is fair to say the dreaded "back, sack, and crack" is, by comparison, about as scary as putting on the wrong color eyeliner.

◼sins of the foreskin

I t might seem surprising, given the ancient Greeks' blasé attitude to male nudity, that they still held *some* notions of modesty. Self-respecting Greeks were quite happy to shed their clothes for nude *symposia* ("drinking parties"), so long as they didn't suffer the mortifying embarrassment of appearing *psolos* ("with glans penis exposed").[20] Greek men so idealized the *posthon* ("long foreskin") that covered the head of the penis that appearing with a short one—leaving one's . . . ahem . . . tip exposed—was considered seriously gross. The playwright Aristophanes, for example, ridicules one character as "an old man who's filthy, hunchbacked, wretched, wrinkled, bald, toothless, and, by God, I think he's *psolos* too."

It was to avoid this shame that naked Greek partygoers, and athletes, tied their foreskins shut with the leather *kynodesme,* "dog leash." For those unfortunates either circumcised or born deficient, a variety of remedies was prescribed: the physician Dioscorides of Anazarbus suggested soaking in honey; his fellow medical man Galen recommended stretching with a hanging lead weight, the *antilipodermos*; or, as a last resort, the philosopher Celsus suggested a brutal surgical procedure in which the skin of the penis was sliced open on the shaft and yanked forward to provide an artificial *posthon.*[20] And to think, all we have to worry about is whether our fly is up.

It's not looking good for our metrosexual champion, David Beckham. His narcissism apparently wouldn't qualify him for the job of backstage testicle-taper in the Wodaabe *gerewol* beauty parade. What about the second leg of the metrosexual trifecta, then: feminization? Coad describes the conventional definition of a feminized male as one who "was comfortable with women and feminine ways" and who "explored the feminine side of his nature." We have

Beckham's quote about his feminine side to indicate that he certainly sees himself as quite feminized. But what are his actual girly-man (to quote Arnold Schwarzenegger) qualifications? Sure, he's comfortable plastering his face with womanly cosmetics, but as we've seen, in that contest he's a poor second to the Wodaabe and other tribal men. What about his habit of draping himself in female clothing—the famed sarongs, sequined tracksuits, and so on? Well, for starters, the sarong is not actually an inherently feminine piece of clothing. Even in the place that gave the garment its name, Malaysia, sarongs are as much masculine as feminine garments. The same problem arises with Becks's tracksuits, which, however sequined, are not indisputably feminine dress items. At the annual *gerewol,* by contrast, Wodaabe men wear *actual* women's dresses—the gorgeous, patterned wraps of Wodaabe women that are fastened around the hips by a very feminine belt of beads, and around the knees by a tight leather or cloth strap (to restrict the wearer to appropriately coy and mincing steps).

Modern metrosexual defenders might protest that wearing just one dress a year hardly qualifies—even Dennis Rodman, for example, has slipped into (of all things) a wedding frock in public. But many ancient and tribal males embraced their feminine selves all year round. Some, indeed, took the embrace so far that they almost *became* women. One such group were the Tahitian *mahus*—men who so feminized themselves that they were often mistaken for women by early European explorers, as described by Captain William Bligh after examining one particular *mahu*:

> . . . *he had the appearance of a Woman, his Yard & Testicles being so drawn in under him . . . from custom of keeping them in that position . . . [that] . . . those [men] who are con-*

nected with him have their beastly pleasures gratified between
his thighs . . . on examining his privates I found them both
very small and the Testicles remarkably so, being not larger
than a boy's of 5 or 6 years old, and very soft as in a state of
decay . . .

The *mahu*'s adoption of a receptive role in sex was one marker of
his feminization, but there were others. *Mahus* also embraced the
everyday aspects of female life, as this missionary's report makes
clear:

> *. . . they [the mahus] go among the women, observe all their*
> *customs, eat & drink & sleep with them & do all the offices*
> *of females in making cloth etc . . .*[21]

A similar eagerness to embrace the world of women's work was
also noted among the *fa'afafine* "women men" of Samoa, encountered by nineteenth-century seafarers. *Fa'afafine* boys could be
picked in childhood by their attraction to women's work such as
cooking, cleaning, and nursing. *Fa'afafine* might, or might not, grow
up to become receptive homosexuals and to wear women's clothing, but their embrace of the feminine was so total that they, like
mahus, sometimes went on to become secondary wives for more
conventional Samoan males. Lest both *mahus* and *fa'afafine* be
thought a Polynesian peculiarity, even one of the most hyper-
masculine tribal societies, the North American Sioux Indians, had
a class of men who lived, and loved, as women. Termed "berdache"
by early anthropologists, these Sioux men renounced the warrior's
life in favor of a womanly life of weaving, nursing, cooking, and
receptive homosexuality. So completely did they adopt their

feminine roles that they, too, might become second or third wives to other Sioux men.

It's difficult to see David Beckham, whatever his feminization credentials, going quite *that* far.

That, apparently, is strike two. What, then, of the final leg in the metrosexual trifecta: eroticization? On that score, it is clear that we modern metrosexuals really are more prone to sexual exhibitionism than our immediate forefathers. A survey by *GQ* magazine, for example, found that while no ads prior to 1984 depicted men semi-nude or in sexually evocative contexts, thirty-seven ads in that year did so. By 1994 that figure had risen to forty-three. Beckham, too, has clearly taken erotic display of his male body to new heights: a 2002 film of him sleeping, commissioned by London's National Portrait Gallery, was described by one critic as an erotic masterpiece in which the viewer is made to feel they are sleeping beside Becks. But what about our more distant forefathers? How does our exhibitionism rate when compared to the Wodaabe, or to that of other tribal or ancient men?

The *gerewol*, for example, is clearly an overtly erotic display. Apart from the womanly wraps covering their thighs, and their gorgeous jewelry and ornamentation, Wodaabe males compete bare-chested in both the *gerewol* and the *yaake*. Even those decorations are profoundly erotic symbols: the strings of cowrie shells that Wodaabe men wear for necklaces at *gerewol* represent female vaginas, and the ostrich plume jutting vertically from their headdresses is a deliberately phallic symbol. The erotic movements Wodaabe dancers make also supplement these sexual emblems. Men dancing at *gerewol* stretch themselves on tiptoe to make themselves more sexually desirable, and snap their heads into exaggerated poses to display the beauty of their necks and profiles. They also widen their eyes and roll them in flirtatious expressions very similar to those of (female) Balinese dancers. Perhaps the clearest proof of the erotic nature of *gerewol* can be seen in who judges it—women. The jury of three *suboybe* ("choosers") is drawn from the most beautiful and nubile of the host tribe's young women. (The girls of highest status are usually, in fact, the daughters of previous *gerewol* winners.) These three young beauties observe the men from a distance, discussing their erotic appeal, then slowly pass up and down the line of dancing males, finally indicating the sexiest by stopping in front of him and giving a ceremonial gesture. The winner is not, contrary to lurid Western reports, entitled to sleep with the three judges—though a good deal of other sex does eventuate at *gerewol*.

In fact, such explicit erotic consequences highlight another failure of modern metrosexuals—follow-through. Despite his constant buffed and bared appearances before the camera shutter, Beckham is clearly a mere click-tease. Dubious media scandals such as the Rebecca Loos affair aside, Becks is, it seems, boringly faithful to his wife, Victoria. The *gerewol,* on the other hand, is explicitly designed for Wodaabe males to hook up with women other than their wives. Two kinds of sexual liaisons result from *gerewol*: assignations and *teegal* marriages. In Western terms, the former is a one-night stand and the latter refers to the taking of a mistress—both outside the official *koobgal* marriage between a Wodaabe man and his primary wife. By rolling their eyes at the watching girls and glancing to indicate a meeting place, the men organize one-night stands with those women, married and unmarried, they have managed to impress. At the conclusion of the dance, they melt into the bush with their partners for a night of bliss on their woven mats. If a man has seriously impressed a conquest with his beauty, he may pull off the envied feat of "wife-stealing"—convincing the woman to leave her husband, if she has one, and stay with him as a second, third, or even fourth wife in a *teegal* marriage.

How's *that* for erotic follow-through?

Even Beckham's exhibitionist eroticization of sport has all been done before, again with much more direct and explicit sexual consequences. Ancient Greek athletics were so infused with eroticism that they often culminated in actual sex, usually homosexual. Athletes were worshipped sexually to such a degree, in fact, that some sportsmen attracted hordes of love-struck gay groupies. Socrates, for example, described the chaos when the handsome young athlete Charmides attended the gymnasium: "amazement and confusion reigned when he entered; and a troop of lovers followed him."[22] Later, when the young hunk took a seat on the bench, his male groupies literally fell over each other to secure a place near him. Nor did the Greeks fail to follow this eroticization through to its logical conclusion. Indeed, surviving artworks show that the Greek gymnasium was a hotbed of homosexual activity. Numerous vase paintings, for instance, show Greek men at the gym approaching young athletes in the standard pose of a seducer—one hand touching the boy's chin, the other his penis. Lest it be thought Greek sports only stimulated homosexual eroticism, though, we also have the outraged words of the Athenian playwright Euripides on the nudity of Spartan women while competing in athletics, to show that the trade swung both ways:

> No Spartan girl could ever live clean if she wanted. They're always out on the street in scanty outfits, making a great display of naked limbs. In those they race and wrestle with the boys too—abominable's the word.[23]

Even *female* Greek athletes, it seems, took their eroticization of sport further than the wannabe efforts of our metrosexual-in-chief, David Beckham.

Dear me—Beckham's attempt, admittedly involuntary, to sweep the Wodaabe *gerewol* seems to have turned to farce. He's fallen short on all three legs of the metrosexual trifecta: narcissism, feminization, and eroticization. While the winners are packing up and fitting their camels with extra saddles for the girls whose hearts they've stolen, Becks is still out there, kicking up dust in a vain attempt to escape the label of Wodaabe wallflower. His wife, Victoria, meanwhile, has disappeared into the desert with a particularly tall and handsome Wodaabe wife-stealer, there to spend her life grinding his millet and milking his cows as his third *teegal* wife—while he pampers his beauty, the better to arrange further liaisons. Not even last ditch attempts to retrieve Beckham's reputation by appealing to his athleticism will save him. Sure, he puts in a solid ninety minutes or more of soccer, but *gerewol* dances last all night for seven grueling days in a row. There is actually some question whether even Beckham would be fit enough to last this distance. Similarly, attempts to uphold the reputation of modern metrosexuals by pointing to our excessive dieting in pursuit of thinness won't wash either. Wodaabe men eat no more than the odd mouthful for the entire duration of *gerewol*—one reason it's such an intense endurance contest.

There is one last aspect of male beauty in which die-hard supporters of modern metros might still insist they claim the winner's mantle, however: body modification. We modern men are, they maintain, quicker to pierce, tattoo, scar, or deliberately mutilate ourselves in pursuit of beauty than any men in history. We are also, according to them, more willing to go under the plastic surgeon's knife than our forefathers ever were. The tide of complaints from conservative commentators about "modern primitives" with Christmas-tree body ornaments, and botoxed boys with liposucked abs, certainly gives some credence to the notion. Once again, though, it is just a bald assertion until we compare the body-modifying habits of ancient and tribal men. And even a quick survey, it turns out, immediately dispels the idea that we could have taught our forefathers a thing about piercing or plasticizing the masculine body.

Take piercing and scarring. True, we modern men do display an astonishing eagerness to mutilate ourselves thus—one survey of European males, for example, found that 27 percent aged fourteen to twenty-four had undergone at least one of these procedures. Yet, as American anthropologist Ted Polhemus has pointed out, in those tribal societies where mutilation was the norm (the greater number of them) *all* the men would be so mutilated. To not decorate oneself thus would, in fact, mean one wasn't a man. Similarly, the actual procedures of our piercings and scarrings, which are mostly undertaken under anaesthetic, pale beside the terrifying ordeals that tribal men underwent to beautify themselves. Piercing, to begin with, was often a brutal exercise in tribal societies. Where modern men might perforate their lower lips, using painkillers, with a small stud or ring, Mura Indian men punctured theirs with the fat tusks of the peccary, or South American wild pig. Nose piercing, similarly, is increasingly popular with modern males, yet it doesn't begin to approach the trauma of "septum piercing" as still practiced by the Asmat tribe of Irian Jaya, whose men perforate their nose-cartilage with the huge *otsj,* an inch-thick bone plug. Some modern males, likewise, stretch their ears with expanding plugs until they dangle halfway to their shoulders, yet this pales alongside the efforts of the Botocudo Indians of South America, so named for the

Portuguese word describing the huge wooden discs their men (and women) wore in their ears and lower lips.

The same situation prevails with intentional scarring. Modern tattoo magazines report a surge in men scarring themselves with designs using tattoo guns without the ink. This is, admittedly, quite painful, because the procedure is usually done sans anaesthetic. Yet a single bout of decorative scarring at the hands of prehistoric Australian Aborigines would probably send those same men screaming for the bandaids and lignocaine. Australian Aboriginal men at the time of European colonization often bore elaborate patterns of thick, raised keloid scars over their entire bodies. To make these they sliced deep cuts into their skin and muscle, forced the lips of the wound apart and packed it with fat, clay, and ashes to irritate the wound and prevent healing.[24] These procedures would be repeated for up to three months, by which time the keloid scars might be over an inch higher than the skin. Explorers reported that the scars of a fully initiated man of the Kimberley region would, if laid end on end, measure thirty yards in length.

If we moderns are wusses in our cosmetic mutilations, then, might we still not take the cake in terms of actual cosmetic *surgery*? That modern men are increasingly prepared to go under the knife to gratify their narcissism is not in doubt—in 2006 American plastic surgeons performed 85,570 male nose jobs and 35,020 male liposuctions. It's also true that ancient and tribal men, the Maasai and Romans excepted, were blocked from performing much cosmetic surgery by their primitive surgical skills. Yet this didn't stop some prehistoric men from carrying out very radical procedures to correct what they saw as their cosmetic deficiencies. Oromo men of Ethiopia several hundred years ago, for example, performed the gynecomastia, or male breast reduction, which is the fifth most commonly requested procedure for modern would-be metrosexuals—in the Oromos' case, however, the operation was a simple amputation with an iron blade (sans anesthetic, of course). More commonly, however, prehistoric men used non-surgical means to correct their bodies' failings. Mayan men, for instance, attached a bead or ball of wax to their head so as to dangle between their eyes and thereby encourage them to go cross-eyed—a very desirable look in their culture. Another non-surgical, but extreme, cosmetic technique was head deformation. This procedure, which took place in a boy's infancy, involved his young head being squashed into either a conical or flat-topped shape by binding it tightly with boards or pressing it between two heavy stones. As a cosmetic procedure, it seems to have had a long history—several Neandertal skulls from 45,000 years ago show evidence of it.[25] Even back in deep prehistory, it seems, men were willing to undergo cosmetic procedures so drastic they would make Joan Rivers blanch.

■prehistoric periodontistry

Modern men are clearly almost as obsessed with the appearance of their teeth as women: a survey by the British Association of Cosmetic Dentists found that over 40 percent of all cosmetic dental procedures are now done on males. Though whitening and capping are the most common, many men now also go for more extreme options such as implants and gum contouring. Even these intrusive procedures, however, pale beside those used by ancient and tribal males to modify their teeth.

Some Southeast Asian tribesmen of precolonial times, for example, actually *blackened* their teeth, supposedly to distance themselves from dogs, which they considered to be white-toothed but unclean animals. The McKenzie River Eskimos apparently filed their canines down for exactly the same reason. Some tribal males, on the other hand, did just the opposite, filing their incisors to points to beautify themselves (though it also seems to reduce cavities). Even the extravagant jewelled "grill" mouthpieces beloved of modern rappers such as Paul Wall, Nelly, and Kanye West would have looked distinctly second-rate in the company of Mayan males: high-born Mayan men not only inlaid their teeth with jade and jewels, they also etched beautiful, convoluted designs directly onto their teeth's surface.

With even these last-ditch defenses breached it should be clear that we modern metrosexuals—and our standard-bearer, Becks—have definitively lost the fight. We are not the most narcissistic, beauty-obsessed males of our species; that honor goes to the Wodaabe, the Tuareg, the Maya, the maccaronis—and every other prehistoric or tribal male who ever touched up his face with ochre and animal fat by the light of a burning brush torch and the reflection of a still pond. The astute reader, however, will notice that while we modern men are proven wannabes in the beautification stakes, we haven't yet said much about actual, natural beauty. What are we physically like—stripped of all cosmetics, mutilations, surgical interventions, hairdos, jewels, and costumes—compared to ancient men? True, even on strict physical grounds, David Beckham wouldn't get a look-in at *gerewol* (he's too short, not red-skinned enough, and his nose is nowhere sufficient in length to satisfy the Wodaabe aesthetic), but their standards are too culturally governed to be reliable. In fact, the state of affairs with our natural, physical beauty is even more galling than our failures as metrosexuals. Beauty-wise modern males have had advantages no prehistoric man could have dreamed of, yet we still managed to blow it and wind up looking like the ugly stepbrothers. What women find beautiful in men is surprisingly easy to predict based on the visual markers of both the male body and the male face. (Physical beauty might well lie in the eye of the beholder, but if it does then every female human eye has damned similar tastes.) And on both counts *Homo masculinus modernus* scores a big fat zero, despite receiving a couple of enormous helping hands.

Body-wise, for example, one of the strongest markers of what women find beautiful is height. Tall men universally report having more lovers, more marriages, and more children than their vertically challenged brothers. On the face of it that should leave us laughing—Western men are, after all, 5 to 10 percent taller today than their European forefathers of two to three centuries ago. (Though, as the impressive stature of Stephen Webb's T8 Australian Aboriginal runner shows (see page 23), very early *Homo sapiens* males, not to mention even earlier giants such as *Homo heidelbergensis,* frequently towered over us.) Yet a quirk of female mate preferences and our own couch-potato habits have conspired to erase this hard-won advantage. It turns out that women's preference for tall men is conditional: attractive men still have to fall within an ideal VHI, or volume-to-height index—in layman's terms, how tubby you are.[26] (Interestingly, there are some exceptions to this rule for ancient men—see below.) Grow too fat, as roughly 30 percent of we Western males now have,[27] and it doesn't matter how tall you are: you'll still be sitting at home with a blow-up love doll and a meal of canned spaghetti on Saturday night. Your romantic target meanwhile would, if she could, be dancing the night away with her shorter, but leaner and sexier, date—a prehistoric Australian Aboriginal, Amerindian, African, or even Inuit man.

◼when fat was the new black

Dieting is undeniably a modern-male obsession; some medical journals report that 10 percent of eating disorder cases from the 1990s onward have been young males. Yet we can't by any means claim to have invented the obsession—Polynesian men were dieting fanatically more than 350 years ago. In their case, however, their obsession was not with *losing* weight, but with *gaining* it—as much as possible, as quickly as possible.

Early Spanish explorers reported that groups of Tahitian youths would occasionally retire to a large canoe shed, there to lie motionless on a carpet of fern-leaves soaked in coconut oil. For the period of their stay they moved as little as possible, all the while being fed vast quantities of extremely fattening food.

When they finally emerged, their first action was to exhibit themselves naked for their tribesmen, who commented approvingly on their now gloriously fat bodies. Usually their period of indolence lasted a month, though some firstborn youths were made to laze and gorge their whole adolescence away as "cherished children." Envious modern couch potatoes can take some comfort, however; life as a "cherished child" wasn't all roses. They often had to be beaten to make them eat more. Even a spot of bulimic purging didn't save them; the Spanish reported that unwilling gorgers were forced to eat their own vomit, too.

The second set of visual markers used by women to determine male beauty are facial characteristics, one of the most important of which is symmetry. Women have evolved to value symmetry in male faces, the theory goes, because it is a good marker of the strength of a man's immune system and health—he is able to maintain symmetrical growth despite obstacles such as disease and parasites, which tend to visibly disrupt the process. Again, we modern men have incredible advantages over our prehistoric counterparts: our medicine and nutrition are now so good that we hardly suffer any insults to our facial symmetry at all. But here, once again, we've managed to fritter away our advantage. Women also value exaggerated facial features such as a large, robust jaw, a wide mouth, prominent cheekbones, and a broad face with wide-set eyes.[28] The growth of all of these is governed by testosterone levels, which, strangely enough, seem to be dropping (for some as yet unknown reason) across the Western world.[29] Although I'm unaware of any research into the area, this possibly means the facial features women find most attractive in men are growing less pronounced. Since these apparently hardwired female preferences will not disappear anytime soon, it seems we modern males are on track to finding yet one more way to leave our womenfolk disappointed—with our physical beauty. Or lack thereof.

Strictly speaking, though, the situation may not turn out to be quite so grim. After all, judgments of beauty are relative, and luckily for us our elders and betters aren't around for women to compare us to. To get the girl, we moderns simply have to convince her we're better than the next *schlub,* not some genuinely swashbuckling he-man from 10,000 BCE. Just to be on the safe side, however, it may be wise to make one last effort to find something, *anything,* positive we have to throw onto the reproductive and desirability scales. Might it not, for example, be time to summon up the last, desperate hope of all those jostling to avoid being the last one standing at the masculine matrimonial ball—our skill as fathers? Such skill has, after all, saved many a sub-optimal man from the genetic oblivion of not breeding, as this joke from comedian Larry Wilde illustrates:

DOCTOR: Mrs. Smith, I don't like the looks of your husband.
MRS. SMITH: Neither do I, doc, but he's good with the kids.

And modern fathers would, as a group, seem to be eminently qualified. The past two decades have seen the rise of the so-called "new father"—the dad who's more sharing, loving, and giving, and who spends more time both with his children and caring for them, than any of our own fathers and grandfathers would have thought possible, desirable, or even sane. Yet how does the "new father" compare, I wonder, with another group of super-dads who made the news recently for their phenomenal parenting abilities: the ancient but still surviving Aka Pygmies of the Western Congo Basin.

I can hardly bear to look.

Babies

Who is this "new father" who is suddenly all over the talk shows and pages of pop-culture mags, supposedly rehabilitating the reputation of modern males with his new-found paternal skills? Where did he come from? According to authors Karen Hansen and Anita Garey in their book *Families in the U.S.*, he's the lineal descendant of several ancestral fathers. Way back in the Middle Ages, when the church ruled supreme, lived "Dad the moral guardian": the father who assumed the main burden of shaping, usually by brute force, the moral character of his offspring. Then, with the advent of industrialization and the rise of the middle class, came "Dad the distant breadwinner": the classic, aloof Western *paterfamilias* of the 1930s and 1940s. Many harassed modern dads might think that's where developments should have stopped, but this glorious escape from responsibility in fact proved temporary. The influx of women into employment in the post-war era prompted entirely reasonable complaints that men weren't pulling their weight domestically—reasonable to everybody except men, that is, who by that time had forgotten they were supposed to be pulling at all. There were also concerns, sparked by the spread of psychoanalytic sex-role theory around the same time, that the absence of men was turning a generation of boys into sissies. Thus was born the "involved father," typified by the *Father Knows Best* sitcom dad, Jim Anderson, who played with his kids, attended recitals and baseball games, and was always available to dispense allowances or paternal advice.

The "involved father," however, tended to limit his involvement to his older children; infant care in general, and diaper changing in particular, were left to the wife and mother. That sufficed for a while, until the women's movement—and its wannabe masculine little brother, the men's movement—finally forced the reluctant hand of the "involved father" into the diaper bucket, too. Thus was born today's model: the "new father," the dad who spent time with his kids, was involved with them during infancy (not just later childhood), was available for actual child-care (not just play), and was as equally involved with his daughters as his sons.[1] The trademark of the "new father" is his determination to share in every aspect of parenthood, bar none. Some "new fathers," for example, go so far as to wear an "empathy belly"—a device that not only simulates a thirty-three-pound weight around the midriff, but also features a rib-belt to constrict the lungs, mobile lead weights that simulate foetal movement, a warm-water pouch to emulate the heat of pregnancy, and a specially positioned weight that mimics a fetal head pressing into the wearer's bladder.

Somewhat less exotic specimens of fatherhood are the Aka Pygmies, who still live in the rainforests of the Western Congo Basin, much as they have done for hundreds, and possibly thousands, of years. These tribal peoples are genuine Pygmies, in that their males average less than 5' in height (compared to our 5'10"). Like their neighbors, the Mbuti Pygmies, they probably get their short stature from a mutation making them resistant to human growth hormones. Their bands of around one hundred people make their living by gathering edible forest plants and insects, and hunting small to medium-sized animal prey in communal "net hunts"— although Aka men, again like the Mbuti, also bring down elephants and wild boar with the spear (see, page 65). The Aka crop up in any discussion of fatherhood thanks to the pioneering fieldwork of Professor Barry Hewlett, from Washington State University, on Aka fathering. After researching the Aka for fifteen years and living with them for some months, Hewlett submitted a Ph.D. thesis that called their men "the best fathers in the world."[2] Aka men, Hewlett reported, not only spent large amounts of time with their children every day, much of that time was in direct physical contact with them, skin-on-skin. They treated their daughters exactly the same as their sons. They also took genuine interest in their infant children, sharing their care substantially with the child's mother, rather than just playing with them. So dedicated to infant care were Aka men, Hewlett reported, that they even, at times, *suckled* their babies. (The skeptical reader, of course, will at this point raise the sensible question of how Aka men could suckle infants when they don't have breasts. Or the ability to lactate. Incredibly, however, it turns out that a substantial minority of Aka Pygmy men *do* grow them. That's all I'll say about that right here, though; if this flash of male cleavage isn't enough and you can't wait for a full explanation, I suggest you leaf forward to page 227.)

It's immediately obvious that these characteristics make the Aka the perfect foil against which to test the claims of the Western "new father." Aka Pygmy men have substantial achievements in all four areas of prowess claimed by the Western "new father": they spend time with their kids, they are involved with them during infancy, they are available for child *care* and not just play, and they seem to treat their daughters the same way they treat their sons.

Thanks to Hewlett's work, we also have precise figures to compare, since he meticulously recorded everything from the percentage of time Aka fathers spent within three feet of their children to how often Aka infants crawled to their dads around the campfire. All we have to do, then, is find comparable figures for the Western "new father" (we'll substitute the TV for the campfire) and we can transport him to a clearing in the Congo rainforest for a "dad-off" with these diminutive super-fathers. True, such an exercise might lay us open to the charge of running an unsavory, exploitative freak show. All I can say, however, is that I will do my best to ensure the Western "new father" is treated with the dignity he deserves and isn't forced to model his "empathy belly" or "man-wrap" baby carrier for amused Aka gawkers too often.

To kick off proceedings, then, just how much time *does* the much-improved Western "new father" spend with his children? And how does that compare to his female partner's efforts? According to the U.S. Bureau of Labor Statistics (BLS), American men still lag considerably behind their women.[3] A married, employed father, for example, spends an average 1.21 hours a day engaged in child-care activities, while his employed wife spends 1.97. The discrepancy between unemployed dads and moms is even more pronounced—1.75 hours compared to 3.21, or almost double. True, these figures are a vast improvement on those of the past forty years: a miserable 17 minutes a day in 1965, 26 minutes in 1985 and 51 minutes in 1998. Yet the true difference between a husband's and wife's time with the kids may remain even greater than those figures suggest. The BLS stats also reveal that a wife still does four times as much housework (which generally *is* childcare in any house peopled with anklebiters) as her husband. It seems, in fact, that the preferred childcare activity of the modern "new father" is simply *being* there. Statistics from another study record that dads these days are within eyesight or earshot of their kids for an average 3.56 hours a day, most of this being on weekends.

Given that numerous other studies show father-presence is an essential element of children's wellbeing, this is an undeniable improvement on the "distant breadwinner" dad of old. In Aka society, however, it would probably be considered child abuse by neglect. Aka Pygmy dads, Hewlett records, are available to their children for an average twelve hours a day, every day of the week.[4] That's not just within earshot, either—Aka dads stick within *arm's length* of their offspring for that entire time. How on earth do they do it? Partly it's through actually holding their kids, which Aka dads do for almost a quarter of their time while in camp. They also sleep with their kids, along with their wives, on incredibly narrow beds (about eighteen inches in width), until well into the kids' early teens. Aka dads also take their children with them just about everywhere. Hewlett reported that he often witnessed drinking parties where Aka fathers downed palm wine (a naturally occurring alcohol) with their children perched in their laps or on their hips.

Outraged Western "new fathers," of course, might justifiably protest that they're not allowed to take their kids to bars anyway. They would also probably take refuge in the claim that the Aka are freaks—one-off exceptions to the no-doubt poor efforts of other ancient and tribal dads. While it *is* true that the Aka are in a class of their own among hunter-gathers (Hewlett records that Aka men hold their kids for five times as long as the men of any other culture), they are by no means the only doting fathers of the tribal world. While figures as meticulous as Hewlett's are rarely available, the great anthropologist Bronislaw Malinowski nonetheless reported that Papuan Trobriand Island men were extremely devoted fathers, carrying their children around for hours at a time.[5] Melanesian Lesu men of New Ireland, similarly, were known for playing with their children daily, often spending hours at a time with them and taking them along when they gathered socially with other men. After hearing this, the Western "new father" might even be tempted into a perverse sulk, stating that if he can't be the best in time spent with his progeny then, by God, he'll be the worst. Even that honor (such as it were), however, would be denied him. The men of numerous ancient and tribal groups outdid us in neglect, too. One example will do: the Rwala Bedouin tribesmen of Saudi Arabia and Syria a century ago spent so little time with their children that a Rwala boy could easily reach adolescence without having spoken to his father more than once or twice.[6]

spare the rod

The phrase "Spare the rod and spoil the child" has its origin in a biblical verse, Proverbs 13:24. It has justified many a savage caning for unfortunate Christian school children, yet some ancient tribal disciplinarians took the advice to even greater extremes. The Tswana people of South Africa, for example, *literally* applied the rod, sometimes with fatal consequences.

The *bogwera* initiation rite of the Tswana featured a disciplinary ritual in which young boys were made to confess their sins and were then punished for them. Punishment was meted out with thorny sticks nicknamed *dichoshwano*, "ants," or *dinotshe*, "bees." Miscreants were whipped on the body until the ants and bees ripped open their skin. Serious wrongdoers were stretched out on their back with their head tilted while their bared throat was repeatedly hit—it was this use of the *dichoshwnne* that sometimes resulted in death.

Just as savage were Rwala Bedouin Arab fathers of the Syrian desert. They disciplined their sons by stabbing them with daggers—or sabers in the case of particularly weighty offences. Crying out was specifically forbidden and prompted further punishment.

Yet even Tswana and Rwala boys, if they survived, eventually escaped their father's control. Ancient Roman men, on the other hand, were subject to their father's total authority for their entire lives. Even elderly Roman senators, grandfathers themselves, might find themselves subject to an autocratic father's whim. Thanks to the legal institution of *patria potestas*, too, this was no joke: Roman dads could seize their sons' properties and income, force them to divorce, and even kill them with impunity. The founder of Rome, Brutus, is reputed to have done exactly that, executing two of his own sons for military incompetence. ■

In the endurance contest of time spent with the kids, it seems, the Aka have it all over the Western "new father." They spend three times as long with their children as Western dads do, and at much closer range to boot. What about the second marker of the "new father" then: involvement with one's infants, rather than just one's older kids? This symbolizes "new fathering" because the earlier "involved father" didn't do it—if a child wasn't old enough to don a baseball mitt or throw a football it was still, by definition, it's mother's concern. A quick glance at the statistics shows that modern dads have indeed jettisoned this attitude: in fact, they've reversed it. The figure of 1.21 hours per day spent caring for their children, given earlier, relates to children under the age of 6; for children over the age of 6 that figure drops to 47 minutes per day. True, the under-6 measure is not a precise one, but it nonetheless indicates that dads these days spend *more* time with their infants than their older kids, not less. The only proviso I would add is that those low levels of housework show that modern dads still aren't quite up to *all* aspects of caring for their infants. Be that as it may, how does the modern dad's improved connection with his infant kids compare to that of his Aka competitors?

Hewlett's figures show that Aka dads are much more intensely involved with their infant children than the Western "new father." In the first four months of their infants' lives Aka dads hold them for 22 percent of their time in camp (the percentage is lower when the men are out on a hunt). This figure declines as the infants get older, but is still at 14.3 percent when the infants are eighteen months old. This is not surprising, given the words of one Aka father quoted by Hewlett: "We Aka look after our children with love, from the minute they are born to when they are much older."[7] Hewlett found, what's more, that this is no idle boast: Aka men really do undertake a lot of infant care. When babies fuss at night it is most often their fathers who take them outside to soothe them. It is also often their fathers who wipe the infants off with leaves after they urinate or defecate (frequently on the father himself). They kiss their infants more often than the children's mothers do. Aka men have no qualms either about assuming other supposedly female duties such as chewing their babies' food for them and feeding them. One might think, of course, that Aka men can't do quite everything for their babies that their mothers can—nurse them, for example. Incredibly, however, it turns out that Aka men *do* suckle their children.

This fact was brought to the world's attention in a newspaper interview with Hewlett in 2005.[8] The paper reported that the professor had occasionally witnessed male breastfeeding during his fieldwork with the Aka. Skeptics raised the sensible question of how men could breastfeed without breasts, but the mystery only deepened with Hewlett's insistence that he had, in fact, witnessed frequent instances of gynecomastia (male breast growth) among young Aka Pygmy men. While this sounds remarkable, it is supported by the reports of frequent gynecomastia among the unrelated Mbuti Pygmy people of Eastern Congo. What's more, male lactation (milk production) is not an unknown phenomenon. It occurs, even in the absence of identifiable breasts, in some groups of Western men suffering from a hormonal imbalance, such as cancer patients and concentration-camp survivors. The two major hormones involved are prolactin, which stimulates milk production in the breast, and estrogen, which in turn stimulates the production of prolactin and the growth of breast tissue. Putting these facts all together, could it be, then, that Aka dads have truly crossed the final frontier into breastfeeding, super-dad stardom?

To find out, I contacted Professor Hewlett directly. He quickly set me straight—yes it's true that Aka dads frequently offer their babies a nipple, but this is simply, he says, for comfort, not for breastfeeding. Given that mechanical stimulation of the nipples, even men's nipples, does generate prolactin production, however, might such suckling not produce lactation in the occasional Aka father? Hewlett had never witnessed this, and after asking several Aka men directly had, in fact, been told that Aka men *couldn't* breastfeed, since their "nipples were too small." So what about the curious male breast growth that Hewlett, and others, had noticed among the Aka and other Pygmy men? Clearly, some Aka men, at least, experience surges of estrogen sufficient to prompt breast growth. But this, Hewlett thought, was probably related to diet or peculiarities of Pygmy growth, rather than Aka fathering and suckling. I'm not so sure, however. A 2001 study by the Mayo Clinic found that Canadian men who were expectant fathers developed elevated levels of estrogen and reduced testosterone. It doesn't seem too far a stretch, then, to theorize that the caring, paternal style of Aka men is a contributing cause of high estrogen levels and gynecomastia among them (though it could just as easily be the other way around). Suffice it to say that, for whatever reason, a substantial minority of Aka men carry a visible symbol of their caring, fatherly abilities on their own bodies.[9]

In any case, although Aka Pygmy men are apparently unique in their suckling behavior, they are not unique among ancient and tribal men in care of infant children. Other tribal fathers took very loving care of their infant children too. Malinowski, for example, made it clear that those Trobriand Island fathers began their devoted attention in their child's early infancy:

> He (the father) will fondle and carry a baby, clean and wash
> it, and give it the mashed vegetable food . . . The father per-
> forms his duties with genuine natural fondness . . . looking

at it with eyes of such love and pride as are seldom seen in
those of a European.[10]

Accounts of Melanesian Lesu fathers, similarly, spoke in glowing terms of their connection with their infant children:

> *The father and mother are equally tender towards the*
> *child . . . A man plays with his child . . . talking pure foolish-*
> *ness to the baby . . . Or they may croon one of the dance songs*
> *to the infant.*[11]

Malinowski pointed out that such tender paternal behavior tended to occur in matrilineal societies (those tracing descent through the female line), since fathers in those societies were not the primary male authority figures (a child's mother's brother was). Patrilineal descent, on the other hand, tended to discourage close paternal affection, as in the case of the African Kipsigis people, whose fathers don't hold their infants at all for their first year of life. Clearly we modern fathers are, to some extent, throwing off our patrilineal roots in moving towards a model of greater infant care. Yet these figures show we still have a long way to go before we get anywhere near the efforts of Aka, Trobriand Island, or Lesu dads.

Rounds one and two, then, seem to have gone to the Aka and their support crew of tribal super-dads. But what of the two remaining markers of the "new father"—child-care rather than play, and equal treatment for sons and daughters? To take the first of these first, why exactly *is* a greater proportion of care as opposed to play considered a desirable trait of the modern "new father"? It's for two reasons: first, it indicates a willingness to do the heavy lifting of childcare (though what was that about the housework?), and second, it shows a high level of intimacy and comfortableness with one's children. At first glance, the figures for the involvement of the "new father" in actual child *care* do seem to have improved dramatically. According to a University of Chicago study, employed, married fathers went from spending seventeen minutes a day caring for their kids in 1965 to fifty-one minutes in 1998 (the latest figures available).[12] Yet the same study also showed that the *ratio* of care to play actually remained the same—that is, play had increased even more dramatically.[13] Sure, dads were giving more time overall to their kids, but they still preferred to spend that time in play, rather than care—diaper changing, feeding, and other tasks. Another study by the University of Michigan, similarly, showed that playing with his kids still takes up 39 percent of a modern dad's total involvement, as opposed to 28 percent for caring activities. For mothers, on the other hand, play takes up just over 21 percent of their total involvement. There is also a marked difference in the nature of mothers' and fathers' play: dads far more frequently engage in vigorous, physical interaction with kids than mothers do.

The comparison with Aka dads here is revealing, for despite their extraordinary levels of involvement with their kids, Aka fathers almost never *play* with them. Hewlett reported that he witnessed just one episode of father–child play in 264 hours of recorded observations. Aka children, when interviewed, also reported that their fathers rarely played with them. We are so conditioned to think of a father's role as a playful one that this would sound distressingly neglectful to us, were it not for all the other figures on Aka dads' superior care. So what's going on? There are two main reasons for the non-playful nature of Aka dads' interaction with their kids. First, that they have a strong role in teaching their children, which Western men have largely surrendered to the state. Aka training is a daily, minute-by-minute affair and starts from a remarkably early age, as Hewlett writes:

> *I was rather surprised to find parents teaching their eight-to-twelve-month-old infants how to use small pointed digging sticks, throw small spears, use miniature axes with sharp metal blades, and carry small baskets.*[14]

Aka dads don't need to invent games to play with their kids, since their whole life with them is, effectively, a teaching game. Beyond that reason however, lies another: the sheer intimacy of the understanding that Aka fathers have for their children. They spend so much time caring for them, Hewlett writes, that they become expert at knowing what their child needs and when. An Aka father can, it seems, read his young child far better than a modern Western father, even a "new" dad, can read his child. Looked at in this way, the preference for play shown by Western fathers is not an inbuilt, biological drive, as is sometimes stated, but a simple product of not knowing exactly what to do. Hewlett points to a major difference between European and Aka fathers in support of this: European men almost always initiate their interactions with their child, he says, while Aka men almost never do. They don't have to—their deep familiarity with their kids allows them to interact comfortably, easily, and naturally.

▣kids on parade

Child beauty contests have had a bad reputation since the tragic murder of JonBenét Ramsay in 1996. Yet they have continued to grow to the level where, according to the Pageant Center Web site, twenty-five thousand such contests are held every year, generating in excess of a billion dollars.[15] The Pageant Center claims that child beauty parades were invented in Florida during the 1960s, yet it might surprise them to know that some tribal peoples had, by that time, already been holding child beauty contests for hundreds of years.

In ancient Hawaii, doting grandparents apparently lined up their *pa'i punahele*, "little favorites," for periodic *ho'okelakela*, "beauty contests." These, however, were quite different from today's extravaganzas of fake spray tan, baby's breath, and pint-sized satin evening gowns. In line with the Polynesian love of corpulence (see "When fat was the new black" box on page 215) *pa'i punahele* were stuffed with food to make them as fat as possible. They also might have had trouble tottering down the catwalk, since *pa'i punahele* were carried everywhere and not allowed to walk for the first few years of their lives. Even so, these arrangements were still probably healthier than modern-day child beauty contests; a study published in the *Journal of Eating Disorders* found that girls who had been contestants in child beauty pageants were more likely to have significant body-dissatisfaction issues.[16] ▣

At this point things are looking grim for the "new father"—3 out of 4 rounds have now gone to his Aka rivals. Can he fight a rearguard action on the last supposed marker of his "new" fatherhood: equal treatment for sons and daughters? Initial signs, once again, seem promising. The Western world has none of the female infanticide that so skews sex ratios in some Asian and African countries (112 boys are born for every 100 girls in South Korea, thanks to the advent of sex selection based on ultrasound). Yet look a little deeper and some intriguing patterns emerge. Despite the absence of any tendency to abort female fetuses, 48 percent of American expectant fathers still say they want a son, as opposed to 19 percent who hope for a daughter. After the child is born, too, subtle differences in treatment set in, possibly not even consciously noted by the dad himself. Fathers are, for example, more motivated to work harder, and for more money, once they have had a son. They spend more time playing with them, too—an hour a day during weekdays as opposed to just half an hour with their daughters.[17] (The discrepancy becomes even more pronounced in the case of stepfathers, who spend more time with sons than daughters in every category of child-care, not just play.) The difference in fathers' attitudes to sons and daughters can even affect the man's marriage. Fathers are more likely to marry the mother of their child, for example, if that child is a son. One study of couples who had learned the sex of their child through ultrasound even found that those couples with sons were more likely to marry before the baby was born. The list goes on: parents with sons are more likely to start a university fund; levels of happiness and marital harmony are higher for couples with male children, and divorce rates lower; when couples *do* divorce, the father is more likely to seek custody if sons are involved, rather than daughters. In each one of these measures the difference is small, but marked. The figures don't lie—the Western "new father," despite his undoubtedly sincere protestations of equal love, does *not* treat his daughters exactly the same as his sons. Do the Aka show the same tendency?

Interestingly, we don't have any data on this problem—not a scrap.[18] Professor Hewlett didn't even address the issue in his fieldwork among the Aka. So completely absent is the question that his excellent book on Aka dads, *Intimate Fathers,* doesn't even carry index entries for sons and daughters. This may, of course, be a simple matter of research focus, but I think something deeper is going on. Hewlett's study does not investigate differences in Aka dads' treatment of sons and daughters, I'd suggest, because there are none. Aka society is so blind to status differences between men and women that the idea of treating boys differently to girls doesn't occur to them. The evidence lies in Hewlett's descriptions of male and female roles in Aka life. These are, he writes, characterized by an extremely high level of equality:

> *Aka women challenge men's authority on a regular basis and are influential actors in all kinds of decision making. Women participate in decisions about camp movement, extramarital affairs, bad luck on the hunt, and sorcery accusations . . . the capabilities of men and women are very similar, and therefore tasks can be reversed easily.*

Aka women participate actively in supposedly male activities such as net hunting, and are, in fact, responsible for killing the small antelopes and other prey that the men chase into the net (they don't, however, take part in the rarer spear hunts for elephant and wild boar). The high status of Aka women is shown through the lyrics of one of their popular *dingboku,* "women's dance songs": "the penis is not a competitor, it has died already! The vagina wins!" It is also evidenced by the fact that neither Hewlett nor any of the other anthropologists who have worked with the Aka witnessed incidents of male violence toward women. (Interestingly, there *was* some female-on-male violence, generally from wives who cut their husbands' faces with knives or hit them with burning logs for sleeping with another woman. Even here, though, a more usual female tantrum involved simply tearing their shared hut down.) So while I admit that we have no direct data on Aka dads' treatment of daughters compared to sons, I'm still, regrettably, able to award them probable victory in this round, too.

On every defining measure of "new" fatherhood, then, we modern men have proven to be deadbeat dads. Despite our national fatherhood institutes, parenting programs, dads' clubs, and birthing classes, we've been out-fathered by a bunch of forest dads who couldn't even read a "Prepared for Pregnancy" pamphlet, let alone Bill Cosby's *Fatherhood.* At this point, however, the humiliated "new father" might well protest that the comparison is unfair. Fathering these days presents special challenges, he would argue, ones of which the Aka could never have dreamed. What about those innovations the "new father" has dreamed up to meet those challenges, such as his embrace of stepfathering? Or being present at his child's birth? Or bringing his kids up without any discipline (a favorite complaint of right-wing radio shock jocks)? How could the Aka possibly match the Western "new father" in those, since he, presumably, invented them?

Well, let's see.

Stepfathering, it's true, is often considered a speciality of modern families in the post-sexual-revolution era. Yet our self-proclaimed skills in inclusive parenting seem to evaporate whenever the census-taker comes around: in 2004 less than 6 percent of American children lived with their mother and a stepfather, as opposed to almost 25 percent who resided with just their single mother.[19] What's more, outcomes for children living with those stepdads are sometimes less than best. Research carried out by Margo Wilson and Martin Daly in the 1980s showed that stepfathers were responsible for higher rates of (and more severe) child assault and murder than biological fathers.[20] Direct maltreatment is, thankfully, rare even among stepfathers, but neglect in favor of one's biological children, unfortunately, isn't. Another study of American stepfathers showed that on four measures of investment in children—financial support from birth, time spent with them, children's university attendance, and financial support while studying—they lavished fewer resources on their stepchildren than on their own kids.[21] The distinction held even when a man's stepchildren were living in the same family as his biological kids. While most modern stepdads make genuine efforts to love their stepchildren just as much as their own, it seems they're simply not particularly good at doing so.

The Aka, by contrast, seem to manage better. Stepfathering is, for a start, much more common in Aka society than among Western "new fathers." Due to the early age at which Aka parents die, and their surprisingly high divorce rate, over 40 percent of Aka children live with at least one stepparent by the age of sixteen. Every stepchild Hewlett interviewed said their stepfather had treated them well, sometimes even better than their own father had. True, Hewlett notes that stepfathers didn't seem to provide as much direct care as biological dads did, but he also cautioned that his data was too limited from which to draw valid conclusions. In

Aka society there certainly seems to be *some* benefit in having a stepfather—Hewlett states that almost every child in his survey who had lost a father also died within months, unless their mother remarried. This is probably due to the dangerous conditions in the Aka's jungle home, coupled with the loss of the father's substantial contribution to child care. Other tribal societies in jungle habitats proved even more skilled at sharing custody and stepfathering. Some, indeed, extended their sharing to the mother herself. Men of the South American Bari, Canela, Mundurucu, and the Mehinaku Indian tribes believed that it took the semen of several men to make a child, and that each then carried the responsibilities of a father. Remarkably, kids lucky enough to score such multiple dads had better survival rates than children with a single father.[22] (Although we must not, of course, idealize all ancient tribal fathering: Aché Indians of Paraguay, for example, actually killed children whose fathers either died or left the group.[23]) The Western "new father," by comparison, seems rather selfish—a study done in 2004 showed we tend to save our best fathering efforts for those children who physically resemble us.[24]

If our stepfathering boasts have proven mere bombast, then, what about our presence at our children's births? This is certainly a new development—fifty years ago husbands weren't even allowed inside many U.S. maternity wards during their child's birth; these days more than 90 percent attend.[25] It's also something Aka fathers *don't* do, so it seems we've finally scored at least *one* victory over those smug, super-paternal show-offs. Aka fathers don't have particular taboos against fathers attending childbirth (Hewlett records at least one father who did assist when his wife went into labor alone in the forest). Most other ancient tribal societies, though, did. The fluids associated with childbirth were often considered so polluting that fathers avoided a woman's labor on pain of death. That doesn't mean, however, that they played no part in their child's birth. Some tribal males were required to build a special hut for their wife to give birth in. Others had to observe extensive restrictions, such as the Mehinaku of Brazil, whose fathers had to abstain from sex, isolate themselves in a secluded hut, and avoid certain foods (such as fish) for months after the birth. Among the Garifuna people of Honduras, this period could last three years.[26] Some tribal fathers, on the other hand, *did* attend their child's birth. Their activities there, however, weren't limited to holding their wife's hand and uttering the occasional "Push!" Among the Aka's pygmy neighbors, the Mbuti, fathers were (and still are) required to strip naked and expose their penis (try doing *that* in the maternity ward and see how far you get). Among precolonial Burmese mountain people, not just the father but *all* the men of the tribe stripped off and assumed a variety of obscene postures, supposedly to scare off evil spirits. Even more extreme, however, were those societies that practiced couvade, "sympathetic pregnancy," rituals. Some of these simply mimicked the wife's pregnancy, as in the case of those South American Indians among whom, according to anthropologist Yves d'Evreux:

> He [the husband] lies-in instead of his wife who works as usual; then all the women of the village come to see and visit him in his bed, consoling him for the trouble and pain he had in producing his child; he is treated as if he were sick and very tired without leaving his bed.[27]

Others, however, involved the sadistic infliction of pain on the father to *make* him empathize with his wife's suffering. Some ancient Brazilian tribes, for example, slashed the father all over his body with the teeth of an agouti (a rodent with teeth so sharp they pierce Brazil nuts) and poured tobacco juice mixed with pepper into the cuts. An even more directly empathic experience, though, was required of the Mexican Huichol Indian father in the olden days, who:

> During traditional childbirth . . . sits above his laboring wife on the roof of their hut. Ropes are tied around his testicles and . . . each time she feels a painful contraction, she tugs on the ropes so that her husband will share some of the pain of their child's entrance into the world.[28]

Now if that doesn't make any "new father" slink off to discard his "empathy belly" in shame, he'll have to add self-delusion to his list of shortcomings.[29]

It seems cruel to continue, but for the sake of the exercise, what about our supposed invention of noncorporal discipline of children? The past few decades have, it's true, seen a march away from physical discipline. Corporal punishment is now illegal in all European schools and most European homes, schools in three Australian states, and schools in twenty-three American ones. This is certainly an improvement from the barbarism of earlier times. As late as the 1820s Alfred Lord Tennyson was flogged so severely for forgetting his lines while reciting a school text that he was confined to bed for six weeks. And medieval punishments, of course, had been even worse, as when disrespectful Saxon children in early England were fastened to walls with the *joug* ("metal collar") for passersby to pelt and abuse.[30] Yet not all ancient and tribal societies have been as cruel as ours. It's probable that the Aka Pygmies, for example, have *never* used such brutal punishments. Pygmy fathers today rarely hit their children; Hewlett says he only witnessed it once in fifteen years of research among the Aka. (In fact, in Aka culture hitting children can constitute grounds for divorce.) Aka fathers don't even attack their children verbally; Hewlett records that he almost never heard a Pygmy father, or mother, say the word "no" to a misbehaving child. (They generally just shift them away from the object of misbehavior.) Nor do Aka dads demand an overly high level of respect from their children. Hewlett reports with some amusement the words of an outraged villager of the Ngandu (a neighboring people who treat their children more strictly than the Aka):

> *Young pygmies have no respect for their parents; they regard their fathers as their friends . . . they always use their first names. Once I was in a pygmy camp . . . and a son said to his father, "Etobe your balls are hanging out of your loincloth" and everyone started laughing. No respect, none, none, none . . .*[31]

I may be misjudging him, but I'd wager many a "new father" would be tempted to foreswear his noncorporal punishment principles when Timmy comes out with *that* little number!

■Here's to you, Mrs. Robinson

We often brag that our children receive the most enlightened sex education of any children in history, in contrast to the dark ignorance of medieval and Victorian times. Teachers in most American states (those that haven't gone the "abstinence only" route) provide what they call "comprehensive" sex education, but it might well astonish those educators to find that sex ed in the ancient world was sometimes so comprehensive it even included on-the-job training. On the island of Tongareva, for example, a boy's first growth of pubic hair:

> ...marked his introduction to copulation: a mature woman was appointed by his father to press back his foreskin over the glans and to instruct him, by actual demonstration, how to copulate. After that the boy began for the first time to wear a loincloth (i.e., to conceal his genitals) and was deemed ... ready for actual (in contrast to playful) copulation ... [32]

This sounds almost like abuse, to our ears, but it is worth remembering that attitudes to children's bodies could be very different in ancient societies. Manchu mothers of ancient northern China, to give one of numerous examples, might often be seen in public sucking their infant son's penis (for pacification), though they would never dream of kissing his cheek—an explicitly erotic gesture in Manchu culture. ■

Why *should* we modern fathers be so much worse than the Aka, despite our fantastic riches in resources and self-help books? In our defense, it isn't entirely our fault. Anthropological studies of good fathering (defined as intimate and emotionally warm) have found that it is far more common in hunter-gatherer societies. The studies have also identified the conditions that seem to inhibit this approach in other cultures. One of those, as mentioned, is the patrilineal-descent system, but there are others. Researchers have discovered, for example, that the most distant fathering tends to take place in pastoral, or herding, societies. This is mostly because such societies allow the accumulation of enormous private wealth. This in turn encourages men to adopt promiscuous mating strategies like polygamy in which their number of offspring goes up, since they can now support them, but their investment in each goes down. There's also the problem that herding takes a man away—often a long way away—from his family and thus removes him from the fathering scene. It's also the case, finally, that herding societies tend to be quite violent ones. The fact that so much wealth is tied up in a mobile, easily stolen resource means herders often have to employ extreme violence as a deterrent. The drawback, of course, is that such aggression is not conducive to warm and empathic fathering (see, the "Spare the rod" box on pages **224–25,** for sobering evidence of this).

It is immediately obvious, too, that our society—that of the "new father"—satisfies at least two of these conditions. True, we no longer have to resort to hyperaggression to deter our foes (the justice system now does that for us), but we are still very much like a pastoralist society in that our workplaces usually take us away—again, often *far* away—from our homes and any opportunity for sustained fathering. We are also quite an acquisitive society, which, as we have seen, encourages promiscuity and inhibits paternal investment. (True, we don't always father the huge broods that those polygamist pastoral fathers do, but it's not just the extra children that dilute those fathers' paternal investment. It's also the weakened attachment to any particular woman that results from having multiple sexual partners—which high-status males in our society also report.) Similarly, the fact that employed fathers who take "the daddy track"—forgoing work time to care for their children—suffer worse career outcomes, and are considered less conscientious employees by their employers, demonstrates that there is a cost placed on paternal investment in our society.[33]

Clearly our fathering fundamentals need some attention.

Remarkably, though, even the superpaternal Aka also have their fathers who don't dig the daddy track. The Aka don't have many high-status positions to strive for, but they do have some, among them the posts of *kombeti*, "headman," *nganga*, "healer," and *tuma*, "elephant hunter." Hewlett found that men who had held those positions generally showed less intimate fatherly care than those who had not. Just like their Western counterparts, this was probably because they devoted most of their effort to status-seeking activities, rather than fathering.[34]

But these men are the exception, rather than the rule, and a small one at that. For most Aka men, their unique culture allows them to nourish their fathering instincts free of such poisonous influences. What conditions allow this? Hewlett identifies three, the first of which is equality between men and women. Aka husbands, Hewlett writes, spend a lot of time with their wives, enjoy their company, and have such a high level of respect for women's work that they see nothing demeaning in helping them perform it. This leads directly into the second condition Hewlett identifies: the fact that men and women work together in activities such as net hunting and caterpillar gathering, putting the father at child-care ground zero all day, every day. This in turns leads into the third condition: the high level of father-child bonding. Aka fathers grow so emotionally close to their young children because they are physically close to them throughout their entire childhoods.

This, Hewlett says, has strong implications for our own society. Not only does it mean that we must find ways to bring fathers' workplaces closer to their homes, be it through workplace child care or flexible paternity leave. It also means that our current focus on ensuring quality time for dads with their kids may be misguided. Quality time, Hewlett says, simply cannot substitute for *quantity* time.

That is the real lesson of the Aka. Following their example may well help us improve in future, but right now we are once more in desperate trouble. *Homo masculinus modernus* has come in second-best, yet again, in a fight over the last possible quality that makes a man worthy of the name: his skill as a dad. On top of our previous failures—see BRAWN, BRAVADO, BATTLE, BALLS, BARDS, and BEAUTY—it is a bitter blow. But since all these aspects of masculinity—strength, courage, beauty, sporting, and literary skill—have proven to be simple ploys in the age-old struggle to mate, and thereby save ourselves from genetic oblivion, our mediocre efforts beg the question: just how well *do* we do, then, with the ladies? How good *are* we in the arts of Venus, especially in comparison to those ancient men who have so soundly thrashed us elsewhere?

Certainly, we are, once again, not short on boasts about it—recall Wilt Chamberlain's unbelievable claim of twenty thousand lovers (see page **146**). Then there are the claims of the "seduction community," immortalized in books such as Neil Strauss's *The Game* and TV shows like *The Pickup Artist,* that they have brought the art of seducing women to heights exceeding even those of the legendary Casanova. Seduction "gurus" in the community insist they can get a woman to sleep with them within seven hours, to pay them for sex, and to have orgasms on vocal command. This last, admittedly, is difficult to believe, but it's merely a more extreme version of our supreme confidence in our ability to satisfy women sexually as never before in history. Who, after all, discovered the clitoris and the female orgasm, complete with their excitingly updated cousins, the G-spot and female ejaculation? What man in history has ever employed the sophisticated techniques we have to induce the same? Who has ever been as sexually liberated, had more adulterous affairs, consumed such explicit pornography, or even been as *gay* as us?

There's only one way to find out. Strap yourselves in, ladies and gentlemen, as we embark on a tour through sex-toy manufacture in the European Palaeolithic; Hawaiian *pili* ("touched by the wand") swingers' parties; and Andean Moche ceramic kettles so pornographic they'd have Larry Flynt firing up his kiln for a piece of the action. Oh, and don't forget to bring some tissues—not for the fluids, but the tears.

Which I have a very strong suspicion it's all going to end in.

I s it conceivable that Wilt Chamberlain really slept with twenty thousand women in the course of his womanizing career? To those unfamiliar with the life of the 7'1" "Wilt the Stilt" (he hated the name, apparently), here is a quick biography: Chamberlain was born in 1936 in Philadelphia, where he took up basketball at Overbrook High School before progressing to a professional career with the Harlem Globetrotters, the Los Angeles Lakers, and the San Diego Conquistadors, eventually retiring in 1974. Chamberlain so dominated basketball in his time that he still holds seventy-two NBA records, such as being the only player to score one hundred points in a game, or to average over fifty points a game for an entire season. What of his score in the bedroom, though? True, certain facts about Chamberlain seem to lend credence to his extraordinary claim. The fabulous pad he built in Bel Air, Los Angeles, during his years with the Lakers *was* known as the venue of Playboy-style parties, and Chamberlain *is* documented as once sleeping with twenty-three women in ten days.[1] Given these appetites, and the fact that a total of twenty thousand would merely require Chamberlain to sleep with an average of one woman per day for fifty years (between the ages of thirteen and his death at sixty-three), the figure seems difficult but perhaps possible. But look a little closer and doubts arise.

First, Chamberlain got off to a late start: his schoolmates reported he was still a virgin at graduation. Second, his mini Playboy mansion, where most of this action took place, wasn't built until Wilt was over thirty. A few years probably have to be taken off, too, at the other end of Chamberlain's life, since he began suffering serious heart trouble in his early fifties, ten years before his death from congestive heart failure in 1999. Then there is the fact that Chamberlain claimed twenty thousand *different* women, when he is known to have had a couple of regular girlfriends—(this may not have stopped his womanizing, but it surely inhibited it somewhat). Taking all this into consideration, Chamberlain's daily average might have had to be as high as two to three women per day, *every day,* to make his total of twenty thousand. We will never really know, of course, but it seems reasonable, given this, to mark Chamberlain down to a *possible* ten thousand conquests over the course of his womanizing career.

This is still an impressive total, in anybody's language, but how does it compare to the famous players of the ancient past? To make it a fair contest, we will have to compare Chamberlain with the only class of man who could equal him in prestige, wealth, and opportunity—those rulers and potentates who were able to accumulate harems. (Athletes such as Porphyrius [see page 145] could, too, of course, but sadly we don't have any information on the famous charioteer's erotic achievements.) A quick survey shows that many of these horny tyrants would have given Chamberlain a serious run for his bunnies. King Tanga of the ancient north Indian kingdom of Varanasi, for example, apparently kept a harem of sixteen thousand maidens. Ghiyath-ud-din-Khilji, who ruled another Indian kingdom, Malwa, in the late sixteenth century, did almost as well with fifteen thousand. True, this is only six thousand and five thousand more, respectively, than Chamberlain's amended total, but it must be remembered that there was also some movement in and out of harems as women aged and were replaced by younger beauties, meaning the true totals for the ancient womanizers could have been even higher. As late as the nineteenth century, King Mongkut of Siam—immortalized for Western audiences through the Rodgers and Hammerstein musical *The King and I*—maintained a harem of six thousand women. Defenders of the sexual prowess of *Homo masculinus modernus* and his womanizing champion Chamberlain, might, however, protest that merely having a harem of several thousand women isn't the same as sleeping with them. Yet we do have evidence that these rulers *did* indulge the gluttonous sexuality that their power allowed. Mongkut, for example, fathered eighty-two children—particularly impressive considering he was a celibate monk until the age of forty-seven, giving him just seventeen years with those six thousand concubines before his death at sixty-four. Then there is the evidence, noted earlier (see page 111), that approximately 32 million people, or 0.5 percent of the world's population, are descended from Genghis Khan and his close male relatives. (The study actually found that 16 million men carry Genghis Khan's Y-chromosome; by extension, that means approximately 16 million daughters probably descend from him, too.) Despite the Mongols' reputation for rape, the greater part of this contribution clearly came from the massive harems Genghis and his successors maintained. Genghis's grandson Kubilai, for example, kept a seraglio of seven thousand women, replenishing them with a yearly intake of a couple of hundred virginal beauties from within his empire.

Clearly, these libidinous lords could well have put even Wilt the Stilt to shame in the womanizing stakes. It could be argued, however, that they, as well as Chamberlain himself, represent an unusual deviation from the norm. More relevant is the experience of the ordinary man, the everyday *Homo masculinus modernus* schmo going about his business—part of which, presumably, includes trying to reproduce himself. How does he fare against his ancient and tribal "ordinary guy" competitors? Any inquiry into this immediately runs into a problem: reliable figures for the number of lovers the average modern Western male has in his lifetime are almost nonexistent. Every survey taken not only gives a different figure, it also shows a logical impossibility—that men average many more partners in their lives than women do.[2] The only logical assumption is that men consistently exaggerate their reported number of sexual partners (and that women underreport theirs).[3] A better strategy, therefore, is to look at their *rate* of romantic success—how often they close the deal in how many attempts. Fortunately, we do have one measure (admittedly a vague one) of the modern ordinary man's success rate in romantic ventures, thanks to those gurus of the seduction community mentioned at the end of the previous chapter. For the uninitiated, the seduction community is a loose conglomeration of male self-help experts, now predominantly Internet-based, who grew out of the movement set off by Eric Weber's 1970 book *How to Pick Up Girls!*[4] These gurus pride themselves on providing, usually for a price, sure-fire pickup advice specifically for the ordinary schmo—no matter, as one pickup instructor's book is subtitled, what he looks like, or how much money he makes. Exact claims of numbers of lovers are again hard to pick out among the general braggadocio, but they certainly are substantial: pickup guru Erik Von Markovik, who calls himself Mystery, tells readers of his book *The Mystery Method: How to Get Beautiful Women into Bed* that he has slept with hundreds of women.[5] This is undeniably noteworthy, yet most pickup gurus will admit that these successful hits also come out of many, many approaches and rejections. So, while these superstars of "ordinary man" romancing do boast reasonably high *numbers* of conquests, their actual *rate* of success is much lower.

But is it better, or worse, than that of ancient and tribal males?

Thanks to the work of anthropologist Thomas Gregor among the Mehinaku, we do have a sample population of tribal men with which to compare. During his years of living in a Mehinaku village, Gregor compiled a list of which men were having affairs with which women. To his astonishment, he discovered that in a village of just thirty-seven adults, eighty-eight extramarital affairs were being conducted.[6] Almost all the men were conducting at least three affairs at any one time, and some were involved in ten. What makes the total so striking is that incest prohibitions severely limited the number of partners from whom a man could choose, meaning that the men of the village were, effectively, having affairs with every single woman that their laws allowed them to. Their success rate, in other words, was almost 100 percent. Apart from simple bribery with gifts (which admittedly played a strong part), Gregor put this down to the erotic courage of Mehinaku men, who sometimes went so far in their pursuit of girlfriends as to simply stick their hand through the thatched walls of her hut in hopes of an intimate touch, regardless of whether her potentially enraged husband was home. They also frequently attempted the ultimate in dangerous infidelities—creeping into a girlfriend's hut at night to copulate with her as her husband slept in his hammock just inches above. (Interestingly, the Tahitians had a very similar custom called *mafera*, "night creeping"—in this case, however, the main threat was from the woman's relatives who shared her communal hut; to evade them the stealthy lothario usually greased himself with coconut oil to slip through their clutching hands.)

rough trade

Sadomasochism is a popular form of sexual fantasy: 14 percent of American men and 24 percent of American women report at least occasional desires to be painfully violated. Once more, however, we lack follow-through—just 5 percent of couples ever graduate to incorporating real pain into their sex lives.[7] Some tribal peoples, by contrast, mixed pleasure with pain in almost every sexual experience.

Lovers in the Trobriand Islands, for example, left the marks of their passion all over each other's bodies. Not only did they frequently draw blood with bites to their lovers' lips, cheeks, and noses, and tear out clumps of hair in their sexual frenzy—they also bit off each other's eyelashes at orgasm and raked each other's skin so deeply they left deep, permanent scars called *kimali*. More serious erotic scarring also took place in the sadistic *kimali kayasa* festival, this time involving weapons. In the *kimali kayasa*, village boys danced and sang while the girls flirted with them—by slashing them with bamboo knives and obsidian axes. Each girl's aim, Bronislaw Malinowski wrote:

> . . . was successively to slash as many men as she
> could; the ambition of the man to carry away as many
> cuts as he could stand, and to reap the reward in each
> case.[8]

Remarkably, the *kimali kayasa* was not even the most violent of the Trobrianders' erotic customs. That honor goes to the *yausa*, an orgiastic assault inflicted on male trespassers by village women. In the *yausa*, Malinowski reported:

> ...the women will defecate and micturate [urinate] all over his body, paying special attention to his face, which they pollute as thoroughly as they can... [causing the man to] vomit, and vomit, and vomit... sometimes these furies rub their genitals against his nose and mouth, and use his fingers and toes, in fact any projecting part of his body, for lascivious purposes.

Considering even a faked version of these activities sent audiences across the modern world into vomiting hysterics (the *2 Girls 1 Cup* viral Web video, in which two actresses ate supposed excrement—actually melted chocolate) it seems doubtful any but the most dedicated of modern masochists would genuinely relish a *yausa* session at the hands of these harpies. ■

Clearly, then, while the seduction-community gurus' pickup techniques *do* work, they lag some ways behind those of our ancient forebears. In terms of bang for their buck (sorry), would-be Casanovas would be better off scanning a few anthropology texts and ordering in some night-vision goggles for a midnight *mafera* run. It isn't just the comparative lack of success that damns the gurus' techniques, though. Examining them in the light of those of our tribal forefathers leaves the distinct impression that the gurus, and by extension the rest of us, are such unchivalrous Romeos that we scarcely deserve the label.

The gurus' use of language in seduction, for example, is rather different from the love talk of the ancient past. Most gurus use language as a weapon to manipulate a woman's emotional state. The aim is to bypass her conscious self and access her deep emotional machinery, effectively removing her ability to consciously evaluate the pickup artist's approach. The pickup artist's language is, accordingly, often calculated, deceptive and full of purpose, but with very little beauty, poetry, or art. Sometimes, indeed, it is not even very nice. Mystery, for example, is famous for inventing the "neg," short for negative. This is a not-quite-insult such as, "Nice nails—are they real?" that "puts the target off-guard and makes her question her own value, increasing yours on a relative basis."[9] Perhaps the most highly developed use of manipulative language, though, can be found in the "speed seduction" product offered by Ross Jeffries. Jeffries, dubbed the "King of Schwing" by *Rolling Stone* magazine, is a devotee of neuro-linguistic programming, a pseudo-scientific motivational program that seeks to trigger emotional states through the use of supposed subliminal commands and keywords. Speed-seduction practitioners will, therefore, pepper their language with subliminal triggers such as "YOU'RE MINE"—as a deliberate mispronunciation of "YOUR MIND"—to implant an attitude of surrender in the target woman's mind. This reaches a height of manipulative crudity in the following suggestive routine—attributed not to Jeffries but to another legendary pickup artist, Bishop—which supposedly allows novice seducers (the PUA: pickup artist) to convince women to fellate them:

PUA: Hey Alicia. What do you love to eat? [What] makes you salivate just by thinking of it?

GIRL: Oh . . . I love fresh ripe mangoes from Hawaii.

PUA: Ripe mangoes . . . IMAGINE SUCKING into one sweet, delicious, juicy mango NOW . . . can you taste the sweetness of the mango . . . INSIDE YOUR MOUTH . . . doesn't that give you lots of pleasure and ha-PENIS . . . I bet, if there were a mango here NOW, you'd WANT IT IN YOUR MOUTH [point subliminally to your penis].[10]

Effective this ludicrous patter may well be,[11] but poetry it isn't.

The language of love in tribal societies, by contrast, often was (and is) richly poetic. Anthropologist Mette Bovin, for instance, writes that among the Wodaabe nomads of Niger:

> A young man who wishes to impress and seduce a young girl must never be too direct. He should develop a refined language, a nonaggressive poetic language called "sweet tongue" . . . The seducer talks in metaphors, in images, almost in poetry. If a young man is too direct, or too fast, the girl may go away and listen to a more polite young man.[12]

A successful ancient Tahitian seducer, similarly, was he who "composes pretty love songs and utters them with a tender voice, tender as the taro leaf softened by the evening breeze."[13] Some tribal males even had to master a completely new language, or a new way of speaking, to engage in love talk. Tribal Mangyan men of the Philippines island of Mindoro, for instance, had to speak in *pahágot*—a specialized love language in which the speaker formed words not by exhaling, but by inhaling. This tricky art (try it yourself and see) was used to disguise the identity of Mangyan Romeos as they serenaded their prospective lovers from the darkness outside their huts.[14]

As it is with saying, so it is with doing. Seduction-community literature is full of urgings for the would-be PUA to "be the alpha male." Tony Clink's book *The Layguide*, in fact, makes this the second of his ten seduction commandments. Actually, though, what he recommends is not that the aspiring PUA *be* the alpha male, but that he *pretend* to be him, as this advice from the book makes clear:

> *Project the image of the alpha male and women will flock to you . . . You do this not by getting muscles and money, but by changing your attitude . . . determine what the model of an alpha male should be . . . then become that model. Again, this has nothing to do with strength, looks, or money . . .* [15]

Note that there is no suggestion here that the PUA actually *do* anything to prove himself as a capable, attractive, alpha man—master a musical instrument, say, or work out, or perform charity work with needy children. Aspiring tribal Don Juans who tried to simply assume the status of alpha males, on the other hand, would have been laughed out of their loincloths, or worse. *They* were judged on what they actually achieved, as this passage from an ancient Tahitian seduction guide makes clear. The man who could become a successful seducer was, the guide states:

> The man who beats the drum well (women will pursue him);
> The one who plays the nose-flute well (they will take him forcibly);

The handsome-faced *Arioi* [dancer] who bathes . . . in the
morning;
The renowned wrestler who . . . will . . . always win;
The warrior . . . whose head has never been struck by his
enemy's club;
The artisan who builds a beautiful canoe;
He who builds a handsome house.[16]

Without wishing to rub it in, one can't help but notice that there is
not a single mention of "He who hasn't really done anything except
pump himself up into a delusional state of masculine self-worth
with constant-rotation neurolinguistic programming on his iPod"
there.

But perhaps that just got left out at the editing stage.

In any case, things seem clear—*Homo masculinus modernus* is
not quite the champion seducer the gurus of the seduction community tell themselves, and us. But what about those times he,
however inexpertly, actually *gets* the girl? How well does he satisfy
her sexually? Reading the letters columns of men's mags such as
FHM and *Maxim* certainly gives the impression there are more satisfied women running around today than ever before. But we don't
have to just take their boasting words for it. There is also considerable scientific evidence that modern heterosexual women really *are*
more sexually satisfied than their sisters of decades past. Forty percent of Finnish women in 1992, for example, reported satisfaction
with their sex lives, as opposed to just 30 percent who had been
thus satisfied in 1971 (mind you, that still leaves 60 percent *un*satisfied).[17] Confirming the boasts of all those men's-mag correspon-
dents, the Finnish women agreed that their men now used more

varied and superior sexual techniques, performed better and for longer in bed, and brought them to orgasm much more frequently than their partners of twenty years before had. This seems conclusive, at least for Finnish women, but a fair comparison again demands that we ask how all three of these categories—modern men's techniques, performance, and ability to bring our partners to orgasm—measure up to those of our ancient and tribal forerunners.

Several lines of evidence show male sexual techniques really have improved over the past few decades. First, those Finnish women reported that their lovers engaged in more caressing and foreplay than before, were more willing to experiment with sex toys, and were also much more likely to take the active role in oral sex. Other figures confirm this: 76.6 percent of American men now report having given their partners cunnilingus at least once.[18] In this case, once again, we don't even have to just take their word for it—it's also proven by the changing patterns of *herpes simplex* infection in the modern world. Two strains of the *herpes simplex* virus infect modern humans: HSV-1 and HSV-2. HSV-1 historically was confined to the mouth, causing cold sores, while HSV-2 was transferred by genital-to-genital contact, causing genital herpes. A 2006 Dutch study, however, found that over 52 percent of genital herpes cases are now caused by HSV-1, and another, Australian, study shows that more than twice as many women have HSV-1 genital infections as men.[19] It seems those American men aren't lying: they really are performing more oral sex on their partners (though that's not, unfortunately, the only gift they're giving them). The fact that the rate of HSV-1 genital infection was as low as 3 percent in some Western countries as late as 1980 shows how uncommon such activities were before.[20]

Remarkably, that's not the only information the twin herpes simplex viruses can give us about past human sexual behavior. The mere fact that there *are* two strains—one associated with the human mouth, and the other with the human genitals—probably shows that male hominins didn't perform oral sex on female hominins for almost the entire 4-million-year period since they split from the lineage of chimpanzees[21]—if they had, the two viral species would not have diverged in the first place.[22] In terms of oral sexual techniques, then, it seems *Homo masculinus modernus* really is a superstar performer compared to earlier species of man, as well as his own species' brothers of thirty years ago.

His brother *Homo sapiens* of one hundred to ten thousand years ago, though, are another story. The explorers who first contacted Polynesian islanders in the Pacific were fascinated and repelled to discover that Polynesian men were experts at stimulating their women using body parts that would, in the explorers' opinion, have been better employed reciting biblical verses. On the Truk Islands, for example, cunnilingus was unabashedly performed by those older men who had lost the ability to otherwise satisfy their voracious young female lovers.[23] Polynesian men even anticipated the infamous food scene in the steamy film *9 1/2 Weeks* with their practice of nibbling delectable morsels of fish direct from their lovers' vaginas. Similarly, the ancient Greeks, as we have seen from the works of Aristophanes (see page **169**), were quite familiar with cunnilingus, however much they decried it. The Romans, as well, depicted the act on numerous artworks, even though they, too, thought it shameful, and likely to cause permanent bad breath. At the same time, on the opposite side of the world, Chinese Taoists had developed an obsession with the practice, viewing it as a means of imbibing the sacred feminine essence necessary to prolong life. Given the frank eroticism of the *Kama Sutra,* it is surprising that Indian sensualists of the same era were not quite as enthusiastic, but in fact that manual mentions cunnilingus just twice   once as a practice of sexually frustrated women in harems, and once to remark that it was "not recommended . . . [but] . . . if it feels good, do it."[24] Remarkably, the Islamized Arabs of the same period were far keener, eagerly obeying the prophet Muhammad's hadith ("official pronouncement") that "every game a person plays is futile except for archery, training one's horse, and playing with one's wife."

■The cave girl's best friend?

For over a century archaeologists have been puzzled by certain implements found in the caves of Stone Age Europe. Averaging around six inches in length, and carved from bone and antler, they resemble nothing identifiable—except possibly a field marshal's baton, leading early archaeologists to label them *bâtons de commandment.* Those same archaeologists were too refined to point out that the tools also look like some other implements used to put men in their rightful place: dildos.

Arguments have raged back and forth ever since about what the implements might be. Based on the handhold at one end, complete with a hole for the index finger, one archaeologist suggested they were spear-throwers. Another, noting the multiple grooves carved in the sides of many *bâtons de commandment,* suggested they were records of lunar cycles. Hardly any have seen fit to ask the obvious question—what if they really *were* dildos?

It's not just their phallic shape that suggests *bâtons de commandment* might have been the playthings of lonely Palaeolithic cave girls. Their dimensions also conform closely to those of modern sex toys. Some have phallic veins and glans penises carved into them. Many even terminate in the same upturned curve that modern G-spot vibrators do. It's all speculation, of course, but if *bâtons de commandment* really *were* dildos, it might open up the remarkable possibility that those incised grooves on their sides aren't some complex form of lunar notation at all, but simply there to provide texture for the stimulation of their discerning users. They would then be, in effect, the Palaeolithic equivalent of the French Tickler.

The picture is even worse for us when it comes to sex toys. True, those satisfied Finnish women *do* vouch for our increased willingness to experiment with devices that pleasure. And a quick stroll down the aisles of any sex store will reveal a bewildering variety of sexual implements—G-spot vibrators, nipple clamps, penis sleeves, and so on. Tribal lovers of our prehistoric past, however, would have laughed at our lily-livered approach to pleasuring women. They turned *their own genitalia* into sex toys, usually through dangerous and painful surgery. For example, the nineteenth-century father of

Italian anthropology, Paolo Mantegazza, recorded that a Dayak tribeswoman of Borneo could legally divorce her husband if he refused to mutilate his penis to accommodate the *ampallang*—a two-inch rod of silver or gold, capped with small balls at either end, which was pushed horizontally through the member so that the balls protruded either side of the glans, thereby stimulating her vaginal walls.[25] Spanish explorers reported that tribesmen in the Visayas Islands of the central Philippines did the same, substituting the balls for a rotating metal star, which "by the prickings of that star . . . [left] their inconceivably voluptuous mates thoroughly satisfied." Neither group of tribesmen, though, went quite as far as those Indian men, described by fifteenth-century Venetian traveler Niccolò de' Conti, who surgically implanted numerous "jingle-bells" in their penises. These men, de' Conti wrote:

> . . . *purchase bells of gold or silver; and the same women who hawk them come to lift up his skin for him in various places. After the jingle-bells have been inserted and the incision has been sewed up, the wound heals in a few days. Some of them put in a dozen or more . . . the men who are thus fitted out are in the greatest grace and favor with the ladies; and many of them, as they go walking down the street, are proud of letting the sound of their bells be heard.*[26]

Technique-wise, then, the picture for modern males is mixed. Though we are certainly more enthusiastic than our grandfathers and great-grandfathers (not to mention earlier *species* of men) about activities such as cunnilingus, it turns out our more ancient forefathers were often even more comfortable with them. We have also proven less than total in our commitment to pleasuring our lovers with sex toys—at least compared to Dayak, Visayan, and Indian tribesmen of five hundred years ago. But what, then, of the second of our claims to prowess—performance?

Again, we have certainly lifted our game, and our stamina, since the pre-sexual-revolution era. Whereas foreplay lasted just twelve minutes on average in the 1950s, and actual intercourse just two, by 1995 the majority of men were reporting at least occasional sexual encounters that lasted over an hour.[27] Men below the age of thirty now also report having sex at least twice a week.[28] Impressively horny this may be, but it still falls short of the sexually supercharged men of earlier days. The nineteenth-century novelist Herman Melville, for example, described the Typee men of the Pacific Marquesas Islands, among whom he was briefly imprisoned, as sexual athletes who had to be at their lovers' disposal for multi-orgasmic adventures at any time of day or night.[29] More precise statistics were recorded by anthropologists on Mangaia, in the Pacific Cook Islands, where young men were found to engage in intercourse until orgasm three times a night, every night. Even men in their late forties copulated at least three times a week, climaxing each time.[30] This is approximately double the rate of men in their late forties today, who average just over one sexual encounter a week. Even the Polynesians, however, were shamed by men of the Pokot tribe in early twentieth century East Africa, whose women commonly demanded sexual fulfillment five to ten times a night.[31]

It seems incredible, finally, that given these apparent failures in our sexual performance we could bring women to orgasm anywhere near as often as we apparently think we do. And the evidence is, in fact, against us on that score. True, the Finnish women mentioned earlier *do* report a higher frequency of orgasm than their sisters of 1971,[32] but the actual figures are still not encouraging. A mere 28.6 percent of American women surveyed reported that they were always able to orgasm during sex with their male partners.[33] This is pathetic when considered in the light of the delusional male responses to the same survey, in which 56 percent of men stated that their female partners always orgasmed during sex. It is doubly pathetic when placed alongside late twentieth-century sexologist Shere Hite's finding that 95 percent of the women in her survey *were* able to orgasm consistently through masturbating. Some women in our tribal past, however, apparently weren't forced to rely on autoeroticism for fulfillment. They really could depend on their men to help them orgasm through intercourse every single time. Trukese men, to give one example, regarded sex as a competition in which the partner who orgasmed first lost. If he was pathetic enough to allow it to be him, he faced not just contempt from his lover, but also from his whole tribe.[34] Malinowski, similarly, wrote that men having sex in the New Guinean Trobriand Islands had to wait for their partner to *ipipisi momona*, "climax," before they could proceed to orgasm themselves. In fact, the example of the Trobriand Islanders shows that yet more of our claims—to have discovered female orgasms and ejaculation—are bogus, too. The Trobriand Islanders were so familiar with both female orgasms and ejaculation that they used the same word to describe them as male orgasm: the *ipipsi momona* mentioned above. Nor were they alone in their precocious knowledge. Not just other Polynesians, but native peoples as diverse as the East African Batoro and the North American Mohave fully understood the existence and mechanism of both female orgasm and ejaculation. More civilized peoples in Asia were also cognizant of it: several medieval Indian temples feature carved statues showing female ejaculation, and an earlier Chinese sex manual, *The Secrets of the Plain Girl*, discusses it, too. Even the ancient Greeks were aware of female ejaculation—no less of an authority than Aristotle described it in detail when he wrote in *On the Generation of Animals* that:

> . . . the pleasure she experiences is sometimes similar to that of the male, and also is attended by a liquid discharge. But this discharge is not seminal . . . The amount of this discharge, when it occurs, is sometimes on a different scale from the emission of semen and far exceeds it.

This is not a bad effort from Aristotle, almost two thousand five hundred years ago, considering that even today some sex researchers *still* don't accept that female ejaculation really exists.

■ a neverending obsession

The ancient Greeks were unique in their preference for small, neatly proportioned penises. Just about all other ancient and tribal men shared our own modern obsession: that their penises should be as large as humanly, or preferably *in*humanly, possible. They only differed in how they went about trying to get them.

Those belligerent men of Truk, for instance, repeatedly struck their penises hard enough to bruise them, on the theory that this would help them grow. The Portuguese explorer Amerigo Vespucci reported that some South American Indian men went a step further and really did enlarge their members by rubbing them with a certain herb (though how permanent the increase was he doesn't say).

South American men in general seem to have been obsessed with penis size. Other explorers reported that Cholomec males in Peru also tied weights to their penises to lengthen them. The most extreme super-sizers, however, were men of the Brazilian Topinama tribe who repeatedly allowed venomous snakes to bite their members in order to enlarge them. We modern men shouldn't come over too superior, however. After all, the Topinama aren't among the four hundred thousand American men who handed over U.S. $66 million in 2001–02 to the spam advertisers of just one (completely useless) penile enlargement pill called "Longitude."[35]

Perhaps it's lucky that we are not the great seducers we imagine ourselves, since we obviously don't know quite what to do with those unlucky women we *do* get our hands on. All is not lost, however. We do have some fallback credits to our name—according to televangelists such as Billy Graham at any rate. He has described modern men as so immoral that they outdo even those of Sodom and Gomorrah in God's disfavor. Our adultery, wife swapping, swinging, threesomes, foursomes, and other orgies of group sex apparently mark us as the most dissolute men ever. Partisans of the sexual revolution, on the other hand, cite the same habits to label us the most liberated and unrepressed men in history. They can't both be right, obviously.

But who is wrong?

Both, as it turns out. We are neither the most shockingly immoral, nor the most refreshingly liberated men to have ever walked God's earth. In fact, our adultery, wife swapping, swinging, and group sex wouldn't have impressed our tribal forefathers one bit.

Our supposed extramarital extravagance, for example, evaporates under even preliminary inspection. Despite Billy Graham's condemnation, modern Western men are actually more faithful than not. A large, anonymous survey done in the early 1990s revealed that just 24.5 percent of married men had cheated on their wives at any time during their marriage—usually with a single extramarital partner. Compare this to the adulterous adventures of the Mehinaku, noted on page 250—100 percent of men cheating, with an average four to five partners *at any one time*, let alone over the course of their marriage.[36] Nor was it the case that the Mehinaku simply weren't jealous. Gregor records that both Mehinaku husbands and wives were strongly angered by each other's affairs, that they "prized each other's genitals highly." Ancient Hawaiian philanderers were slightly less omnivorous than the Mehinaku, but infinitely more creative. The custom on those surfing islands was for any man and woman who successfully rode the same wave together to take "certain liberties with one another" on the beach, whatever their marital status.[37] In some tribal societies, indeed, adultery was such an accepted part of life that different styles of lovemaking were used for extramarital partners, as opposed to spouses. On Truk, for instance, during sex with a lover:

> . . . *vigorous mutual pain infliction, including lacerating scratching, was considered desirable and was conducted as a kind of contest of strong affection. Between spouses however,*

> *convention called for decorous restraint, which was regarded*
> *as less enjoyable and which led most married persons to en-*
> *gage in extramarital affairs.*[38]

Rather than lipstick on the collar, Trukese philanderers apparently had to explain raked scratches on their backs to their furious wives!

An even more heinous offense than cheating on one's wife, according to those outraged morals campaigners of the Billy Graham era, was swapping her. Wife swapping apparently started among American military communities in 1950s California and by the early 1970s was being treated as an epidemic that was sapping the moral fiber of the nation. Yet one study from that era shows that wife swapping occurred in just 2 percent of all marriages.[39] Given this overreaction, one can only wonder how these good gentlemen (they were mostly men) of the church would have reacted to the habits of prehistoric Inuit men. Eskimo men not only traded wives frequently—sometimes for months or even years—they also *lent* them, hospitably, to visitors for sex. Lest it be thought Inuits, too, were free from the jealousy inherent to this remarkable practice, it should be noted that even the practice of Inuit husbands sharing a wife, which was supposed to be an equitable and non-jealous arrangement, often resulted in the murder of one husband by the other, usually with the secret connivance of the woman (see "Crimes of passion" box on page 268). Australian Aboriginal men of Arnhem Land, similarly, shared their wives as a matter of course, making them sexually available to all their "brother cousins"—cousins on their mother's side. Even this promiscuous partner swapping paled beside that of the Ulithi people in the Caroline Islands, however—they boggled the mind of visiting anthropologist William Lessa with their *pi supuhui* ("100 pet-tings") festival, in which:

> . . . *all persons of the village who are not excessively old or young . . . pair off and go into the woods . . . Married couples are not allowed to go off together . . . [and] . . . one does not remain with the same partner throughout the occasion . . . "tagging" is practiced . . . If visitors . . . happen to be present at the time, they are invited to join in . . . The people describe it as "nice play" and make no apologies for it.*[40]

Comparing the Ulithians' rate of partner swapping—almost 100 percent to our paltry 2 percent—is particularly telling, since Lessa's study was undertaken in the late 1960s, supposedly the height of the American wife-swapping craze.

crimes of passion

Crimes of passion are standard filler for modern tabloid news-papers. Hardly an edition goes by without featuring the mur-der of some jilted lover's ex-girlfriend, or a love triangle ending in tragedy. Inuit lovers of one hundred years ago, however, would have laughed at the supposed violence of our passions.

The Danish explorer Peter Freuchen recorded that a headman of the Caribou Eskimo, when rebuffed by the parents of a girl he wanted as his wife, ambushed and harpooned her entire family of eight in revenge, only then marrying her. Love triangles were also a particular danger for Inuit men, since strong hunters could, and did, simply demand to sleep with other men's wives regardless of either party's agreement. In one case of this kind, this time among the Copper Eskimo, a husband who suffered such an indignity took the unchivalrous step of killing his wife, since he didn't dare murder the would-be cuckolder but was still unwilling to share. He himself was then promptly killed.

With behavior like this it is no surprise that another Danish explorer, Knud Rasmussen, found that every single man in a camp of Musk River Eskimo he visited had been involved in a murder over women. It is probably lucky Inuit societies didn't have newspapers—they would have carried nothing *but* tragic tales of love gone wrong.

Of course, Western wife swappers eventually moved on, too, graduating to genuine swinging by the mid 1970s. The swinging scene has been growing steadily ever since: if NASCA, the North American Swing Club Association, is to be believed 15 percent of U.S. couples now dabble in it. A milestone was the advent of "key parties," gatherings in which participants' car keys were pooled in a bowl and then drawn out at random by their partners for the night. Yet it might surprise the daring sexual adventurers who supposedly invented these events that they did nothing of the kind. Key parties had already been invented, over a thousand years before, by those amorous Hawaiians. Nineteenth-century Hawaiian preacher David Malo was basically describing a massive key party when he reported on the *pili* ("touched by the wand") parties his people had once enjoyed. It was, he wrote:

> . . . a pastime that was very popular with all the Hawai-
> ians . . . an adulterous sport . . . played in the following
> manner. A large enclosure, or pa, was made . . . and all the
> people . . . seated in a circle within the enclosure. [Then] a
> man . . . chanted a gay and lascivious song, waving . . .
> a long wand which was trimmed . . . with tufts of bird
> feathers . . . As he made his circuit . . . the man and woman
> whom he indicated by touching them with his wand went
> out and enjoyed themselves together . . . when daylight
> came the husband returned to his own wife and the wife to
> her own husband.[41]

Even the horny Hawaiians, however, were outdone in swinging by the legendary sensual Tahitians of the same era. Young men and women in Tahiti actually had a permanent swinging fraternity known as the *Arioi* cult, whose members worshipped the peace god Oro by literally making love, not war. *Arioi* troupes traveled the island, from village to village, giving performances of erotically charged dance as a prelude to their real mission—"sampling the sexual wares of their hosts and hostesses."[42] They also sampled each other, constantly, with the highest-status members—called "black legs" from their heavy tattooing—having the right of sexual access to all other members on command. Besides beauty and skill at dance, the main qualification for membership was single status—

marriage resulted in instant expulsion. Most members were, accordingly, young, but some stayed active until well into middle age (some by the simple but gruesome expedient of killing the babies that resulted from their promiscuity). Anthropologists estimated there were thousands of *Arioi* across Tahiti at the time of European contact, out of a total population of just fifty thousand (predictably, male *Arioi* outnumbered females five to one). No exact percentage is available, but Tahitian *Arioi* clearly proportionately outnumber American swingers by a long, long shot.

The amorous activities of the *Arioi* also point to problems with the last accusation of those outraged morals campaigners— that modern men have an unsurpassed appetite for threesomes, foursomes, and all manner of group sex. True, group sex in the modern world has moved into the mainstream from its onetime home among "deviant" subcultures such as bikers, yet no more than 6 percent of modern Western men (and women) report having had a threesome, let alone sex with *more* than three participants.[43] This seems to be because we *Homo sapiens* have an instinctual distaste for allowing our copulations to be witnessed by others. So strong is this that even in tribal societies, where members often live in communal one-room huts, couples still strive for privacy by copulating quietly in the darkness, or in unobtrusive spots outside.[44] Yet some tribal men *did* occasionally indulge in public sex, and when they did it was sometimes with far more than two, three, or even ten extra partners. Some Polynesian societies, for example, celebrated sporting triumphs, or even the return of successful fishing expeditions, with a public orgy. In Hawaii, this also took place upon the deaths of important chiefs, when:

As soon as the chief expired . . . the people ran to and fro
without clothes . . . every vice was practised . . . and the
gratification of every base and savage feeling sought without
restraint.[45]

These scenes of sexual excess might involve all the adult members
of a tribe—sometimes hundreds of people. More disturbing examples (to our ears at any rate) of orgiastic excess were the various
tribal sex rituals. The fertility festival of the New Guinean Kiwai
people, for example, involved several nights of erotic dancing and
mass sex involving all the tribe's members, with the semen being
collected from the women and placed in a pot as a fertility elixir.
Other group sex rituals were less offensive (to our taste) but more
deadly. The funerals of Viking chiefs, for example, called for his
warrior comrades to have group sex with his courageous slave girl
(who had usually volunteered to accompany her master into the
afterlife) as in this distressing eleventh-century eyewitness account
from the Arab traveler Ibn Fadlan:

Then six men entered the tent and all of them had intercourse
with her. They then laid her at the side of her master, and two
took hold of her feet and two her hands; the old woman
known as the angel of death put a rope around her neck and
while two men pulled the rope, the old woman stabbed the
girl . . . Thereafter, the relatives of the dead chieftain arrived
with a burning torch and set the ship aflame.[46]

A similarly deadly orgy accompanied the grieving rituals of the
Amazonian Cubeo Indians, as described in this anthropologist's
account:

> . . . *a fine young girl, painted, oiled and ceremonially cos-*
> *tumed, is . . . made to lie beneath a platform of very heavy*
> *logs. With her, in open view of the festival, the initiates co-*
> *habit, one after another; and while the youth chosen to be last*
> *is embracing her, the supports of the logs above are jerked*
> *away, and . . . the dead girl and boy are dragged from the*
> *logs, cut up, roasted and eaten.*[47]

Disturbing stuff, to be sure, but also enough to put even the most debauched modern group-sex enthusiast off his orgies forever more.

Once again things seem to have come to a dreadful pass. *Homo masculinus modernus's* heterosexual reputation lies in tatters. There is *nothing* he does with his women—from getting them, pleasuring them, swapping them, or even cheating on them—that hasn't been done better, more gently, more frequently, and with more satisfying result by his ancient and tribal forefathers. Should he, then, change tack and try to claim line honors in *homo*sexual adventures? After all, another favored accusation of morals campaigners is that we have unleashed an unprecedented assault of same-sexed sin on the already reeling moral order. There is some scientific support for the notion, too: although only 1 percent of U.S. men describe themselves as exclusively homosexual, according to 2003 data from the National Opinion Research Center, another 4 percent describe themselves as bisexual. But are we *really* the gayest guys to have ever donned a leather loincloth?

Well, let's see.

One might argue, for example, that the example of bonobos shows that even our earliest ancestors had a gay streak. Bonobos, as everybody knows, are incredibly sexy apes, and cheerfully indiscriminate in their choice of partner—the majority of bonobo sexual acts are in fact lesbian ones between older females. Male bonobos are slightly less prone to homoeroticism, but they still frequently engage in scrotum-to-scrotum rubbing and penis fencing.[48] Male chimpanzees, by contrast, don't go in for quite as much "bumping of uglies" but they do fondle each other's scrotums as a gesture of reassurance, and clasp each other by the buttocks when reconciling after a fight. What about our more direct hominin ancestors, though? As it happens there is no evidence for gay abandon among early hominin men, not because they were super-straight, but because there is not much evidence of *any* sexual intercourse before about eighteen thousand years ago (apart from our own existence, of course). While we do have plenty of sexy scratchings and daubings among Stone Age rock art (see page 275), strangely we have very few depicting actual sex.[49] There are, however, plenty of examples of homoerotic behavior in the more recent prehistoric past of *Homo sapiens* males. Among the Sambia people of New Guinea, for example, homosexual behavior was (and probably still is) mandatory for males between adolescence and adulthood. From the age of nine, Sambia boys are compelled to repeatedly fellate the older men of their tribe. This sounds like the most dreadful child abuse to us, but the Sambia see it as helping their boys, since semen—the sacred "milk" that they need to become men—is not generated by the boy's own body, but passed down instead through generations of men.[50] Though ritually driven, there is little doubt that many Sambia men, and boys, are eager participants in the erotic homosexual aspects of this semen transmission.

Lest we think this a bizarre notion only tribal men could possibly entertain, it is worth remembering that some of our own ancestors employed homosexual strategies in raising their boys, too. In ancient Sparta, adult males were actually fined for *not* taking a boy-lover under the age of twelve. This was because the institution of the *eromenos*, "boy-lover," and his *erastes*, "lover-teacher," was thought to be the only way the boy could absorb the *agoge*, "training," he needed to become a Spartan man. The relationship was definitely erotic, although Spartans claimed the *erastes* only ever satisfied his lust by intercrural sex (thrusting the penis between the oiled thighs of the *eromenos*). Contradicting that, however, are the graffiti inscriptions occasionally found near ancient Spartan gymnasiums, saying things like, "Krimon f*cked Amotion here." The Athenians, similarly, were in no doubt about the habits of their Spartan enemies: Athenian plays are full of comic references to sex "the Spartan way"—that is, sodomy. Whatever the truth of the accusation, it should be abundantly clear that male homosexuality was *not* invented at the Stonewall Inn in New York, 1969.

The same goes for another frequent criticism of *Homo masculinus modernus*—his supposed proliferation of explicit pornography. True, porn has exploded over the past forty years, going from a total value of $10 million per year in 1970—for films, magazines, books, and live services like phone sex lines and peepshows—to somewhere between $2 billion and $5 billion per year today. It all started back in 1953, of course, with the first publication of Hugh Hefner's *Playboy*. Or did it? Rock art researcher Russell Dale performed an interesting experiment in the late 1970s—he compared selected female figures from Stone Age European cave paintings with centerfolds from the German edition of *Playboy* magazine.[51] He found that the poses of the rock art women were remarkably similar to those of the centerfolds, emphasizing hips, waists, breasts, and legs. In particular, a large number of paintings show female figures from the rear, an unlikely angle unless the intention is to emphasize the sex appeal of her buttocks. Rock art paintings also often featured explicit images of the vulva, a step too far even for *Playboy*. Of course, modern pornography did eventually move on from Hugh Hefner's tamer offerings, graduating to genuinely hardcore titles such as *Hustler,* the magazine famous for crossing the vulval Rubicon with the distastefully titled "split beaver" shot. Yet so, too, did prehistoric erotic art. The Moche people of ancient northern Peru, for example, can justly be called the original inventors of the sexpot. Their sculptured ceramic kettles, thousands of which have been recovered, often depict hardcore sex acts such as fellatio, as well as vaginal and anal sex, all fashioned in fine, realistic detail.[52] Particularly impressive are the gynecologically accurate genitals of the female figures; the Moche clearly had the jump on *Hustler* by some one thousand five hundred years. Moche pots even sometimes featured disturbing images—such as masturbating skeletons—that would be considered illegal, necrophilic pornography in most Western countries today.[53] Nor were the Moche pots under-the-counter items, as most Western porn is still legally required to be. Every Moche sexpot was not just an explicit sculpture, but also a fully functional kettle, meaning they could probably be found on nonchalant public display in many Moche dwellings. In our society, by contrast, public display of pornography is still so frowned upon that the sitcom *Seinfeld* once built the subplot of a whole episode around the disturbing presence of a stack of *Penthouse* magazines in a dentist's office.[54]

After all this, it really seems that *Homo masculinus modernus* has but one choice: to retire from the field and give up sex completely. Some modern men, indeed, *have* taken that route, most notably the adherents of the "radical celibate" movement that flourished briefly in the 1980s. One prominent abstainer was the British actor Stephen Fry, who outed himself as a celibate in a memorable 1980s magazine article. Yet even in the matter of restraint we modern males seem distinctly second-rate. Fry's celibacy, for example, apparently lasted for the sixteen years between 1979 and 1995. This is a long dry spell, to be sure, but compared to the heroic abstention of some ancient men it looks positively promiscuous. Early Christian monks known as the "desert fathers," who lived as hermits in the Egyptian wastelands, foreswore sex for their entire lives, even though at that time there was no religious rule that they do so. Simeon Stylites, the famous fifth-century ascetic, for instance, lived for sixty-nine years without ever feeling the caress of a woman (helped enormously by the fact that he spent thirty-seven of them living atop a fifty-foot pillar). Predictably, the lengths the desert fathers went to in order to suppress their lust far outstripped those of modern celibates, too. Victorian-era doctors recommended a bland diet and plentiful cold showers to douse the fires of lust; some early Christians preferred to literally fight fire with fire, searing themselves with red-hot irons when troubled by erotic thoughts. They also put themselves on starvation diets to "dry the body"—malnutrition being an effective means of preventing both semen production and any interest in sex. Some placed poisonous snakes in their loincloths, while one intrepid hermit, troubled by the memory of a recently deceased beauty, dug up her corpse and rubbed his clothing in her rotting flesh to curb his longings.[55]

It could be argued, of course, that the desert fathers were extreme individuals against whom it is unfair to measure ourselves.[56] Some ancient societies, however, included whole populations of men who spent their lives in total chastity. One such, apparently, was the Celtic pre-Anglo-Saxon population of England. A 2002 genetic analysis of Y-chromosome variations among English and Welsh men found that the majority of English males carry Y-chromosomes that are very similar to one another, but very different to those of the Welsh.[57] Since Y-chromosomes are passed down unchanged from father to son, this would seem to indicate that the original Celtic inhabitants of Britain, represented today by the surviving Welsh, were all slaughtered and replaced in England by the invading Angles and Saxons of the fifth century. It would, that is, were it not for the intriguing fact that studies of British female mitochondrial DNA, which is likewise passed down unchanged from mother to daughter, show much smaller differences between England and Wales, indicating that Celtic women *weren't* slaughtered and replaced by invading Angles and Saxons.[58] Then there is the linguistic evidence for survival of at least some Celtic males. Rural folk in some parts of England until very recently employed Celtic systems of counting their livestock, indicating that some Celtic men, at least, survived for long enough, possibly as pastoral slaves, to pass on their shepherding habits.[59] One possible explanation of all this is that Celtic men *did* live through the Anglo-Saxon invasion but were deprived of reproductive access to their women by their new overlords. Male Celtic Britons, it seems, may never have had sex again after the Anglo-Saxons invaded their turf.

How's *that* for radical celibacy?

▢The unkindest
cut of all

Newspaper reports of the 1996 demise of the world's last living eunuch, China's Sun YaoTing, were, to paraphrase Mark Twain, greatly exaggerated. According to a recent medical study published by Johns Hopkins University, a current Web site for self-castrators claims 3,500 members, 166 of whom have actually neutered themselves.[60] Motives ranged from sexual fetishism to a desire to diminish their own sex drive. The recommended tool was the burdizzo, a farmyard castration clamp that severs the testicular blood vessels. The procedure causes 30 to 60 seconds of excruciating pain (sufficient to induce vomiting), yet the ordeal is still, predictably, mild compared to those of ancient eunuchs.

Italian castrati (boys castrated to preserve their soprano voices), for example, had their testicles *crushed* to destroy them, after the lads were first soaked in a scalding bath to soften them. Many didn't survive the procedure. So lethal could testicle crushing be that it was actually used as a method of execution by the Turkish Ottoman emperors.[61]

Even the Turks, though, had it easy compared to Chinese eunuchs. They had their genitals and testicles bathed in hot peppered water, supposedly to numb them, then crushed by a tight, silk bandage, after which they were sliced off at the base with a hooked blade. A metal plug was then jammed into the wound and the boy

> forced to walk around for several hours, before being confined to
> bed without liquids for three days. If he was then able to urinate he
> stood a chance of living, if not he was certain to die horribly.
>
> Korean eunuchs, however, had it worst of all. In ancient times
> they were castrated by having their genitals smeared with human
> feces and then being exposed to packs of hungry dogs.

What a disaster! Even at *not* having sex *Homo masculinus modernus*
runs a distant second to his male ancestors. It could be argued, of
course, that this is not a failing at all in evolutionary terms, since
the genes' mission is to transmit themselves, not set abstinence endurance records. Looked at in this light the most serious of the
failings raised here by far is our lackluster sexual performance. It
is, after all, the one that could imperil our transmission of those
genes. That being the case, let's look a little closer at this particular
shortcoming. What *causes* our deficient sexual performance?

The good news is that, in the West at least, it's partly cultural.
Ever since the early Christians (taking their lead from Platonism)
decided the body was the prison of the soul, and its desires mere
links in the chain, Christendom has been the domain of a sexual
ignorance so profound that Henry VIII's fourth wife, Anne of Cleves,
failed to realize the reason she wasn't getting pregnant was because her fat husband wasn't sleeping with her. Such ignorance
clearly couldn't fail to retard male sexual techniques, and retard
them it did. Thirteenth-century German church father Albertus
Magnus, for example, wrote that of the five sexual positions known

to man (five!) only one, the missionary position, was approved by God.[62] Reliance on this sexual position may, though, partly explain the disappointing figures for orgasm frequency among modern women during intercourse. Studies seem to show that those sexual positions (of which the missionary position *isn't* one) that stimulate the front wall of a woman's vagina, location of the fabled G-spot, are far more likely to result in female orgasm.[63] Interestingly, among those tribal societies with high rates of female orgasm, such as Malinowski's Trobriand Islanders, these positions were common, and the missionary position rarely used. In fact, it was mocked— Malinowski records that a favorite activity of Trobriand Island boys who had worked with Europeans was imitating, for the amusement of their fellows, their masters' strange and ineffective sexual position.

Though humiliating, this at least holds out hope for improvement. Even we, after all, can't resist learning new tricks forever. More troubling is the fact that Malinowski also reported his teenage informants mocking their employers' limited stamina:

> . . . the brevity and lack of vigour of the European performance were caricatured . . . the white man achieves orgasm far too quickly . . . the Melanesian takes a much longer time and employs a much greater amount of mechanical energy to reach the same result.[64]

Here Malinowski's subjects had put their finger on a disturbing (for us, at any rate) prospect: that there might be *physical* deficiencies in the sexual abilities of European men. Compare, for example, the frequency of our two major current sexual problems—premature ejaculation and erectile dysfunction. Even the lowest figures given in modern studies show that 26 percent of modern men ejaculate within two minutes of entering the vagina.[65] (Kinsey's figures from the 1940s and 1950s were even worse, with an amazing 75 percent of men lasting less than two minutes.) The evidence of the men of Truk and the Trobriand Islands, on the other hand, suggests that premature ejaculation was much rarer among at least some tribal men. The same applies to erectile dysfunction. The United Kingdom's National Health Service estimates that more than 50 percent of Western men aged over forty experience at least occasional failure to achieve or maintain an erection. Contrast that with those middle-aged Mangaian womanizers of the Cook Islands, with their thrice-weekly romps and consistent orgasms. The only extenuating circumstance for us is that the environmental stressors of modern life are clearly often to blame. Premature ejaculation, for instance, is often caused by stress and anxiety. Erectile dysfunction, similarly, is often the result of high blood pressure, arteriosclerosis, alcoholism, and smoking, all products of a modern lifestyle largely unavailable to tribal men.

Disturbingly, however, not *all* our performance problems can be sheeted home to environmental factors. Some appear to be genetic. A 1999 study of male identical twins compared with male non-identical twins[66] found that around 23.3 percent of problems in *getting* an erection had a hereditary origin, and 26.7 percent of problems *maintaining* an erection did. A 2007 Finnish twin study found roughly the same genetic correlation for premature ejaculation.[67] Anthropological accounts, on the other hand, indicate that genetic impotence and sexual dysfunction were very rare among tribal men. What few cases there were appear to have been caused by disease or injury.[68]

What accounts for the difference? How can there even *be* one, given that we are talking about sex, the very mechanics of natural selection? How could sexual incompetence have been selected *for* in Western societies, but *against* in tribal ones? It's all wild speculation, of course, but I suspect it's a case of culture changing the selective landscape. Think of it—in which selective environment are the premature ejaculators and non-erectors going to thrive (or slip through the cracks, at any rate)? The promiscuous environs of an ancient Polynesian island, peopled with sexually demanding and discriminating women with the power to choose between multiple, virile partners? Or the backward realm of a medieval Europe where sex is the fumbling, shameful business of clueless peasant men and women barred from even saying the word "sex," let alone comparing notes about its performance?

I think we all, sadly, know the answer to that one.

I t has been a long day's journey into the night. Nor has morning brought succor: the harsh light of dawn has broken on us blinking, naked, shivering, and exposed. Nothing is left to us but to gather the last remaining shreds of our masculine self-respect, clothe our nakedness, and figure out what is to be done.

That is, of course, if anything even *can* be done.

Well, that depends. The dismal results outlined in this book can be traced to three causes: culture, ontogenetics, and genetics. The first two we can do something about; it's the third that's the problem. If our shortcomings should turn out to be genetic in origin there would be very little, short of extensive gene therapy, that we could do about them.

Is there any evidence, then, that they are?

Unfortunately, there is. Those findings on the partial heritability of premature ejaculation and impotence are just the start. A clearer example of one of our deficiencies that is at least partially genetic in origin is our shortsightedness. Charles Darwin was one of the first to highlight this modern physical failing. In his 1839 account of his voyage on HMS *Beagle* he noted the phenomenal eyesight of the two native Fuegian men, Jemmy and York, who were being returned to their South American homeland via the *Beagle*:

> . . . *sailors are well known for their good eyesight, & yet the Fuegians were as superior as another almost would be without a glass. When Jemmy quarrelled with any of the officers, he would say "me see ship, me no tell." Both he & York have invariably been in the right; even when objects have been examined with a glass.*[1]

This had to be hereditary, Darwin remarked, because even in cases where Europeans were brought up among native peoples, and thus exposed to the same environmental influences, their eyesight still seemed less acute.[2] Early nineteenth-century whalers in Australia, similarly, soon learned not to contradict their Australian Aboriginal shipmates, who could spot whales unaided at ranges far beyond those of European capabilities. A famous half-caste Australian Aboriginal whaler, Tommy Chaseland, for example, amazed Captain J. Lort Stokes of the *Acheron* by not just spotting a dead whale floating outside telescope range but also accurately describing the harpoon and fathoms of rope attached to it. Another shipmate wrote that Chaseland could spot land from thirty miles away and see a mile underwater. This difference is still evident today: the Australian ophthalmologist Hugh Taylor reported in 1981 that Australian Aboriginal men in Western Australia had 20/5 vision—they saw clearly at twenty feet what European Australian men could only see at five.[3]

Why *should* the eyesight of Australian Aboriginal men be genetically so much better than that of European males? Clearly it is because of their only recently abandoned hunting lifestyle. The selective landscape in which Australian Aboriginal men lived until just one hundred to two hundred years ago exerted great selective pressure in favor of sharp eyesight. European males, by contrast, have lived in a farming environment for at least eight thousand years, where the plants and animals on which sustenance, and therefore reproductive success, depended were never more than yards away. This apparently led to a relaxation of selective pressure for visual acuity, allowing our eyesight to deteriorate to its current level over the course of several thousand years.

Some of our shortcomings really *are*, therefore, genetic in origin. This is dispiriting, to be sure, but it's some comfort, at least, that they seem to be in the minority. We have the evidence of our bones to prove it; recall from BRAWN that the articular ends of our long bones—the component whose growth is most directly under genetic control—are still roughly as robust as those of our relatives of a million years ago. We can, therefore, breathe a belated sigh of relief. The causes of our multiple shortcomings seem to be more cultural and ontogenetic, which we *can* do something about.

Even some of those deficiencies that *are* genetic in origin, for example, can be tackled through cultural changes. Premature ejaculation, to quote one, is often treated with sexual training to habituate the sufferer to sexual arousal. Perhaps it's time for all of us—pathetic, two-minute wonders that we are—to be put through an urgent crash course on remedial sexual technique. Perhaps a UN task force of any remaining Pokot, Mangaian, Trobriand Islander, and Tahitian men who have managed to resist our slovenly influence can be immediately dispatched to all corners of the Western world—to show us how it's done.

More seriously, knowledge of the foibles revealed here does give us scope for recapturing lost masculine virtues such as bravery and paternal instinct by instituting simple cultural changes. Suitable outlets for the instinctual bravado of young males, for example, can be created; this is one reason diversionary sports programs are so successful in reducing crime rates among young males.[4] Extensive paternity leave arrangements and flexible workplace practices, similarly, could help us strive for the quantity, rather than quality, time so essential to the superior fathering of those remarkable Aka dads.

The deeper message of the bones, though, is that we are, quite simply, traitors. We are traitors to the countless generations of male humans and proto-humans who lived and died—mostly died—to hone the genetic heritage we so signally fail to live up to. Recall that the reduced robustness of those bone shafts, compared to those of *Homo erectus* and other earlier species, is an ontogenetic, or developmental, phenomenon. It is entirely the product of our modern sloth and inactivity. We never give our bodies or minds the stimulation—be it mechanical or intellectual—they need to fully realize the potential encoded in our genotypes, though opportunities to do so surround us every day. True, it is no longer in our power to retrieve the strength of our chimpanzee—or even, probably, our Neandertal—cousins. But we *could* regain the strength of those work-hardened laborers of the early Industrial Revolution, if only we were prepared to exert ourselves as they did. We *could* row as fast as the Greek trireme rowers, run as fast as the Ice Age runners of prehistoric New South Wales, jump as high as the *gusimbuka-urukiramende* high jumpers, and shoot with both the phenomenal accuracy of the Mongol horse archers and the stamina of the medieval Japanese *tōshiya* archers—if only we were willing to put in the grueling training to do so. We could even rap—*really* rap—just like Homer and the Slavic *guslars* if we would but test ourselves with the same fire of words they did.

We are doubly traitorous because our sloth betrays not just our own genetic potential, but that of our sons, too. Recall that the male body is most responsive to the mechanical stresses that stimulate growth between the ages of eight and fourteen. By inducing our sons to follow in our own less-than-glorious footsteps we are sentencing them to a lifetime of brittle bones, weak tendons, and softened bodies and brains. We do our children a real disservice by imagining them as incapable as we ourselves are; without such negativity who knows what heights they might reach? They might even, God forbid, stand a shot at realizing the potential that *ought* to be their birthright—the promise encoded in their twenty-three pairs of chromosomes.

Fixing the problem then, for both ourselves and our sons, would seem to require nothing more than sheer will. Is there any chance we will muster it?

The signs, unfortunately, are not good.

The first step to *solving* the problem is *facing* it, and even here, it seems, we are somewhat lacking. Think back to our happy self-delusion when reporting (actually over-reporting) the sexual satisfaction of our partners, our bravery in facing medical procedures, or the ferocity of our hand-to-hand combat. Self-deception, in fact, seems to define us as a species. It even has its own evolutionary logic—many an evolutionary psychologist has pointed out that the bluffing so essential to threatening behavior in males is much more effective when the male himself believes it, regardless of how true it is. If such self-deception seems a strangely ignoble outcome of evolution, well, so what? Even Darwin never claimed the process necessarily tended toward morally satisfying results. It has, after all, just as readily produced the cowardly hyena as the noble lion.

An interesting primate parallel is the case of the orangutan. Most orangutan males are fearsomely macho, with huge bodies weighing up to 260 pounds and deep calls that boom through their rainforest homes. It is expensive to grow so imposing, but they have to, since only the largest males win the fights necessary for sexual access to females. Orangutan females also flatly refuse to mate with males who are too puny. Yet evolution has also hit on another, less noble, solution to the male orangutan's problem of how to pass on his genes. Some orangutan males forgo the dangerous business of growing big and fighting, instead choosing to live out their lives as small-bodied adolescents. These cowardly "small males" use the energy they save through not fighting to chase females, whom their reduced body size also allows them to catch more quickly than the big males can. Though the females strenuously resist the mating attempts of these inferior specimens, the "small males" strength is still usually sufficient to force them.

Evolution has, effectively, turned orangutan "small males" into sneaky little rapists. It doesn't get much more ignoble than that.

Fortunately, most modern human males retain enough decency to shun such violatory activities. In so many other respects, though, as I hope this book has shown, we are the "small males" of our genus Homo—only without the orangutans' honesty. Orangutan "small males" at least have the courage to embrace and exploit their second-best status; we instead persist in masquerading as "big males." One can only wonder what our Homo erectus ancestors— real "big males"—would have made of our behavior. If we plucked a male Homo erectus, circa 1,000,000 BCE, off the African savannah and set him down in a modern Western all-male event—say a NASCAR rally, or a supposed couples' gathering in a swingers' club—what would he say? It's a matter of some debate, of course, whether he would say anything at all, since it's still unclear if *Homo erectus* even could talk. Yet *if* he could, surely he would be moved to protest our betrayal of the genotype he fought, suffered, and died for. Surely he would paraphrase the words of the deity whose very existence wouldn't even be conceived of for a million years to come—

"My sons, my sons, why have you forsaken me?"

endnotes

Brawn

1. Leit, 2001.
2. Kouri, 1995.
3. Olivardia, 2004.
4. Willoughby, 1970.
5. Huenemann, 1966.
6. Ogawa, 1997.
7. Scholz, 2006.
8. Bauman, 1926.
9. Some commentators have questioned Bauman's findings citing a 1943 paper that found a much lower margin of chimp superiority [Finch, G. (1943). "The Bodily Strength of Chimpanzees." *Journal of Mammalogy* 24(2): 224–28]. Finch's study, however, is anomalous; every later study has confirmed Bauman's findings.
10. Wrangham, 1996.
11. Walker, 2009.
12. Pain, 2007.
13. Haapasalo, 1995.
14. Hawks, 2007.
15. Ricciardellia, 2007.
16. Campbell, 2005.
17. Frederick, 2007.
18. Parkin, 2007.

Bravado

1. Strauch, 1998.
2. Sutton-Smith, 1995.
3. Farthing, 2005.
4. Kruger, 2006.
5. Ember, 1971.
6. Furuichi, 1994.

7. de Waal, 1982.
8. Cambria, 2004.
9. Briggs, 2007.
10. Hurley, 2006.
11. Ellsworth, 2004.
12. Finkel MD, 2002.
13. Motte-Florac, 2004.
14. Takahashi, 1998.
15. Welbourn, 1968.
16. Newman, 1982.
17. Posey, 2004.
18. Welbourn, 1968.
19. Pounder, 1981.
20. Cowen, 2000.
21. Blomberg, 2008.
22. Coe, 1993.
23. Chinnery, 1919.
24. Guilaine, 2005.
25. Sturtevant, 1980.
26. Knowles, 1940.
27. Knowles, 1940.
28. Barnes, 1983.
29. Coleman, 1990.
30. Oliver, 2002.
31. Taylor, 2007.
32. Oliffe, 2004.
33. Ball, 2003.
34. Leake, 1925.
35. Prioreschi, 1996.
36. Arnott, 2002.
37. Webb, 1995.
38. O'Connor, 1997.
39. Guilaine, 2005.
40. Churchill, 2005.
41. Churchill, 1990.
42. Glazier, 2000.
43. Putnam, 1948.

Battle

1. Dunning, 2000.
2. Pappas, 2007.
3. Ngai, 2008.
4. Downey, 2007.
5. Svinth, 2007.
6. Hall, 2003.
7. Rodriguez, 1998.

8. Brophy, 1985.
9. Poliakoff, 1987.
10. Brophy, 1985.
11. Poliakoff, 1987.
12. Brophy, 1985.
13. Brophy III, 1978.
14. Brophy III, 1978.
15. Brophy, 1985.
16. Shadrake, 2005.
17. Kanz, 2006.
18. Knuckey, 1992.
19. Ford, 2005.
20. MacRae, 2006; Sivarajasingam, 2002.
21. Marshall, 1979.
22. Conley, 1999.
23. Hurley, 2007.
24. Burnham, 2006.
25. Murphy, 2006.
26. My personal feeling is that it is far too high, based simply on the evidence of the death certificates: the authors' claim that 92 percent of the deaths they report are confirmed by official death certificates seems impossible to square with Iraqi Ministry of Health records of approximately 50,000 issued certificates. On the other hand, at least one other reputable estimate of Iraqi casualties is even higher.
27. Keeley, 1996.
28. Two, indeed, are almost double. The indigenous Kato people of northwestern California, for example, suffered a death rate from war of 1.45 percent during the 1840s. Fiji in the 1860s, similarly, lost almost 1.25 percent of its population per year through vicious and incessant fighting (the death rate in the past had probably been even higher, since by 1860 Christianity was already reducing violence on the Fijian islands). Incidentally, my calculation of annual Fijian warfare casualty rates (1.25 percent) exceeds Keeley's (0.87 percent) due to our apparently different data on Fiji's total population in 1860. My data shows 160,000, Keeley's 200,000.
29. Haas, 1990.
30. Haas, 1990.
31. Vayda, 1960.
32. Man, 2007.
33. Oliver, 1974.
34. Gabriel, 1991.
35. Oliver, 1974.
36. Kilner, 2000.
37. Polo, 1993.
38. Weber, 2006.
39. Godelier, 1986.
40. Crowther, 2007.
41. Benario, 1986.
42. Warry, 1980.

43. Peers, 2005.
44. Lewis, 1967.
45. Turnbull, 2007.
46. Martin, 2004.
47. Saunders, 1971.
48. Anon, 2006.
49. Lane, 2006.
50. Large male-size among primate species, for instance, is closely (though not perfectly) correlated with polygyny, or the pursuit of multiple sexual partners by males. This is because of the simple logic of natural selection: since mating opportunities with females are a scarce resource that the biggest, strongest males monopolize, their male descendants tend to grow ever larger and meaner. (In extreme cases, like that of elephant seals, among whom males weigh four times as much as females, the largest 5 percent of males produce 85 percent of the offspring each season.) Le Boeuf, 1988.
51. Newburn, 1995.
52. Brunner HG, 1993.
53. Caspi, 2002.
54. Wendland, 2006.
55. Price, 1999.
56. Sadalla, 1987.
57. Van Patten, 2007.
58. As measured by their number of decorations. McEllistrem, 2003.

Balls

1. Paul, 2003.
2. Atyeo, 1979.
3. Yiannakis, 2001.
4. Cantu, 2000.
5. King, 1996.
6. King, 1996.
7. Martin, 2003.
8. Vennum, 1994.
9. Vennum, 1994.
10. Elyot, 1544.
11. Magoun Jr., 1931.
12. Elias, 1986.
13. Atyeo, 1979.
14. Barker, 2003.
15. Guttmann, 1981.
16. Miller, 2006.
17. Mangan, 1997.
18. Kautz, 2000.
19. Blanchard, 1995.
20. Elias, 1986.
21. Carlson, 2004.
22. Carlson, 2004.

23. Nabokov, 1981.
24. Balke, 2003.
25. Nabokov, 1981.
26. Sears, 2001.
27. Critics sometimes claim these results are obviated by the Rwandan jumpers' use of "jumping-off" mounds. The sources show, however, that these were not so much mounds as marks—usually less than two inches in height [see Bale, 1996].
28. Cameron Hurst III, 1998.
29. Guttmann, 2001.
30. Butterwick, 2002.
31. Guttmann, 1996.
32. Freedman, 2008.
33. Anon, 2008.
34. Gregor, 1987.
35. Shadrake, 2005.
36. Crowther, 2007.
37. Shadrake, 2005.
38. Crowther, 2007.
39. Boxill, 2003.
40. Barker, 2003.
41. Nabokov, 1981.
42. Segal, 1984.
43. Rees, 1984.
44. Boxill, 2003.
45. Segal, 1984.
46. Sweet, 1987.
47. Blanchard, 1995.
48. Luschen, 1970.
49. Golden, 2004.
50. Vennum, 1994.
51. Sweet, 1987.
52. Treimel, 2001.
53. Bogin, 1998.
54. McDonald, 2008.
55. May, 2006.
56. Karpowicz, 2007.

Bards

1. There are, of course, many talented and successful *female* rappers, but I'm not talking about them for two reasons: first, even they will readily admit rap is a heavily masculinized art form (that's one of the major challenges they face), and second, women in general are simply not the focus of this book.
2. Lord, 1991.
3. Lord, 1991.
4. Pihel, 1996.
5. Such improvisation does, of course, lighten the burden of what the poet must memorize.

But Homer still had to remember everything in the poems, including every narrative element, and the descriptions and actions of twenty-four major characters and almost one hundred minor ones. Reciting the two poems probably became even more demanding for those bards who lived after Homer, since written copies would then have existed for audiences to compare.

6. Herndon, 1971.
7. Foley, 2007.
8. Garzia, 2007.
9. Armstrong, 2001.
10. Sahlas, 2001.
11. Armstrong, 2001.
12. Rosen, 1999.
13. Parker, 1988.
14. Henderson, 1991.
15. Lucile Hoerr, 1945.
16. Levy, 1975.
17. Adamson Hoebel, 1941.
18. Avorgbedor, 1994.
19. Johnson, 2008.
20. Avorgbedor, 1994.
21. Hunt, 2001.
22. Haselton, 2006.
23. Morgan, 1999.
24. Locke, 2007.
25. Oliver, 1974.
26. Locke, 2007.
27. Marshall, 1961.
28. Lord, 1991.

Beauty

1. Simpson, 1994.
2. Coad, 2008.
3. Simpson, 2003.
4. Bovin, 2001.
5. Rasmussen, 1991.
6. Oliver, 1974.
7. Carlyle, 1997.
8. Bovin, 2001.
9. Brain, 1979.
10. Jaoyti, 2008.
11. Brain, 1979.
12. Rey, 1924.
13. Mageo, 1996.
14. Oliver, 2002.
15. Kardiner, 1974.
16. Mathews, 1900.

17. Gusinde, 1961.
18. Kilmer, 1982.
19. Athenburg, 2007.
20. Hodges, 2001.
21. Oliver, 1974.
22. Guttmann, 1996.
23. Guttmann, 1996.
24. Dyall-Smith, 1999.
25. Trinkaus, 1982.
26. Fan, 2005.
27. Ogden, 2007.
28. Grammer, 1994.
29. Travison, 2007.

Babies

1. Hansen, 1998.
2. Hewlett, 1992a.
3. Anon, 2008.
4. Hewlett, 1992a.
5. Hewlett, 1992b.
6. Lamb, 1976.
7. Hewlett, 1992a.
8. Anon, 2005.
9. I feel duty-bound to point out, however, that the situation may not be as simple as that. According to the medical literature, gynecomastia occurs in 50 to 70 percent of Western adolescent males, too, Singh Narula, 2007. I find it difficult to believe this is the same level of breast growth (three in four Western boys have breasts?), but I suppose it is possible that the reports of Aka and Mbuti gynecomastia simply stem from the fact that Pygmy boys and men walk around without shirts more often than Western men.
10. Hewlett, 1992b.
11. Lamb, 1976.
12. Sayer, 2004.
13. Sayer, 2004.
14. Hewlett, 1992a.
15. *www.pageantcenter.com.*
16. Wonderlich, 2005.
17. The astute reader will no doubt notice these figures differ from those in the section on time spent with children (see page 226). That's because they come from different studies, both of which use slightly different parameters.
18. There is, though, related data showing that the nutrition of Aka daughters under the age of five is marginally better than that of Aka sons. While this doesn't directly bear on fathers' treatment of daughters, it obviously tends to indicate their treatment is at least equal, and possibly better.
19. Kreider, 2008.
20. Parmigiani, 1994.
21. Anderson, 1999.

22. Marlowe, 2000.
23. Irons, 2000.
24. Apicella, 2004.
25. Kiernan, 2003.
26. Valsiner, 2000.
27. Valsiner, 2000.
28. Tabori, 1961.
29. For skeptics who doubt references like these, see the Huichol yarn tapestry held by the Fine Arts Museum of San Francisco, which clearly shows a Huichol dad being encouraged to express his support for his wife by the application of a cord around his genitals.
30. Illingworth, 1968.
31. Hewlett, 1992a.
32. Oliver, 2002.
33. Winters, 2001.
34. In this case, however, Hewlett doesn't record whether they were more promiscuous than lower-status males, making it unclear whether they also diverted effort from fathering to pursuit of multiple sexual partners. Given the high mortality of Aka children without a strong connection to a father, though, it seems doubtful that neglectful promiscuity could be a particularly successful mating strategy in the dangerous conditions of the Aka habitat.

Babes

1. Cherry, 2006.
2. A quick mental exercise shows why this must be the case, even though individual men may have had many more lovers than individual women, and vice-versa. Imagine a sample population of ten men and ten women. Even if just one man has sex with each of the women while the others have none, the average number of lovers for each group will be identical—one man has had ten lovers, nine have had none, and ten women have had one. The average is still one lover per man, and one per woman.
3. Kolata, 2007.
4. Weber, E., 2000.
5. Mystery, 2007.
6. Gregor, 1987.
7. Brannigan, 1987.
8. Malinowski, 1932.
9. Mystery, 2007.
10. Anon, 2008b.
11. Apparently it is—Jeffries, for example, offers his buyers an "If you don't get laid . . . with at least three hot women within ninety days . . . I'll refund every penny" guarantee.
12. Bovin, 2001.
13. Oliver, 1974.
14. Conklin, 1949.
15. Clink, 2005.
16. Oliver, 1974.
17. Haavio-Mannila, 1997.

18. Laumann, 2000.
19. Nieuwenhuis, 2006.
20. Haddow, 2006.
21. Gentry, 1988.
22. A male chimpanzee will frequently apply his fingers and lips to a female chimp's genitals to investigate her fertility status. This constant contact means there is not the same opportunity for herpes virus to become isolated in either the oral or genital region among chimps as there is among humans. Chimpanzee herpes is, accordingly, a single virus in both oral and genital areas.
23. Oliver, 1989.
24. Long, 2006.
25. Mantcgazza, 2001.
26. Mantegazza, 2001.
27. Laumann, 2000; Miller, 2004.
28. Rao, 1995.
29. Heath, 1988.
30. Oliver, 1989.
31. Edgerton, 1964. This is particularly remarkable given that women among the Pokot were apparently also universally subjected to clitoridectomy.
32. Haavio-Mannila, 1997.
33. Laumann, 2000.
34. Marshall, 1979.
35. Brunker, 2003.
36. Gregor, 1987.
37. Houston, 1996.
38. Oliver, 1989.
39. Jenks, 1998.
40. Oliver, 1989.
41. Oliver, 1989.
42. Oliver, 2002.
43. Gammon, 1997.
44. The view is sometimes expressed that this wish for sexual privacy cannot really be an instinct, since watching explicit pornography seems to violate it. Yet I suspect that this is partly why witnessing other people's sex acts is exciting in the first place: because it violates our instinctual sense of propriety. Most other primates, who copulate without concern in public, would probably find the idea of hardcore pornography both boring and incomprehensible.
45. Oliver, 1989.
46. Duczko, 2004.
47. Kirby, 1981.
48. True, other species of chimp *don't* show this behavior, suggesting it may be something that has arisen separately in bonobos since they split from chimps around 1.5 million years ago. It is equally possible, however, that chimps are the ones who have changed, and that our common ancestor behaved with decidedly bonobo-like erotic abandon.
49. Guthrie, 2005. My thanks go out to Dr. Paul Bahn here, who kindly provided his expert knowledge on this.

50. Herdt, 1999.
51. Why he chose the German edition, I'm afraid I don't know.
52. Weismantel, 2004.
53. Anthropologist Mary Weismantel, in her excellent journal article on the Moche sex-pots (see Bibliography), theorizes that the masturbating-skeleton motif is intended to show the continuity of reproduction across generations; even death does not stop the sacred essence of life—semen—being passed down.
54. *Seinfeld* episode, "The Jimmy."
55. Abbott, 2001.
56. It has to be said, however, that not all desert fathers succeeded in conquering their lust. In fact, so many indulged in affairs with peasant lasses that it became customary for village girls to blame any unexplained pregnancy on them.
57. Weale, 2002.
58. Forster, 2004.
59. Gay, 1999.
60. Wassersug, 2007.
61. Miles, 2000.
62. Interestingly, the term itself was invented by Alfred Kinsey, apparently as a misreading from Malinowski's work on the Trobriand Islands. There is no evidence that any missionary ever tried to teach the position to their native congregation. Priest, 2001.
63. Alzate, 1984.
64. Malinowski, 1932.
65. Metz, 1997.
66. Studies of the difference between identical and non-identical (fraternal) twins are important because they allow us to isolate the effects of heredity. Because twins are usually brought up in the same household, and undergo the same environmental influences, any consistent difference between identical and non-identical twins is probably hereditary.
67. Jern, 2007.
68. Simmons, 1960.

epilogue

1. Darwin, 2001.
2. Darwin, 2007.
3. Taylor, 1981.
4. Sherman, 1997.

Bibliography

Abbott, E. (2001). *A History of Celibacy*. Cambridge, James Clarke & Co.

Adamson Hoebel, E. (1941). "Law-Ways of the Primitive Eskimos." *Journal of Criminal Law and Criminology* 31(6): 663–83.

Alzate, H. and Ladi Londono, M. (1984). "Vaginal Erotic Sensitivity." *Journal of Sex and Marital Therapy* 10(1): 49–56.

Anderson, K. G., Kaplan, H., and Lancaster, J. (1999). "Paternal Care by Genetic Fathers and Stepfathers I: Reports from Albuquerque Men." *Evolution and Human Behaviour* 20: 405–31.

Anderson, M. M. (1990). *Hidden Power: The Palace Eunuchs of Imperial China*. Buffalo, NY, Prometheus.

Anon (1987). "The Use of Historical Data in the Assessment of Combat Degradation." *The Journal of the Operational Research Society* 38(2): 149–62.

Anon (2005). "Are the Men of the African Aka Tribe the Best Fathers in the World?" *The Guardian*. London.

Anon (2006). "Country Reports on Terrorism 2005," Statistical Annex. U.S. Department of State. National Counterterrorism Center.

Anon (2008). "Consumer Expenditures in 2007." Bureau of Labor Statistics.

Anon (2008a). "Married Parents' Use of Time, 2003–06." U.S. Department of Labor. Washington, Bureau of Labor Statistics.

Anon (2008b). "Patterns, Poems and Stories." http://www.scribol.com/doc/3856782/Patterns-and-Stories-Like-Bishops-Journal.

Apicella, C. L. and Marlowe, F. W. (2004). "Perceived Mate Fidelity and Paternal Resemblance Predict Men's Investment in Children." *Evolution and Human Behavior* 25: 371–78.

Armstrong, E. G. (2001). "Gangsta Misogyny: A Content Analysis of the Portrayals of Violence Against Women in Rap Music, 1987–1993." *Journal of Criminal Justice and Popular Culture* 8(2): 96–126.

Arnott, R., Finger, S., and Upham Murray Smith, C. (2002). *Trepanation: History, Discovery, Theory*, Taylor & Francis.

Athenburg, K. (2007). *The Dirt on Clean*. New York, North Point Press.

Atyeo, D. (1979). *Blood and Guts: Violence in Sports*. London, Paddington Press.

Avorgbedor, D. K. (1994). "Freedom to Sing, License to Insult: The Influence of Haló Performance on Social Violence Among the Anlo Ewe." *Oral Tradition* 9(1): 83–112.

Baghurst, T., Hollander, D. B., Nardella, B., and Gregory Haff, G. (2006). "Change in Sociocultural Ideal Male Physique: An Examination of Past and Present Action Figures." *Body Image* 3: 87–91.

Bale, J. and Sang, J. (1996). *Kenyan Running: Movement Culture, Geography and Global Change,* London, Routledge.

Balke, B. and Snow, C. (2003). "Anthropological and physiological observations on Tarahumara endurance runners." *American Journal of Physical Anthropology* 23(3): 293–301.

Ball, C. and Westhorpe, R. (2003). "Local Anaesthesia—Before Cocaine." *Anaesthesia and Intensive Care* 31(1): 3.

Barker, J. R. V. (2003). *The Tournament in England, 1100–1400,* Woodbridge, Boydell Press.

Barnes, J. (1983). "Four Choctaw Songs." *MELUS* 10(4): 56.

Bauman, J. E. (1926). "Observations on the Strength of the Chimpanzee and Its Implications." *Journal of Mammalogy* 7(1): 1–9.

Benario, H. W. (1986). "Legionary Speed of March Before the Battle with Boudicca." *Britannia* 17: 358–62.

Berg, S. and Wynne-Edwards, K. (2001). "Changes in Testosterone, Cortisol, and Estradiol Levels in Men Becoming Fathers." *Mayo Clinic Proceedings.*

Berger, T. D. and Trinkaus, E. (1995). "Patterns of Trauma Among the Neandertals." *Journal of Archaeological Science* 22: 841–52.

Blanchard, K. (1995). *The Anthropology of Sport: An Introduction.* Westport, Greenwood Publishing Group Inc.

Bledsoe, G. H. H., Edbert, B., Grabowski, J. G., Brill, J., and Li, G. (2006). "Incidence of Injury in Professional Mixed Martial Arts Competitions." *Journal of Sports Science and Medicine* 5 (Combat Sports Special Issue): 136–42.

Blomberg, S. B., Hess, G. D., and Raviv, Y. (2008). "Where Have All the Heroes Gone? A Self-Interested, Economic Theory of Heroism." *Robert Day School Working Paper* No. 2008–1

Bogin, B. (1998). "The Tall and Short of It: Range of Heights in Humans Demonstrates Plasticity of Human Species." *Discover,* February.

Bovin, M. (2001). *Nomad Who Cultivate Beauty: Wodaabe Dances and Visual Arts in Niger.* Uppsala, Nordiska Afrikainstitutet.

Boxill, J., Ed. (2003). *Sports Ethics: An Anthology.* Oxford, Blackwell Publishing.

Brain, R. (1979). *The Decorated Body.* New York, Harper and Row.

Brannigan, A. (1987). "Pornography and Behavior: Alternative Explanations." *The Journal of Communication* 37(3): 185–89.

Briggs, G. V. (2007). "White Masculinity in the American Action Film Pre and Post 9/11." *School of Film and the College of Fine Arts.* Athens, Ohio University. Master of Arts: 83.

Brophy III, R. H. (1978). "Deaths in the Pan-Hellenic Games: Arrachion and Creugas." *The American Journal of Philology* 99(3): 363–90.

Brophy, R. and M. (1985). "Deaths in the Pan-Hellenic Games II: All Combative Sports." *The American Journal of Philology* 106(2): 171–98.

Brunker, M. (2003). "Anatomy of a Penis Pill Swindle." http://www.msnbc.msn.com/id/3077050/.

Brunner HG, N. M., Breakefield, X. O., Ropers, H. H., and van Oost, B. A. (1993). "Abnormal behavior associated with a point mutation in the structural gene for monoamine oxidase A." *Science* 262(5133): 578–80.

Burnham, G. L., Riyadh, Doocy, S., and Roberts, L. (2006). "Mortality After the 2003 Invasion of Iraq: a Cross-Sectional Cluster Sample Survey." *The Lancet* October 21: 1421–28.

Butterwick, D., Hagel, B., Nelson, D. S., LeFave, M. R., and Meeuwisse, W. H. (2002). "Epidemiologic Analysis of Injury in Five Years of Canadian Professional Rodeo." *The American Journal of Sports Medicine* 30(2): 193–99.

Cambria, R. (2004). "Inside the World of a Rock Roadie." *Spin Magazine Online.*

Cameron Hurst III, G. (1998). *Armed Martial Arts of Japan: Swordsmanship and Archery.* New Haven, Yale University Press.

Campbell, B. C., Pope, H. G. et al. (2005). "Body Image among Ariaal Men from Northern Kenya." *Journal of Cross-Cultural Psychology* 36(3): 371–79.

Cantu, R. C., M. D. and Mueller, F. O. Ph.D. (2000). "Catastrophic Football Injuries: 1977–1998." *Neurosurgery* 47(3): 673–77.

Carlson, L. (2004). "Giant Patagonians and Hairy Ainu: Anthropology Days at the 1904 St. Louis Olympics." *The Journal of American Culture* 12(3): 19–26.

Carlyle, T. (1997). *Sartor Resartus: The Life and Opinions of Herr Teufelsdröck.* Project Gutenberg.

Carrier, D. R. (1984). "The Energetic Paradox of Human Running and Hominid Evolution." *Current Anthropology* 25(4): 483–495.

Caspi A., M. J., Moffitt, T. E., Mill, J., Martin, J., Craig, I. W., Taylor, A., and Poulton, R. (2002). "Role of genotype in the cycle of violence in maltreated children." *Science* 297(5582): 752.

Chagnon, N. A. (1983). *The Fierce People.* New York, Holt, Rinehart and Winston.

Cherry, R. (2006). *Wilt: Larger Than Life.* Chicago, Triumph Books.

Chinnery, E. W. P. (1919). "The Application of Anthropological Methods to Tribal Development in New Guinea." *Journal of the Royal Anthropological Institute of Great Britain and Ireland* 49: 36–41.

Choi, H., and Hee, Y. L. (1970). "Hormonal Therapy on Eunuchism and Eunuchoidism." *Korean Journal of Urology* 11(4): 9–15.

Churchill, S. and Trinkaus, E. (1990). "Neandertal Scapular Glenoid Morphology." *American Journal of Physical Anthropology* 83: 147–60.

Churchill, S. (2005). "Calorie Count Reveals Neandertals Out-Ate Hardiest Modern Hunters." *Science* 307: 840.

Clink, T. (2005). *The Layguide: How to Seduce Women More Beautiful Than You Ever Dreamed Possible.* Bowden, East Street Publications.

Coad, D. (2008). *The Metrosexual: Gender, Sexuality and Sport,* SUNY Press.

Coe, K., Harmon, M. P., and Verner, B. (1993). "Tattoos and Male Alliances." *Human Nature* 4(2): 199–204.

Coleman, K. M. (1990). "Fatal Charades: Roman Executions Staged as Mythological Elements." *The Journal of Roman Studies* 80: 44–73.

Collins, W. J. (1958). *To Work in the Vineyard of Surgery.* Cambridge, Massachusetts, Harvard University Press.

Conklin, H. C. (1949). "Preliminary Report on Field Work on the Islands of Mindoro and Palawan, Philippines." *American Anthropologist* 51(2): 268–73.

Conley, C. (1999). "The Agreeable Recreation of Fighting." *Journal of Social History* 33(1): 57–72.

Costa-Paz, M., Apunte-Tinao, L., and Muscolo, D. L. (1999). "Injuries to Polo Riders: a Prospective Evaluation." *British Journal of Sports Medicine* 33(5): 329–31.

Cowen, T. (2000). *What Price Fame?* Cambridge, Massachusetts, Harvard University Press.

Crowther, N. B. (2007). *Sport in Ancient Times*. Westport, Connecticut, Praeger.

Daly, G. (2003). *Cannae: The Experience of Battle in the Second Punic War*. New York, Routledge.

Darwin, C. and Keynes, R. D. (2001). *Charles Darwin's Beagle Diary*. Cambridge, Cambridge University Press.

Darwin, C. (2007). *Descent of Man*. Sioux Falls, NuVision Publications.

de Waal, F. (1982). *Chimpanzee Politics: Power and Sex Among Apes*. London, Jonathan Cape.

Downey, G. (2007). "Producing Pain: Techniques and Technologies in No-Holds-Barred Fighting." *Social Studies of Science* 37(2): 201–26

Doyle, D. (2005). "Ritual Male Circumcision: A Brief History." *Journal of the Royal College of Physicians of Edinburgh* 35: 279–85.

Duczko, W. (2004). *Viking Rus: Studies on the Presence of Scandinavians in Eastern Europe*. Leiden-Boston, BRILL.

Duffy, K. (1984). *Children of the Forest*. New York, Dodd and Mead.

Dunning, E. (2000). "Towards a Sociological Understanding of Football Hooliganism as a World Phenomenon." *European Journal on Criminal Policy and Research* 8: 141–62.

Dyall-Smith, D. and Marks, R. (1999). "Dermatology at the Millennium: the Proceedings of the 19th World Congress of Dermatology," Sydney, Australia, June 15–20, 1997, Informa Health Care.

Eckert, P. and Newmark, R. (1980). "Central Eskimo Song Duels: A Contextual Analysis of Ritual Ambiguity." *Ethnology* 19(2): 191–211.

Edgerton, R. B. and Conant, F. P. (1964). "Kilapat: The 'Shaming Party' among the Pokot of East Africa." *Southwestern Journal of Anthropology* 20(4): 404 18.

Elias, N. and Dunning, E. (1986). *Quest for Excitement: Sport and Leisure in the Civilizing Process*. Oxford, Basil Blackwell Ltd.

Ellsworth, C. W. (2004). "Definitions of Hazing: Differences Among Selected Student Organizations." Faculty of the Graduate School. Catonsville, University of Maryland. Master of Arts.

Elyot, T. (1544). *The Boke Named the Governour*. London, Thomas Berthelet.

Ember, M. and Ember, C. R. (1971). "The Conditions Favoring Matrilocal versus Patrilocal Residence." *American Anthropologist, New Series* 73(3): 571–94.

Enattah, N. S., Sahi, T., Savilahti, E., Terwilliger, J. D., Peltonen, L., and Järvelä, I. (2002). "Identification of a Variant Associated with Adult-Type Hypolactasia." *Nature Genetics* 30: 233–37.

Evenhouse, E. and Reilly, S. (2006). "Multiple-Father Families, Child Support Enforcement, and Welfare." Unpublished.

Fan, J., Dai, W., Liu, F., and Wu, J. (2005). "Visual Perception of Male Body Attractiveness." *Proceedings of the Royal Society* B 272: 219–26.

Farthing, G. W. (2005). "Attitudes Toward Heroic and Nonheroic Physical Risk Takers as Mates and as Friends." *Evolution and Human Behavior* 26: 171–85.

Finkel MD, M. A. (2002). "Traumatic Injuries Caused By Hazing Practices." *American Journal of Emergency Medicine* 20: 228–33.

Fischer, M. E., Vitek, M. E., Hedeker, D., Henderson, W. D., Jacobsen, S. J., and Goldberg, J. (2004). "A Twin Study of Erectile Dysfunction." *Archives of Internal Medicine* 164: 165–68.

Foley, J. M. (2007). "Basque Oral Poetry Championship." *Oral Tradition* 22(2): 3–11.

Ford, R. (2005). "Drink Fuels 'Stranger Danger' of Rising Violence on Streets." *TimesOnline*.

Forster, P., Romano, V., Calì, F., Röhl, A., and Hurles, M. (2004). "MtDNA Markers for Celtic and Germanic Language Areas in the British Isles." *Traces of Ancestry: Studies in Honour of Colin Renfrew*, ed. Martin Jones (Cambridge, 2004): 99–111.

Frederick, D. A. and M. G. Haselton (2007). "Why Is Muscularity Sexy? Tests of the Fitness Indicator Hypothesis." *Personality and Social Psychology Bulletin*: 33(8): 1167–1183.

Freedman, J. (2008). "The Fortunate 50." *SI.com*.

Furman, A. (2006). "Juggling with the Sharks, Hopping with the Owls." http://www.ashrita.com/stories/juggling=sharks=hopping=owls.

Furuichi, T. and Ihobe, H. (1994). "Variations in Male Relationships in Bonobos and Chimpanzees." *Behaviour* 130(3–4): 213–28.

Gabriel, R. A. and Metz, K. S. (1991). *From Sumer to Rome: The Military Capabilities of Ancient Armies*. Westport, Greenwood Press.

Gammon, L. and Strong, B. (1997). *Threesome: How to Fulfill Your Favorite Fantasy*. West Palm Beach, Triad Press.

Garzia, J. (2007). "History of Improvised Bertsolaritza: A Proposal." *Oral Tradition* 22(2): 77–115.

Gay, T. (1999). "Rural Dialects and Surviving Britons." *British Archaeology* 46.

Gentry, G. A., Lowe, M., Alford, G., and Nevins, R. (1988). "Sequence Analyses of Herpesviral Enzymes Suggest an Ancient Origin for Human Sexual Behavior." *Proceedings of the National Academy of Sciences. USA* 85: 2,658–61.

Gibbons, J. (2008). "The Stages of a Witch Trial." Retrieved 07/01/08, from http://www.summerlands.com/crossroads/remembrance/_remembrance/stages_witch_trial.htm#The%20Stages%20of%20a%20Witch%20Trial.

Gilmore, D. (1990). *Manhood in the Making: Cultural Concepts of Masculinity*. New Haven, Yale University Press.

Gislén, A., Dacke, M., Kröger, R. H. H., Abrahamsson, M., Nilsson, D. E., and Warrant, E. J. (2003). "Superior Underwater Vision in a Human Population of Sea Gypsies." *Current Biology* 13: 833–36.

Glazier, P. S., Giorgos, P., and Cooper, S. M. (2000). "Anthropometric and Kinematic Influences on Release Speed in Men's Fast-Medium Bowling." *Journal of Sports Sciences* 18: 1,013–21.

Godelier, M. (1986). *The Making of Great Men: Male Domination and Power Among the New Guinea Baruya*. Translated by Rupert Swyer. Cambridge, Cambridge University Press.

Golden, M. (2004). *Sport in the Ancient World from A to Z*. London, Routledge, Taylor and Francis Group.

Goldman, L. (1999). *The Anthropology of Cannibalism*. Westport, Connecticut, Greenwood Publishing Group.

Grammer, K. and Thornhill, R. (1994). "Human (Homo sapiens) Facial Attractiveness and Sexual Selection: The Role of Symmetry and Averageness." *Journal of Comparative Psychology* 108(3): 233–42.

Gregor, T. (1987). *Anxious Pleasures: The Sexual Lives of an Amazonian People*. Chicago, University of Chicago Press.

Griskevicius, V., Cialdini, R. B., and Kenrick, D. T. (2006). "Peacocks, Picasso, and Parental Investment: The Effects of Romantic Motives on Creativity." *Journal of Personality and Social Psychology* 91(1): 63–76.

Grulich, Andrew E., de Visser, R. D., Smith, Anthony M. A., Rissel, Chris E., and Richters, Juliet (2003). "Sex in Australia: Homosexual experience and recent homosexual encounters." *Australian and New Zealand Journal of Public Health* 27(2): 155–63.

Guilaine, J. and Zammit, J. (2005). *The Origins of War: Violence in Prehistory.* Malden, Massachusetts, Blackwell.

Gusinde, M. (1961). "Somatology of the Ayom Pygmies of New Guinea." *Proceedings of the American Philosophical Society* 105(4): 394–411.

Guthrie, R. G. (2005). *The Nature of Paleolithic Art.* Chicago, University of Chicago Press.

Guttmann, A. (1981). "Sports Spectators from Antiquity to the Renaissance." *Journal of Sport History* 8(2): 5–27.

Guttmann, A. (1996). *The Erotic in Sports.* New York, Columbia University Press.

Guttmann, A., Thompson, L., and Thompson, L. A. (2001). *Japanese Sports: A History.* Honolulu, University of Hawaii Press.

Haapasalo, H., Kontulainen, S., Sievanen, H., Kannus, P., Jarvinen, M., and Vuori, I. (1995). "Exercise-induced bone gain is due to enlargement in bone size without a change in volumetric bone density: a peripheral quantitative computed tomography study of the upper arms of male tennis players." *Bone* 27(3): 351–57.

Haas, J., Ed. (1990). *The Anthropology of War.* Cambridge, Cambridge University Press.

Haavio-Mannila, E. and Kontula, O. (1997). "Correlates of Increased Sexual Satisfaction." *Archives of Sexual Behavior* 26(4): 399–419.

Haddow, L. J., Dave, B., Mindel, A., McPhie, K. A., Chung, C., Marks, C., and Dwyer, D. E. (2006). "Increase in Rates of Herpes Simplex Virus Type 1 as a Cause of Anogenital Herpes in Western Sydney, Australia, Between 1979 and 2003." *Sex Transm Infect* 82(3): 255–9.

Haggins, B. (2007). *Laughing Mad: The Black Comic Persona in Post-soul America.* Chapel Hill, Rutgers University Press.

Hall, J. (2003). "The Death of Douglas Dedge." *Fightsport* February.

Halperin, D., Winkler, J. J., and Zeitlin, F. I. (1991). *Before Sexuality: The Construction of the Erotic in the Ancient Greek World.* Princeton, New Jersey, Princeton University Press.

Hansen, K. V. and Garey, A. I. (1998). *Families in the U.S.: Kinship and Domestic Politics.* Philadelphia, Temple University Press.

Haselton, M. G. and Miller, G. F. (2006). "Women's Fertility Across the Cycle Increases the Short-Term Attractiveness of Creative Intelligence." *Human Nature* 17(1): 50–73.

Hawks, J., Wang, E. T., Cochran, G. M., Harpending, H. C., and Moyzist, R. K. (2007). "Recent Acceleration of Human Adaptive Evolution." *PNAS* 104(52): 20,753–58.

Hayes, S. K. (1981). *The Ninja and Their Secret Fighting Art.* Rutland, Vermont, Charles E. Tuttle Company.

Hays-Gilpin, K. (2004). *Ambiguous Images.* Walnut Creek, California, Rowman Altamira.

Hazzah, L. N. (2006). "Living Among Lions (Panthera Leo): Coexistence or Killing? Community Attitudes Towards Conservation Initiatives and the Motivations Behind Lion Killing in Kenyan Maasailand." *Conservation Biology and Sustainable Development.* Madison, University of Wisconsin: 153.

Heath, W. (1988). "Melville and Marquesan Eroticism." *The Massachusetts Review* 29(1): 43–65.

Henderson, J. (1991). *The Maculate Muse*. Oxford, Oxford University Press.

Herdt, G. (1999). *Sambia Sexual Culture: Essays from the Field*. Chicago, University of Chicago Press.

Herndon, M. A. (1971). "Singing and Politics: Maltese Folk Music and Musicians." *Anthropology*, Tulane University.

Hewlett, B. (1992a). *Intimate Fathers: The Nature and Context of Aka Pygmy Paternal Infant Care*. Ann Arbor, University of Michigan Press.

Hewlett, B. (1992b). *Father-Child Relations: Cultural and Biosocial Contexts*. New York, Aldine de Gruyter.

Hoag, H. (2008). "Sex on the Brain." *New Scientist* 2665: 28–31.

Hodges, F. (2001). "The Ideal Prepuce in Ancient Greece and Rome: Male Genital Aesthetics and Their Relation to Lipodermos, Circumcision, Foreskin Restoration, and the Kynodesme." *The Bulletin of the History of Medicine* 75: 375–405.

Houston, J. D. and Finney, B. R. (1996). *Surfing: A History of the Ancient Hawaiian Sport*. Rohnett Park, California, Pomegranate Artbooks.

Huenemann, R. L., Shapiro, L. R., Hampton, M. C., and Mitchell, B. W. (1966). "A Longitudinal Study of Gross Body Composition and Body Conformation and Their Association with Food and Activity in a Teen-Age Population: Views of Teen-Age Subjects on Body Conformation Food and Activity." *American Journal of Clinical Nutrition* 18: 325–338.

Hunt, C. (2001). "McGonagall Online." Retrieved 02/22/09, from http://www.mcgonagall online.org.uk/.

Hurley, C., Kiragu, A. W. MD FAAP, and Peltier, G. L. MD FACS (2006). "The Media and 'Copy-Cat' Burn Injuries: 21st Century Impediments to Burn Prevention." *The Journal of Trauma, Injury, Infection and Critical Care* 60(6): 1,382.

Hurley, J. W. (2007). *Shillelagh: The Irish Fighting Stick*. Pipersville, Caravat Press.

Ikai, M. and Fukunaga, T. (1968). "Calculation of Muscle Strength per Unit Cross-Sectional Area of Human Muscle by Means of Ultrasonic Measurement." *Int. Z. angew. Physiol. einschl. Arbeitsphysiol.* 26: 26–32.

Illingworth, R. S. (1968). "Punishment: A Personal View and Historical Perspective." *Clinical Pediatrics* October: 577–82.

Irons, W. and Chagnon, N. A. (2000). *Adaptation and Human Behavior: An Anthropological Perspective*. New York, Aldine.

Jaoyti, T. and DeLoach, S. B. (2008). "Mirror, Mirror on the Wall: The Effect of Time Spent Grooming on Wages." *Department of Economics Working Papers Series* 2008–01.

Jenks, R. (1998). "Swinging: A Review of the Literature." *Archives of Sexual Behavior* 27: 507–21.

Jern, P., Santtila, P., Witting, K., Alanko, K., Harlaar, N., Johansson, A., von der Pahlen, B., Varjonen, M., Vikström, N., Algars, M., and Sandnabba, K. (2007). "Premature and Delayed Ejaculation: Genetic and Environmental Effects in a Population-Based Sample of Finnish Twins." *Journal of Sexual Medicine* 4(6): 1739–49.

Johnson, S. (2008) "Rap Music Originated in Medieval Scottish Pubs, claims American Professor." *Telegraph.co.uk*.

Kamen, H. (1968). "The Economic and Social Consequences of the Thirty Years' War." *Past and Present* 39: 44–61.

Kanz, F. and Grossschmidt, K. (2006). "Head Injuries of Roman Gladiators." *Forensic Science International* 160: 207–16.

Kardiner, A. and Linton, R. (1974). *The Individual and His Society: The Psychodynamics of Primitive Social Organization.* Greenwood Press.

Karpowicz, A. (2007). "Ottoman Bows—an Assessment of Draw Weight, Performance and Tactical Use." *Antiquity* 81: 675–85.

Kautz, P. (2000). "The Gripping History of Glima." *Journal of Western Martial Art* 2000. Retrieved from http://ejmas.com/jwma/jwmaframe.htm.

Keeley, L. H. (1996). *War Before Civilization.* New York, Oxford, Oxford University Press.

Kelly, E. (1974). "A New Image for the Naughty Dildo?" *Journal of Popular Culture* VII(4): 804–09.

Kiernan, K. and Smith, K. (2003). "Unmarried parenthood: new insights from the Millennium Cohort Study." *Population Trends*, 114, 26–33.

Kilmer, M. (1982). "Genital Phobia and Depilation." *The Journal of Hellenic Studies* 102: 104–12.

Kilner, C. P. (2000). *Military Leaders' Obligation to Justify Killing in War.* The Joint Services Conference on Professional Ethics, Washington.

King, S. (1996). *A History of Hurling.* Dublin, Gill and MacMillan.

Kirby, E. T. (1981). "Ritual Sex: Anarchic and Absolute." *The Drama Review* 25(1): 3–8.

Knowles, N. (1940). "The Torture of Captives by the Indians of Eastern North America." *Proceedings of the American Philosophical Society* 82(2): 151–225.

Knuckey, G. (1992). "Patterns of Fracture Upon Aboriginal Crania from the Recent Past." *Proceedings of the Australasian Society for Human Biology* 5: 47–58.

Kolata, G. (2007). "The Myth, the Math, the Sex." *The New York Times, Week in Review.* Aug. 12. Retrieved from http://www.nytimes.com/2007/08/12/weekinreview/12kolata.html.

Kouri, E. M., Pope, H. G. J. et al. (1995). "Fat-Free Mass Index in Users and Nonusers of Anabolic-Androgenic Steroids." *Clinical Journal of Sport Medicine* 5(4): 223–28.

Kreider, R. (2008). "Living Arrangements of Children: 2004." U.S. Department of Commerce, U.S. Census Bureau.

Kruger, F. (2006, 27 June 2006, 11:57 GMT 12:57 UK). "Dicing with Death on South Africa's Trains." Retrieved 07/09/08, from http://news.bbc.co.uk/2/hi/africa/5117318.stm.

Lamb, M. E. (1976). *The Role of the Father in Child Development.* New York, Wiley and Sons.

Lamb, M. E. (2003). *The Role of the Father in Child Development.* Fourth Edition. Hoboken, New Jersey, John Wiley and Sons.

Lane, G. (2006). *Daily Life in the Mongol Empire.* Westport, Connecticut, Greenwood Press.

Laumann, E. O., Gagnon, J. H., Michael, R. T., and Michaels, S. (2000). *The Social Organization of Sexuality: Sexual Practices in the United States.* Chicago, University of Chicago Press.

Le Boeuf, B. J. and Reitrr, J. (1988). "Lifetime Reproductive Success in Northern Elephant Seals." *Reproductive Success.* T. H. Clutton-Brock. Chicago, University of Chicago Press: 344–62.

Leake, C. D. (1925). "The Historical Development of Surgical Anesthesia." *The Scientific Monthly* 20(3): 304–28.

Leit, Richard A., Pope, H. G., and Gray, J. J. (2001). "Cultural expectations of muscularity in men: The evolution of playgirl centerfolds." *International Journal of Eating Disorders* 29(1): 90–93.

Levy, B. S. a. S., Victor, W. (2000). *War and Public Health.* New York, American Public Health Association.

Levy, R. and Heyman, P. (1975). *Tahitians: Mind and Experience in the Society Islands*. Chicago, University of Chicago Press.

Lewis, B. (1967). *The Assassins: A Radical Sect in Islam*. London, Weidenfeld and Nicolson.

Lisowski, F. P. (1967). "Prehistoric and Early Historic Trepanation." *Diseases in Antiquity: A Survey of the Diseases, Injuries and Surgery of Early Populations*. Brothwell, D. and Sandison, A. T. Springfield, Charles C. Thomas: 651–72.

Locke, J. L. (2007). "Cost and Complexity: Selection for Speech and Language." *Journal of Theoretical Biology* 251: 640–52.

Long, L. L. (2006). *The Little Black Book of the Kama Sutra: The Classic Guide to Lovemaking*. White Plains, New York, Peter Pauper Press.

Lord, A. B. (1991). *Epic Singers and Oral Tradition*. Ithaca, London, Cornell University Press.

Lucile Hoerr, C. (1945). "The Clown's Function." *The Journal of American Folklore* 58(227): 25–34.

Luschen, G., Ed. (1970). *The Cross-Cultural Analysis of Sport and Games*. Champaign, Illinois, Stipes Publishing Company.

MacRae, F. (2006). "Binge Drinking to Blame for Half of all UK Violence." *Mailonline*.

Mageo, J. M. (1996). "Hairdos and Don'ts: Hair Symbolism and Sexual History in Samoa." *Frontiers*.

Magoun Jr., F. P. (1931). "Scottish Popular Football, 1424–1815." *The American Historical Review* 37(1): 1–13.

Mah, K. and Binik, Y. M. (2001). "The Nature of Human Orgasm: A Critical Review of Major Trends." *Clinical Psychology Review* 21(6): 821–56.

Malinowski, B. (1932). *The Sexual Life of Savages in North-Western Melanesia*. London, Routledge & Kegan Paul Ltd.

Man, J. (2007). *Genghis Khan*. New York, St. Martin's Press.

Mangan, J. A. (1997). "Sport in Society: the Nordic World and Other Worlds." *International Journal of the History of Sport* 14(3): 173–97.

Mantegazza, P. V. R. (2001). *The Sexual Relations of Mankind*. Honolulu, Hawaii, Minerva Group, Inc.

Marlowe, F. (2000). "Paternal Investment and Human Mating System." *Behavioural Processes* 51: 45–61.

Marshall, L. (1961). "Sharing, Talking and Giving: Relief of Social Tensions among !Kung Bushmen." *Africa: Journal of the International African Institute* 31(3): 231–49.

Marshall, M. (1979). *Weekend Warriors: Alcohol in a Micronesian Culture*. Mountain View, Mayfield Publishing Company.

Marshall, S. L. A. (2000). *Men Against Fire: The Problem of Battle Command*. Norman, University of Oklahoma Press.

Martin, G. (2004). *The New Era of Terrorism: Selected Readings*. Thousand Oaks, California, Sage.

Martin, J. D. (2003). "Sva lykr her hverju hesta[eth]ingi: Sports and Games in Icelandic Saga Literature." *Scandinavian Studies* 75(1).

Masakatsu Kondo, T. A., Ikegawa, S., Kawakami, Y., and Fukunaga, T. (1994). "Upper limit of fat-free mass in humans: A study on Japanese Sumo wrestlers." *American Journal of Human Biology* 6(5): 613–18.

Mathews, R. H. (1900). "Phallic Rites and Initiation Ceremonies of the South Australian Aborigines." *Proceedings of the American Philosophical Society* 39(164): 622–38.

May, T. (2006). "The Training of an Inner Asian Nomad Army in the Pre-Modern Period." *The Journal of Military History* 70: 617–36.

Mays, S. (1998). *The Archaeology of Human Bones*. London, Routledge.

McCall, G. E., Byrnes, W. C., Dickinson, A., Pattany, P. M., and Fleck, S. J. (1996). "Muscle Fiber Hypertrophy, Hyperplasia, and Capillary Density in College Men after Resistance Training." *Journal of Applied Physiology*, 81: 2,004–12.

McDonald, D. (2008). "Sky's the Limit for Australian Archery Team." *Sydney Morning Herald*, July 7. Retrieved from http://www.smh.com.au/news/archery/skys-the-limit-for-australia. Sydney.

McEllistrem, J. E. (2003). "Affective and Predatory Violence: A Bimodal Classification System of Human Aggression and Violence." *Aggression and Violent Behavior* 10: 1–30.

Metz, M. E., Pryor, J. L., Nesvacil, L. J., Abuzzahab Sr., F., and Koznar, J. (1997). "Premature Ejaculation: A Psychophysiological Review." *Journal of Sex & Marital Therapy* 23(1): 3–23.

Miles, M. (2000). "Signing in the Seraglio: Mutes, Dwarfs and Jestures at the Ottoman Court 1500–1700." *Disability and Society* 15(1): 115–34.

Miller, G. F. (2000). "Sexual selection for indicators of intelligence." *The Nature of Intelligence*. Bock, G., Goode, J., and Webb, K. New York, John Wiley.

Miller, S. A. and Byers, E. S. (2004). "Actual and Desired Duration of Foreplay and Intercourse: Discordance and Misperceptions Within Heterosexual Couples." *The Journal of Sex Research* 41(3): 301–09.

Miller, S. G. (2006). *Ancient Greek Athletics*, New Haven, Connecticut, Yale University Press.

Miller, W. B. (2001). "The Growth of Youth Gang Problems in the United States: 1970–1988." U.S. Department of Justice. Office of Juvenile Justice and Delinquency Prevention.

Moffitt, R. A. (1997). "The Effect of Welfare on Marriage and Fertility: What Do We Know and What Do We Need to Know?" *The Effect of the Welfare System on the Family and Reproductive Behavior*. Washington D.C.

Morgan, J. (1999). *When Chickenheads Come Home to Roost: A Hip-Hop Feminist Breaks it Down*. New York, Simon and Schuster.

Motte-Florac, J. and Thomas, M. C. (2004). *Les Insectes Dans La Tradition Oral*. Rebecq, Peeters Publishers.

Murphy, D. (2006). "Iraq Casualty Figures Open up New Battleground." *Christian Science Monitor* October 13.

Mystery (2007). *The Mystery Method: How to get Beautiful Women into Bed*. New York, St. Martin's Press.

Nabokov, P. (1981). *Indian Running: Native American History and Tradition*. Santa Barbara, Capra Press.

Newburn, T. and Stanko, E. A. (1995). *Just Boys Doing Business?: Men, Masculinities and Crime*. New York, Routledge.

Newman, P. L. and Boyd, D. J. (1982). "The Making of Men: Ritual and Meaning in Awa Male Initiation." *Rituals of Manhood*. Herdt. G. Berkeley, University of California Press.

Ngai, K. M, Levy, F., and Hsu, E. B. (2008). "Injury trends in sanctioned mixed martial arts competition: a 5-year review from 2002 to 2007." *British Journal of Sports Medicine* 42: 686–89.

Nieuwenhuis, R. F., van Doornum, G. J., Mulder, P. G. H., Neumann, H. A. M., and van der Meijden, W. I. (2006). "Importance of Herpes Simplex Virus Type-1 (HSV-1) in Primary Genital Herpes." *Acta Derm Venereo* 86: 129–34.

O'Connor, E. (1997). "Fractions of Men: Engendering Amputations in Victorian Culture." *Comparative Studies in Society and History* 39(4): 742–47.

O'Malley, Z. (2008). "Hip-Hop's Cash Kings 2008." *Forbes.com*.

Odem, M. E. and Clay-Warner, J. (1998). *Confronting Rape and Sexual Assault*. New York, Rowman and Littlefield.

Ogawa, K. M. U. and Michimasa MD (1997). "Humeral Shaft Fracture Sustained during Arm Wrestling: Report on 30 Cases and Review of the Literature." *The Journal of Trauma: Injury, Infection, and Critical Care* 42(2): 243–46.

Ogden, C. L., Carroll, M. D., Curtin, L. R., McDowell, M. A., Tabak, C. J., and Flegal, K. M. (2007). "Prevalence of Overweight and Obesity in the United States, 1999–2004." *Journal of the American Medical Association* 295(13): 1,549–55.

Oliffe, J. (2004). "Anglo-Australian Masculinities and Trans Rectal Ultrasound Prostate Biopsy (TRUS-Bx): Connections and Collisions." *International Journal of Men's Health* 3(1): 43–60.

Olivardia, R. (2001). "Mirror. Mirror on the Wall, Who's the Largest of Them All? The Features and Phenomenology of Muscle Dysmorphia." *Harvard Review of Psychiatry*, 9:5, 254–59.

Olivardia, R., Pope Jr., H. G., Borowiecki III, J. J., and Cohane, G. H. (2004). "Biceps and Body Image: The Relationship Between Muscularity and Self-Esteem, Depression, and Eating Disorder Symptoms." *Psychology of Men & Masculinity* 5(2): 112–20.

Oliver, D. (1974). *Ancient Tahitian Society*. Honolulu, The University of Hawaii Press.

Oliver, D. (1989). *Oceania: The Native Cultures of Australia and the Pacific Islands*. Honolulu, University of Hawaii Press.

Oliver, D. L. (2002). *Polynesia in Early Historic Times*. Bess Press.

Pain, S. (2007). "Histories: When Men Were Gods." *New Scientist Magazine* 2590: 46–47.

Pappas, E. (2007). "Boxing, wrestling, and martial arts related injuries treated in emergency departments in the United States, 2002–2005." *Journal of Sports Science and Medicine* 6(CSSI-2): 58–61.

Parker, W. H. (1988). *Priapea: Poems for a Phallic God*. New York, Croom Helm in association with Methuen, Inc.

Parkin, D. J. and Ulijaszek, S. J. (2007). *Holistic Anthropology: Emergence and Convergence*, New York, Berghahn Books.

Parmigiani, S. and Vom Saal, F. S. (1994). *Infanticide and Parental Care*. New York, Taylor and Francis.

Paul, R. J. (2003). "Variations in NHL Attendance: The Impact of Violence, Scoring, and Regional Rivalries." *American Journal of Economics and Sociology* 62: 345–64.

Peers, C. and Raffaele, R. (2005). *Warrior Peoples of East Africa*. Oxford, Osprey Publishing.

Peterkin, A. (2001). *One Thousand Beards: A Cultural History of Facial Hair*. Vancouver, Pulp Press.

Pihel, E. (1996). "A Furified Freestyle: Homer and Hip Hop." *Oral Tradition* 11(2): 249–69.

Poliakoff, M. (1987). *Combat Sports in the Ancient World*. New Haven and London, Yale University Press.

Polo, M., Yule, H., and Cordier, H. (1993). *The Travels of Marco Polo: The Complete Yule-Cordier Edition*, Mincola, New York, Courier Dover Publications.

Posey, M. (2004). "Burning Messages: Interpreting African American Fraternity Brands and Their Bearers." *Voices: The Journal of New York Folklore* 30, 1–3.

Potts, M. and Short, R. V. (1999). *Ever Since Adam and Eve: The Evolution of Human Sexuality.* Cambridge, Cambridge University Press.

Pounder, D. J. (1981). "Ritual Mutilation: Subincision of the penis among Australian Aborigines." *The American Journal of Forensic Medicine and Pathology* 4(3): 227–29.

Price, E. O. (1999). "Behavioral Development in Animals Undergoing Domestication." *Applied Animal Behavior Science* 65: 245–71.

Priest, R. J. (2001). "Missionary Positions." *Current Anthropology* 42(1): 29–68.

Prioreschi, P. (1996). *A History of Medicine: Greek Medicine.* Omaha, Horatius Press.

Putnam, P. (1948). "The Pygmies of the Ituri Forest." *A Reader in General Anthropology.* C. S. Coon, H. Holt.

Raley, S. and Bianchi, S. (2006). "Sons, Daughters, and Family Processes: Does Gender of Children Matter?" *Annual Review of Sociology* 32: 401–21.

Rao, K. V. and Demaris, A. (1995). "Coital Frequency Among Married and Cohabiting Couples in the United States." *Journal of Biosociological Science* 27: 135–50.

Rasmussen, S. J. (1991). "Veiled Self, Transparent Meanings: Tuareg Headdress as Social Expression." *Ethnology* 30(2): 101–17.

Rauser, A. (2004). "Hair, Authenticity and the Self-Made Macaroni." *Eighteenth-Century Studies* 38(1): 101–18.

Rees, C. R. and Miracle, A. W. (1984). *Conflict Resolution in Games and Sports.* Olympic Scientific Congress, Eugene, Oregon, Sage.

Rey, C. F. (1924). "The Arussi and Other Galla of Abyssinia." *Journal of the Royal African Society* 23(90): 85–95.

Ricciardellia, L. A., McCabe, M. P., Mavoa, H., Fotu, K., Goundar, R., Schultz, J., Waqa, G., and Swinburn, B. A. (2007). "The Pursuit of Muscularity Among Adolescent Boys in Fiji and Tonga." *Body Image* 4(4): 361–71.

Rice, X. (2007). "Herdsman Fights off Lion but Dies After Hyena Attack." *The Guardian* November 21.

Richters, J., de Visser, R., Rissel, C., and Smith, A. (2006). "Sexual Practices at Last Heterosexual Encounter and Occurrence of Orgasm in a National Survey." *The Journal of Sex Research* 43(3): 217–26.

Robinson, M. E., Riley III, J. L., Myers, C. D., Papas, R. K., Wise, E. A., Waxenberg, L. B., and Fillingim, R. B. (2001). "Gender Role Expectations of Pain: Relationship to Sex Differences in Pain." *The Journal of Pain* 2(5): 251–57.

Rodriguez, G. V. P. and Nobili, F. (1998). "Long-term effects of boxing and judo-choking techniques on brain function." *Italian Journal of Neurological Science* 19(6): 367–72.

Rosen, R. M. and Marks, D. R. (1999). "Comedies of Transgression in Gangsta Rap and Ancient Classical Poetry." *New Literary History* 30(4): 897–928.

Russell, L. (2008). "'A New Holland Half-Caste': Sealer and Whaler Tommy Chaseland." *History Australia* 5(1): 08.1–08.16.

Rutter, M. (1980). *Developmental Psychiatry.* London, Heinemann Medical Books.

Sadalla, E. K., Kenrick, D. T., and Vershure, B. (1987). "Dominance and Heterosexual Attraction." *Journal of Personality and Social Psychology* 52(4): 730–38.

Sahlas, Demetrios J. M. D., M.Sc. (2001). "Functional Neuroanatomy in the Pre-Hippocratic Era: Observations from the *Iliad* of Homer." *Neurosurgery* 48(6): 1,352–57.

Saunders, J. J. (1971). *The History of the Mongol Conquests.* London, Routledge and Kegan Paul.

Sayer, L. C., Bianchi, S. M., and Robinson, J. P. (2004). "Are Parents Investing Less in Children? Trends in Mothers' and Fathers' Time with Children." *American Journal of Sociology* 110(1): 1–43.

Schmitt, D. and Churchill, S. E. (2003). "Experimental Evidence Concerning Spear Use in Neandertals and Early Modern Humans." *Journal of Archaeological Science* 30: 103–14.

Scholz, M. N., D'Aout, K., Bobbert, M. F., and Aerts, P. (2006). "Vertical Jumping Performance of Bonobo (Pan paniscus) suggests Superior Muscle Properties." *Proceedings of the Royal Society of Biological Sciences* 273: 2,177–84.

Sears, E. S. (2001). *Running Through the Ages.* Jefferson, North Carolina, McFarland.

Segal, E. (1984). "To Win or to Die: A Taxonomy of Sporting Attitudes." *Journal of Sport History* 11(2): 25–31.

Shadrake, S. (2005). *The World of the Gladiator.* Stroud, Gloucestershire, Tempus.

Sherman, L. W., Gottfredson, D., MacKenzie, D., Eck, J., Reuter, P., and Bushway, S. (1997). "Preventing Crime: What Works, What Doesn't, What's Promising. A Report to the United States Congress." Department of Justice, National Institute of Justice.

Sherrow, V. (2006). *Encyclopedia of Hair: a Cultural History.* Westport, Connecticut, Greenwood Publishing.

Simmons, D. C. (1960). "Sexual Life, Marriage, and Childhood among the Efik." *Africa: Journal of the International African Institute* 30(2): 153–65.

Simpson, M. (1994). "Here Come the Mirror Men." *The Independent,* 15 November, London.

Simpson, M. (2003). "Beckham, the Virus." *Salon.com.*

Singh Narula, H. and Carlson, H. E. (2007). "Gynecomastia." *Endocrinology and Metabolism Clinics of North America* 36: 497–519.

Sivarajasingam, V. S. J., Matthews, K., and Jones, S. (2002). "Trends in Violence in England and Wales 1995–2000: an Accident and Emergency Perspective." *Journal of Public Health Medicine* 24(3): 219–26.

Spector, I. P. and Carey, M. P. (1990). "Incidence and Prevalence of the Sexual Dysfunctions: A Critical Review of the Empirical Literature." *Archives of Sexual Behavior* 19(4): 389–408.

Strauch, H., Wirth, I., and Geserick, G. (1998). "Fatal accidents due to train surfing in Berlin." *Forensic Science International* 94: 119–27.

Sturtevant, W. and Axtell, J. (1980). "The Unkindest Cut, or Who Invented Scalping." *The William and Mary Quarterly, Third Series* 37(3): 451–72.

Sutton-Smith, B. and Pellegrini, A. (1995). *The Future of Play Theory.* New York, SUNY.

Svinth, J. R. (2007). "Death Under the Spotlight: The Manuel Velazquez Boxing Fatality Collection." *Journal of Combative Sport,* 1–20.

Sweet, W. (1987). *Sport and Recreation in Ancient Greece.* New York, Oxford University Press.

Tabori, P. (1961). *The Art of Folly.* London, Prentice-Hall International.

Takahashi, M. L. (1998). "Adolescence and Identity Transformation: A Cross-cultural Analysis of Puberty Initiations." *Department of Anthropology.* Ottawa, Carleton University. Master of Arts.

Taylor, H. R. (1981). "Racial Variations in Vision." *American Journal of Epidemiology* 113(1): 62–80.

Taylor, S., Field, D., and Annandale, E. (2007). *Sociology of Health and Health Care.* London, Blackwell Publishing.

Toroyan T., P.M.E. (2007). *Youth and Road Safety.* Geneva, World Health Organization.

Travison, T. G., Araujo, A. B., O'Donnell, A. B., Kupelian, V., and McKinlay, J. B. (2007). "A Population-Level Decline in Serum Testosterone Levels in American Men." *The Journal of Clinical Endocrinology & Metabolism* 92(1): 196–202.

Treimel, J. (2001). *Dreams and Magic in Sport of the Ancient World*. 9th International Postgraduate Seminar on Olympic Studies, The International Olympic Academy.

Trinkaus, E. (1982). "Artificial Cranial Deformation in the Shanidar 1 and 5 Neandertals." *Current Anthropology* 23(2): 198–99.

Tsunenari, S., Idaka, T., Kanda, M., and Koga, Y. (1981). "Self- Mutilation: Plastic spherules in Penile Skin in Yakuza, Japan's racketeers." *The American Journal of Forensic Medicine and Pathology* 2(3): 203–7.

Turnbull, S. (2007). *Warriors of Medieval Japan*. Osprey Publishing.

Valsiner, J. (2000). *Culture and Human Development: an Introduction*. Thousand Oaks, California, Sage.

Van Patten, T. (2007). Soprano Home Movies. *The Sopranos*. United States.

Vayda, A. P. (1960). *Maori Warfare*. Wellington, A. H. & A. W. Reed.

Vennum, T. (1994). *American Indian Lacrosse: Little Brother of War*. New York, The Smithsonian Institution.

Walker, A. (2009). "The Strength of Great Apes and the Speed of Humans." *Current Anthropology* 50(2): 229–34.

Walker, P. L. (2001). "A Bioarchaeological Perspective on the History of Violence." *Annual Reveiw of Anthropology* 30: 573–96.

Warry, J. (1980). *Warfare in the Classical World*. New York, St. Martin's Press.

Wassersug, R. J. and Johnson, T. W. (2007). "Modern-Day Eunuchs: Motivations for and Consequences of Contemporary Castration." *Perspectives in Biology and Medicine* 50(4): 544–46.

Weale, M. E., Weiss, D. A., Jager, R. F., Bradman, N., and Thomas, M. G. (2002). "Y Chromosome Evidence for Anglo-Saxon Mass Migration." *Molecular Biology and Evolution* 19(7): 1,008–21.

Webb, S. (1995). *Palaeopathology of Aboriginal Australians*. Cambridge, Cambridge University Press.

Weber, E. (2000). *How to Pick Up Girls*. Tenafly, NJ, Symphony Press.

Weber, G. (2006). *The Terrible Islands*. Retrieved www.andaman.org/Book/Chapter3/text3 .htm.

Weismantel, M. (2004). "Moche Sex Pots: Reproduction and Temporality in Ancient South America." *American Anthropologist* 106(3): 495–505.

Welbourn, F. B. (1968). "Keyo Initiation." *Journal of Religion in Africa* 1(2): 212–32.

Wendland, J. R., Hampe, M., Newman, T. K., Syagailo, Y., Meyer, J., Schempp, W., Timme, A., Suomi, S. J., and Lesch, K. P. (2006). "Structural variation of the monoamine oxidase A gene promoter repeat polymorphism in nonhuman primates." *Genes, Brain and Behavior* 5: (40–45).

Willoughby, D. P. (1970). *The Super-Athletes*. New York, A. S. Barnes and Company.

Winters, J. (2001). "The Daddy Track." *Psychology Today* Sep/Oct. Retrieved from http://www.psychologytoday.com/rss/pto-20010901-000006.html.

Wonderlich, A. L., Ackard, D. M, and Henderson, J. B. (2005). "Childhood Beauty Pageant Contestants: Associations with Adult Disordered Eating and Mental Health." *Eating Disorders* 13(3): 291–301.

Wong (Ph.D.), M. A. (2008). "Male initiation rites—Introduction to a Special Focus." *The Society for the Psychological Study of Men and Masculinity Bulletin* 11: 1–13.

Wrangham, R. and Peterson, D. (1996). *Demonic Males: Apes and the Origins of Human Violence.* Boston, Houghton Mifflin Company.

Yiannakis, A. and Melnick, M. J., Ed. (2001). *Contemporary Issues in Sociology of Sport.* Champaign, Human Kinetics.

index